CHAPTER 14	THE BREEDING PROCESS	58
Section 14.1	The Covering Season	58
Section 14.2	Definitions: Breeding Season, Breeding Cycle	58
Section 14.3	The Stallion	59
Section 14.4	Sex Drive of the Stallion	59
Section 14.5	Semen Quality	59
Section 14.6	Overuse of Stallion	60
Section 14.7	Stallion Subfertility	60
Section 14.8	Artificial Insemination Prohibited	60
Section 14.9	Broodmares	60
Section 14.10	Mares Serviced at Stud	60
Section 14.11	Veterinary Services to Mares	61
Section 14.12	The Oestrous Cycle	61
Section 14.13	Teasing Mares	61
Section 14.14	Optimum Time for Coitus	62
Section 14.15	Mating	62
Section 14.16	Conception	62
Section 14.17	Twin Conceptions	63
Section 14.18	Pregnancy Diagnosis	63
Section 14.19	Gestation	63
Section 14.20	Foaling	64
Section 14.21	Covering at Foal Heat	64
Section 14.22	Rearing the Foal	64

CHAPTER 15	BEHAVIOUR OF THE RACEHORSE	66
Section 15.1	Equine Intelligence	66
Section 15.2	Factors Influencing Equine Behaviour	66
Section 15.3	Horse a Reflex Animal	66
Section 15.4	Herding Instinct	66
Section 15.5	Horse is Non-Aggressive	67
Section 15.6	Horse — A Creature of Instinct	67
Section 15.7	Peculiar Equine Senses	68
Section 15.8	Individuality of Horses	68

CHAPTER 16	CONFORMATION GENERALLY	70
Section 16.1	Bones, Joints and Muscles	70
Section 16.2	Points	70
Section 16.3	Conformation Important, but Not an End in Itself	70
Section 16.4	Presence	71
Section 16.5	Size and Proportional Compatibility	71
Section 16.6	Measurement of Height	71
Section 16.7	Balance	72
Section 16.8	Nearside/Offside	72
Section 16.9	Variation in Conformation of Sprinters and Stayers	72

CHAPTER 17	DETAILED CONFORMATION	73
Section 17.1	Ideal Marks of Quality of Racehorse	73
Section 17.2	Comment on Above by a Renowned Horseman	78

CHAPTER 18	THE FOOT AND THE FARRIER	79
Section 18.1	The Foot	79
Section 18.2	The Farrier	79

79
79
81
81
81

CHAPTER 20	COLOURS AND MARKINGS	83
Section 20.1	Skin and Coat	83
Section 20.2	Evolution of Colours	83
Section 20.3	Instability of Early Colour	83
Section 20.4	Colour of the Thoroughbreds	83
Section 20.5	Horsemen's Colour Preference	85
Section 20.6	Markings	85

CHAPTER 21	FOOD AND NUTRITION	88
Section 21.1	Feeding — a Balance of Art and Science	88
Section 21.2	The Equine Digestive System	88
Section 21.3	Food Classifications	88
Section 21.4	Bulk Foods	89
Section 21.5	Energy Foods	89
Section 21.6	Vitamins and Minerals	89
Section 21.7	Daily Feed Intake	90
Section 21.8	Feeding Requirements of Thoroughbred Stock	90
Section 21.9	Feeding the Racehorse	90
Section 21.10	Stable Visitors' Titbits	91
Section 21.11	Unhygienic and Faulty Feeding	91
Section 21.12	Poisonous Plants	91
Section 21.13	Watering — an Important Part of Feeding	91

CHAPTER 22	HEALTH AND MEDICINE	92
Section 22.1	Health and its Signs	92
Section 22.2	Veterinary Medicine	92
Section 22.3	Horse Doctors	92
Section 22.4	Disease and its Signs	92
Section 22.5	Disease Producing Organisms	93
Section 22.6	Disease-Producing Parasites	93
Section 22.7	Control of Parasites	94
Section 22.8	Preventive Medicine or Hygiene	94
Section 22.9	Duty of Trainer and Handler to Sick Horses	94
Section 22.10	Bleeders	94
Section 22.11	Care of the Sick Horse	95
Section 22.12	Temperature, Respiration, and Pulse	95
Section 22.13	Weight	95
Section 22.14	Death or Destruction of Racehorse	96

CHAPTER 23	LIFE SPAN	97
Section 23.1	Uniformity of Age of Thoroughbreds	97
Section 23.2	Dental Age Chart	97
Section 23.3	Age Comparison — Equine and Human	98

CHAPTER 24	REGISTRATION OF PEDIGREES	100
Section 24.1	Development of the Thoroughbred in Australia	100

Section 24.2	The Australian Stud Book (ASB)	100
Section 24.3	Eligibility for Admission to the ASB	101
Section 24.4	Bases of Entries in ASB or Non-Stud Book Register	101
Section 24.5	Broodmare Records	101
Section 24.6	Female Families	102
Section 24.7	Foal Identification	102
Section 24.8	Freezebranding	103
Section 24.9	Blood-Typing	103
CHAPTER 25	**REGISTRATION OF RACEHORSES**	**104**
Section 25.1	The Registrar of Racehorses	104
Section 25.2	Registration Prerequisite to Racing	104
Section 25.3	Naming of Horse	104
Section 25.4	Certificate of Registration	105
Section 25.5	Document of Description	105
Section 25.6	Transfer of Ownership	105
CHAPTER 26	**OWNERS AND LESSEES**	**108**
Section 26.1	Who May Own or Lease	108
Section 26.2	Partnerships	108
Section 26.3	Syndicates	108
Section 26.4	Promoters	108
Section 26.5	Leases	109
Section 26.6	Assumed Names of Owners and Lessees	109
Section 26.7	Racing Colours	109
Section 26.8	Racehorse Owners' Association	109
CHAPTER 27	**FINANCIAL VIABILITY OF OWNERSHIP**	**110**
Section 27.1	Ownership Costs	110
Section 27.2	Ownership Income	110
Section 27.3	Ownership Not Financially Viable	110
Section 27.4	Owners — The Keystone of the Racing Industry	111
Section 27.5	Auxiliary Ownership Purposes	111
CHAPTER 28	**BUYING AND SELLING A RACEHORSE**	**112**
Section 28.1	Contract of Sale	112
Section 28.2	Sale with Engagements	112
Section 28.3	Insurance	113
CHAPTER 29	**SOUNDNESS OF HORSE FOR RACING**	**114**
Section 29.1	Soundness	114
Section 29.2	Examination as to Soundness	114
CHAPTER 30	**TRAINERS**	**118**
Section 30.1	Licensing of Trainers	118
Section 30.2	Services Provided by Trainers	118
Section 30.3	Skill and Competence of Trainers	119
Section 30.4	Trainers' Association	119
Section 30.5	Stablehands	120
Section 30.6	Stable Returns	120
Section 30.7	Prohibited Substances	121
Section 30.8	Sampling and Testing for Prohibited Substances	121
Section 30.9	Use of Batteries	122
CHAPTER 31	**FINANCIAL VIABILITY OF TRAINING**	**123**
Section 31.1	Income of Trainers	123
Section 31.2	Expenses of Trainers	123
Section 31.3	Average Cost of Training a Horse	123
Section 31.4	Financial Viability of Trainers	124
CHAPTER 32	**TRAINING**	**125**
Section 32.1	Early Education of Youngsters	125
Section 32.2	Early Racetrack Training	126
Section 32.3	Training Programs	126
Section 32.4	Conditioning of Horses Resuming from Spelling	127
Section 32.5	Trackwork	127
Section 32.6	Barrier Trials	128
Section 32.7	Conditioning Runs	128
Section 32.8	First Uppers	129
Section 32.9	Races Won by Fit Horses	129
Section 32.10	Horses on the Decline	130
Section 32.11	Letting-Down	130
Section 32.12	Spells	130
Section 32.13	Length of Spell	131
Section 32.14	Let-Ups	131
CHAPTER 33	**FITNESS**	**134**
Section 33.1	Fitness and its Components	134
Section 33.2	Musculo-Skeletal Fitness	134
Section 33.3	Cardiovascular Fitness	134
Section 33.4	Respiratory Fitness	135
Section 33.5	Psychological Fitness	135
Section 33.6	Inherent Courage	135
CHAPTER 34	**ABILITY**	**136**
Section 34.1	Fitness/Ability Relativity	136
Section 34.2	Ability	136
Section 34.3	Class By Race Eligibility	136
Section 34.4	Class by Ability	137
Section 34.5	Ability Classifications	138
Section 34.6	Horses from Overseas	139
CHAPTER 35	**SEX IN RELATION TO RACING**	**140**
Section 35.1	Description of Horses According to Sex	140
Section 35.2	Castration	140
Section 35.3	The Effect of the Mating Season	140
Section 35.4	Fillies and Mares Versus Colts and Horses	141
Section 35.5	Sex Allowance in Mixed-Sex Races	141
CHAPTER 36	**AGE IN RELATION TO RACING**	**142**
Section 36.1	Two-Year-Olds	142
Section 36.2	Over-Racing of Two-Year-Olds	142
Section 36.3	Three-Year-Olds	142
Section 36.4	Four- and Five-Year-Olds	143
Section 36.5	Six-Year-Olds	143
Section 36.6	Aged Horses	143

GALLOPERS AND GAMBLERS

GALLOPERS AND GAMBLERS

A Guide to Thoroughbred Racing in Australia

Pat Craven

HALBOOKS PUBLISHING

HALBOOKS PUBLISHING

Published 1997 by Halbooks Publishing
30 Elouera Road Avalon NSW 2107 Australia

Copyright © 1997 Pat Craven

This work is copyright. All rights reserved. Apart from any fair dealing for the purposes of study, research, criticism or review, as permitted under the Copyright Act, no part of this book may be reproduced by any means without the prior written consent of both the copyright owner and publisher.

National Library of Australia
cataloguing-in publication data:

    Craven, Patrick Noel 1924–
    Gallopers and Gamblers
    A guide to thoroughbred racing in Australia

Bibliography.
ISBN 0 646 32197 8

1. Horse racing - Australia. 2. Horse racing - Betting - Australia. 3. Race horses - Australia. I. Title.

Page design by Lucy Michalewska
Computer page composition by ID Studio, Sydney
Cover design by Richard Tabaka
Printed and bound in Hong Kong by South China Printing Company

FOREWORD

BY
MR. R. L. (BOB) CHARLEY, CHAIRMAN,
NSW THOROUGHBRED RACING BOARD

I was captivated by racing's charms from a very early age. To satisfy my thirst for knowledge of this great sport and industry I was obliged to devour both folk lore and fact by reference to a range of journals as well as experience passed on by others.

Nowhere to be found was a comprehensive guide to the many facets of this complex pastime.

In recent years books galore have been published on racing. The careers of champions have been catalogued, both equine and human. There have been reference books on the breeding, training and management of horses, as well as all manner of guides to riches through punting manuals. This comprehensive reference book deals broadly with all facets of the industry and outlines, without veneration or criticism, the principles, systems and procedures upon which industry customs and regulations are based.

I commend this book to all industry participants as well as those newcomers who wish to unlock the vault of racing experience.

ROBERT CHARLEY
16 June, 1997

TABLE OF CONTENTS

PART 1	THE PRELIMINARY	11
Chapter 1	Provision of Consolidated Reference Book on Flat Racing	12

PART 2	THE FAMILY OF THE HORSE	15
Chapter 2	Evolution of First True Horse	16
Chapter 3	Recent Ancestry of Modern Horse	19
Chapter 4	Modern Horse	21

PART 3	USE OF THE HORSE	25
Chapter 5	Use of the Horse Before Mechanisation	26
Chapter 6	Use of the Horse in Australia	30
Chapter 7	Use of the Horse in Modern Life	32

PART 4	EARLY HISTORY OF THE THOROUGHBRED	35
Chapter 8	Development of the Thoroughbred	36

PART 5	BLOODSTOCK (THOROUGHBRED) BREEDERS	41
Chapter 9	Breeders	42
Chapter 10	Stud Farms	45

PART 6	BLOODSTOCK (THOROUGHBRED) BREEDING	47
Chapter 11	Breeding Methods	48
Chapter 12	Basic Genetic Concepts	50
Chapter 13	Improvement Through Genetics	53

PART 7	THE BREEDING PROCESS	57
Chapter 14	The Breeding Process	58

PART 8	BEHAVIOUR OF THE RACEHORSE	65
Chapter 15	Behaviour of the Racehorse	66

PART 9	THE BODY OF THE RACEHORSE	69
Chapter 16	Conformation Generally	70
Chapter 17	Detailed Conformation	73
Chapter 18	The Foot and the Farrier	79
Chapter 19	Gaits of the Horse	81
Chapter 20	Colours and Markings	83

PART 10	FOOD AND HEALTH OF THE RACEHORSE	87
Chapter 21	Food and Nutrition	88
Chapter 22	Health and Medicine	92
Chapter 23	Life Span	97

PART 11	REGISTRATION OF THOROUGHBRED PEDIGREES AND RACEHORSES	99
Chapter 24	Registration of Pedigrees	100
Chapter 25	Registration of Racehorses	104

PART 12	OWNERS AND OWNERSHIP	107
Chapter 26	Owners and Lessees	108
Chapter 27	Financial Viability of Ownership	110
Chapter 28	Buying and Selling a Racehorse	112
Chapter 29	Soundness of Horse for Racing	114

PART 13	TRAINERS AND TRAINING	117
Chapter 30	Trainers	118
Chapter 31	Financial Viability of Training	123
Chapter 32	Training	125

PART 14	FITNESS AND ABILITY OF RACEHORSES	133
Chapter 33	Fitness	134
Chapter 34	Ability	136
Chapter 35	Sex in Relation to Racing	140
Chapter 36	Age in Relation to Racing	142

PART 15	STABLES AND STABLECRAFT	145
Chapter 37	Stables and Stablecraft	146
Chapter 38	Saddlery	149
Chapter 39	Stable and other Vices of the Racehorse	152

PART 16	JOCKEYS AND JOCKEYSHIP	155
Chapter 40	Jockeys	156
Chapter 41	Financial Viability of Jockeyship	160
Chapter 42	Jockeyship	162

PART 17	CLASSES OF RACES ON THE FLAT	165
Chapter 43	Classes and Types of Races	166
Chapter 44	Weight-for-Age Scale	174

PART 18	RACETRACKS	177
Chapter 45	Racetracks Generally	178
Chapter 46	Metropolitan Racetracks and Barrier Guides	184

PART 19	RACE MEETINGS	205
Chapter 47	Race Meetings Generally	206
Chapter 48	Pre-Race Day Procedures	208

PART 20	RACE DAY PROCEDURES	215
Chapter 49	Race Day Procedures Before the Race	216
Chapter 50	The Race	220
Chapter 51	Post Race Meeting Procedures	224

PART 21	BOOKMAKERS AND BOOKMAKING	227
Chapter 52	Bookmakers	228
Chapter 53	Bookmaking	230
Chapter 54	Betting With Bookmakers	235
PART 22	TOTALISATORS AND THE TABS	239
Chapter 55	Totalisators	240
Chapter 56	Totalisator Administration Boards (TABs)	246
PART 23	PUNTERS AND PUNTING	249
Chapter 57	Punters and Punting	250
PART 24	WEIGHT RATINGS	253
Chapter 58	Introduction to Weight Rating	254
Chapter 59	Calculation and Recording of Weight Ratings	256
Chapter 60	Data Not Included in Weight Ratings But Noted for Future Selection Procedure	264
PART 25	APPLICATION OF WEIGHT RATINGS	267
Chapter 61	Preliminary Selection Procedure	269
Chapter 62	Selection Procedure	271
Chapter 63	Framing a Market on Weight Ratings	282
Chapter 64	The Flow of Weight Rating Data From Source to User	284
PART 26	ADMINISTRATION OF THE RACING INDUSTRY	287
Chapter 65	Origin of Racing and Racing Administration	288
Chapter 66	Structure of Racing Control	291
Chapter 67	The Role of Principal Clubs	293
Chapter 68	The Role Of District Racing Associations	298
Chapter 69	The Role Of Race Clubs	299
	APPENDIX	301
	BIBLIOGRAPHY	302

PART 1
THE PRELIMINARY

Chapter	1	Provision of Consolidated Reference Book on Flat Racing
Section	1.1	Book Published to Meet a Need
	1.2	Acknowledgments
	1.3	Profit Payable to Charity
	1.4	Meanings of Certain Terms

PART I THE PRELIMINARY

CHAPTER 1 **PROVISION OF CONSOLIDATED REFERENCE BOOK ON FLAT RACING**

Section 1.1
Book Published to Meet a Need

> Do they know? At the turn to the straight
>   Where the favourites fail,
> And every atom of weight
>   Is telling its tale;
> As some grim old stayer hard-pressed
>   Runs true to his breed,
> And with head just in front of the rest
>   Fights on in the lead;
> When the jockeys are out with the whips,
>   With a furlong to go;
> And the backers grow white to the lips –
>   Do you think *they* don't know?
>
> Do they know? As they come back to weigh
>   In a whirlwind of cheers,
> Though the spurs have left marks of the fray,
>   Though the sweat on the ears
> Gathers cold, and they sob with distress
>   As they roll up the track,
> They know just as well their success
>   As the man on their back.
> As they walk through a dense human lane,
>   That sways to and fro,
> And cheers them again and again,
>   Do you think *they* don't know?

Our great bard A.B. "Banjo" Paterson in his 1902 poem "Do they know?" quoted above, raised the question: Do racehorses know what racing is all about and, do the winners know what applause is about? He answered by way of retort: Do you think they don't know?

So much for the animal knowledge. But what about the human knowledge? In his treatise "Racehorses and Racing", Banjo stated that, with the exception of racing experts, very few persons who patronise racing have any practical knowledge of the racehorse or racing. They know that they lose their money when sometimes they should have won; they know that bookmakers offer them what seem to be unreasonably short odds, and so on.

The position that existed in 1914 when Banjo wrote his classical treatise has not changed in this modern age. Where then can those who don't know, or who only think they know, learn the rudiments of thoroughbred racing? Where can they find the answers to the many questions that arise? Questions about the breeding, ownership, training and riding of racehorses; the conduct of race meetings; the design of racetracks; the types and distances of races; the methods of selecting the chances in a race and ascertaining their relative prices; the control of betting transactions; and so on and on.

There has not been a convenient consolidated reference book to supply in simple terms the information sought.

This book has, therefore, been published to meet a need and that is to assist those many people who wish to acquire a broad knowledge and understanding of the many and varied facets of the whole spectrum of thoroughbred flat racing. Explanations have been set forth herein in as simple terms as practicable — by a novice for novices. The book does not pretend to be an authoritative document for specialists.

As indicated, the book deals only with thoroughbred flat racing, that is to say, racing in which competing thoroughbreds do not have to overcome obstacles in running. The subjects of hurdle racing, steeple-chasing, harness racing, or the racing of any type or breed of horse other than the thoroughbred, are not dealt with here. Broad reference may be made here to such subjects and certain of the material may be common to all forms of racing, or may, with necessary adaptation, be applied to such other forms of racing.

A very broad brush has been taken to paint in the book a very broad picture about the evolution of the horse species; life of the horse in the wild; domestication and use of the horse by humans; and the development of types and breeds of horses, particularly the thoroughbred breed. Through such background knowledge we can better understand the modern horse — its behaviour and interaction with the environment that we have created around it. For those so interested there is an abundance of specialised material available about the story of the past — a story of fascination and wonder.

Section 1.2
Acknowledgments

About 30 years ago a new system was developed for analysing, measuring and recording of past performances of racehorses, and the use of those records for pre-race selection and pricing. The Late Rem Plante was a pioneer in this and in 1964 he published a book titled *Australian Horse Racing and Punters' Guide* which I studied with great interest.

Although Rem's book contained a wealth of knowledge, it puzzled me — not in what it said, but rather in what it didn't say! For business reasons in those days, Rem didn't disclose everything.

After my retirement from office I found it necessary to establish some fresh interest. I had always been interested in horses and horse racing and Rem's puzzles were intriguing. My interests heightened and my research began.

In carrying out my research, I necessarily had recourse to information contained in: Acts of State Parliaments and Regulations made thereunder dealing with racing and betting; the Australian Rules of Racing; Local Rules of Racing; Racing Calendars; annual reports, public documents, or papers issued by State governments, statutory bodies (including TABs), principal clubs, race clubs, and bodies or associations of persons connected with the breeding or racing industries; to information sought directly from various persons as individuals or as representatives of bodies or associations; to relevant works in public or club libraries; to various publications — papers, periodicals and books.

Sincere thanks are extended to every person who rendered assistance and co-operation in any way in the production of this book. Special thanks of course are extended to Rem's son, Marcel Plante, for permitting me to draw so heavily on his father's book. Indeed this guide is in essence an updating and expansion of Rem's book.

Section 1.3
Profit Payable to Charity

Distributions from any profits made by me, the author of this book, as the result of its publication and sale, will be made on a proportionate basis to principal clubs for the credit of funds established for the welfare of persons who are in needy circumstances as the result of accident or injury incurred in the hazardous racing industry.

Section 1.4
Meanings of Certain Terms

In this book, unless the context otherwise indicates:

(a) where the term *man, men, he, his, him, horseman, horsemen, sportsman, sportsmen,* or the like, has been used it is intended for reasons of simplicity to denote any member of the human family, male or female; and

(b) the term State means any State of the Commonwealth of Australia and, where necessary, includes the Australian Capital Territory and the Northern Territory.

PART 2
THE FAMILY OF THE HORSE

Chapter	2	Evolution of First True Horse
Section	2.1	The Forest Browsing Ancestors
	2.2	The Plain Grazing Ancestors
	2.3	The First True Horse
	2.4	Summary of Evolutionary Changes
Chapter	3	Recent Ancestry of Modern Horse
Section	3.1	Restriction of Horses to Regions
	3.2	Exclusive Ancestors of Modern Horse
	3.3	Adaptation of Horses to Regional Environment
	3.4	Many Types and Breeds But Only One Ancestral Type
Chapter	4	Modern Horse
Section	4.1	Members of the Horse Family
	4.2	Domestic Horses
	4.3	The Heavy Horse
	4.4	The Light Horse
	4.5	The Pony
	4.6	Hot Bloods, Cold Bloods, Warm Bloods

PART 2 THE FAMILY OF THE HORSE

CHAPTER 2 EVOLUTION OF FIRST TRUE HORSE

Section 2.1
The Forest Browsing Ancestors

Most authorities have indicated that from the vast amount of palaeontological information available about the horse species, they are able to trace the development of the species during the past period of some 55 million years. The story is briefly set forth below.

Fossil remains of what are known, or presumed, to be evolving horses have been discovered in various parts of the world.

The remains of the first known ancestors of modern horse are referred to as fossil genus *Eohippus*. That term derives from the Greek words *eos* meaning "the dawn" and *hippus* meaning "horse". The particular animal is thus referred to as the "dawn horse".

We are told, among other things, that *Eohippus* stood at between 25cm and 35cm high; had broad, padded feet with four toes on each forefoot and three toes on each hindfoot (with vigital splints); had a small hoof on each of its toes; had short, low crowned, and simply arranged teeth, suitable for browsing on the soft and leafy herbage of the dense and steamy jungles of that time; had small eyes set low to the side of the head indicating that it was a hunted animal; and was enabled by its phalanges and its conformation to run efficiently over the soft, marshy ground and so flee from the large predators of the period.

Those "dawn horses" are said to have first appeared during the Eocene geological epoch (55 to 40 million years ago) in North America. They are said to have been followed late in the Eocene by *Orohippus*, a genera that was very similar to *Eohippus,* but slightly larger.

Two like genera, *Epihippus* and *Mesohippus*, followed *Orohippus*. The fossil records indicate that *Mesohippus* stood at between 50cm and 70cm high; had three toes on each foot and while all toes were functional, the lateral toes of each foot were slightly smaller than the middle toe, and, as a consequence , the animal's weight was borne more on the middle toe; had teeth that were still suitable for browsing, rather than grazing, but there were early signs of modification.

Other browsing groups followed *Mesohippus* and some of them travelled from the North American region to Europe and Asia. However, they all gradually became extinct.

Section 2.2
The Plain Grazing Ancestors

The gradual extinction of the browsing ancestors of modern horse and the emergence of the grazing ancestors was the result of the significant changes in climate and vegetation during the Miocene geological epoch (25 to 11 million years ago). Forests became larger and the plains more lush with grass.

The transition from browser to grazer was first discerned in fossil genera *Parahippus*, and was more clearly perceived in its descendant *Merychippus*.

Records indicate that *Parahippus* stood on average about 95cm high and had a long, straight back. Compared with its ancestors, there was a marked change in the lower leg. The central toe on each foot had become enlarged and the external or lateral toes had become smaller. Dentition had changed to allow for grazing on the grasslands in addition to browsing in the forests.

Merychippus evolved from *Parahippus* and horses of the genera were the first ancestors of modern horse to take to the plains and become predominantly grazing animals. From the records we are told that *Merychippus* was larger than its ancestor; bore its weight on the middle toe of each foot; had small and useless lateral toes; and had dentition suitable for grazing.

Merychippus was followed down the evolutionary line by *Pliohippus* which appeared in the Lower Pliocene Age (11 to 2 million years ago). *Pliohippus* stood at about 115cm; was more angular than its ancestors; had a single hoof on each foot with the lateral toes reduced to almost vestiges; had a longer neck than its ancestors; and its eyes were located further back in its skull.

Section 2.3
The First True Horse

The next evolutionary step was from *Pliohippus* to *Equus* the first true horse.

Equus emerged at the beginning of the Pleistocene Age about 2 million years ago. During that age there were alternating ice ages and warm periods until planet Earth's present climate and landscape gradually developed. *Equus* was an adaptive species and withstood the extremes of climate.

Equus is thought to have originated in North America and migrated to South America. It also migrated across the land bridge that then connected North America and Asia, to parts of Asia, Europe, and Africa.

Section 2.4
Summary of Evolutionary Changes

There are no fossil records of ancestors of the dawn horse, *Eohippus*, but it is presumed to have evolved from stock having the mammalian type appendages of five fingers and five toes.

Fossil records from *Eohippus* to modern horse, *Equus* (in fact more than 260 species are said to have been identified and named), indicate the changes that occurred in the bodily structure of horse species during "cause and effect" processes spread over 55 million years.

Included in the changes in body structure were the following: the size of the body increased; the limb structure developed and became elongated; the neck and skull lengthened; the extremities of the limbs simplified; the body weight was transferred to the centre toe pad which became greatly strengthened and formed into a hoof; and the teeth and their arrangement distinctly altered. All such changes were designed to benefit the functions of the horse — its fleetness of foot, its ingestion of food, and so on.

PART 2 THE FAMILY OF THE HORSE

CHAPTER 3 RECENT ANCESTRY OF MODERN HORSE

Section 3.1
Restriction of Horses to Regions

During the millions of years of evolution, species of animals that were developing into true horses, and later, true horses themselves, undertook long and treacherous migrations. These migrations would not have been for adventure, but rather as a consequence of sheer necessity, for example, the need for young animals to move from over-populated areas and seek their own less populated areas, or for animals to move from areas where climatic conditions were unsuitable and to seek warmer climates.

Progressive immense changes to the Earth's surface established natural boundaries (mountains, deserts, or seas) that acted as barriers to migration and so restricted animals to the region of their origin, or to the region to which they had migrated. Some of the significant changes in this regard were as follows: the sinking about 2 million years ago of the isthmus between Asia and North America that had existed for 90 million years; the formation of the Himalayas about 25 million years ago; the formation of the Sahara Desert; the sinking and later rising of land linking North and South America; separation of Australia from Asia; and so on.

Regions to which animals were confined by natural boundaries are referred to as zoogeographical regions, each being distinguished from others in the nature of its fauna and flora. The zoogeographical regions are as follows:

Nearctic Region: Greenland and North America down to central Mexico.

Neotropical Region: South America, Central America, and the Antilles.

Palearctic Region: Europe, Africa north of the Sahara Desert, and Asia north of the Himalayan Mountains.

Oriental Region: Asia south of the Himalayan Mountains and the archipelagos of Sunda, Borneo, and the Phillipines.

Ethiopian Region: Africa south of the Sahara Desert.

Australasian Region: Australia, New Zealand, New Guinea, and other neighbouring islands of the South Pacific Ocean.

Such scientific subdivision of the Earth into zoogeographical regions is based on a scheme documented by Alfred Russel Wallace who was a contemporary of the English naturalist, Charles Darwin, during the mid-nineteenth century.

Section 3.2
Exclusive Ancestors of Modern Horse

As indicated earlier, genera *Equus*, the first true horse, originated in what is now called the Nearctic Region, but its descendants became extinct in that region and also in the Neotropical Region some 10000 years ago. Neither *Equus*. nor any of its descendants, migrated to the Australasian Region. Hence the exclusive ancestors of modern horse were the descendants of *Equus* that inhabited the Palaearctic, Oriental, and Ethiopian regions.

Section 3.3
Adaptation of Horses to Regional Environment

The changes that established natural boundaries to regions of the world and restricted the migration of animals between regions, also brought about changes in regional environmental elements, particularly in climate, terrain, altitude, soil, vegetation, and nutritious value of such vegetation. Animals therefore adapted and evolved according to the environment of the region to which they were restricted.

Long before man domesticated the horse there would have been many types and variations of the horse species. Physical differences would have been due to adaptation of different ecotypes of horses to local environment and also to natural breeding — all types of horses can successfully interbreed.

Section 3.4
Many Types and Breeds, but Only One Ancestral Type

After domestication, man interfered with natural breeding by breeding for specific purposes, that is, selective breeding.

Today there are many types and breeds of horses and there are some significant differences in size, shape, colour, performance, temperament, and so on among them. It is generally accepted that all such types and breeds descended from one ancestral type being a descendant of *Equus*, the first true horse.

PART 2 THE FAMILY OF THE HORSE

CHAPTER 4 **MODERN HORSE**

Section 4.1
Members of the Horse Family

All hoofed, herbivorous mammals, including the horse, are zoologically grouped into a division of order *Herbivora*, called *Ungulata*. Ungulates typically have only one or two toes, the even-toed group being called *Artiodactyla*, and the odd-toed group (including the horse) *Perissodactyla*. Species of *Perissodactyla* are subclassified as follows:

- suborder   *Ceratomorpha*, with the families *Tapirdae* (tapirs) and *Rhinocerotidae* (rhinoceroses).
- suborder   *Hippomorpha*, with the single family *Equidae* (horses, asses, and zebras).

The many members of the horse family, *Equidae*, are descendants of *Equus*, the first true horse. Having originated in a particular country or countries, they may today be found throughout the world. They are called by various common, colloquial, or vernacular, names according to the country of location. However, for scientific purposes, they are grouped and identified as follows:

Horses:	Domestic horses	*Equus caballus*
	Mongolian wild horses	*Equus caballus przewalski*
	Tarpans	*Equus caballus gomelini*
Asses:	Asian asses	*Equus hermionus*
	East African asses	*Equus asinus*
	Onagers	*Equus hermionus onager*
Zebras:	South African mountain zebras	*Equus zebra*
	African common zebras	*Equus burchelli*
	Central East African zebras	*Equus grevyi*
	South African quaggas	*Equus quagga*

All species of *Equidae* referred to in the above table are capable of successful crossbreeding but because the various species have different numbers of chromosomes in body cells, some crossbred offspring are sterile (for example, the mule and the hinny).

Section 4.2
Domestic Horses

The species *Equus caballus* includes all breeds and types of domestic horse in existence today.

The term "breed" means a relatively homogeneous (essentially alike) group of animals within a species, developed and maintained by man along strict blood-lines, and registered in a stud book. It may also mean a group of animals indigenous to a particular country and having purebred bloodlines and characteristics constant throughout generations.

All modern breeds must trace from the primitive prehistoric horses but the division of horses into pedigreed breeds, that is, into breeds in which individuals have a recorded line of descent from purebred ancestry, is comparatively recent, say, up to a century ago.

The term "type" means a group of horses developed and maintained by man, through a mixture of selected bloodlines, for a particular purpose, but perhaps not meeting strict definitions of a stud book. Some types may become breeds and, indeed, in the past have done so.

Long before domestication of the horse there would have been many variations of the species. Since domestication man has, by selective breeding, developed an enormous range of horses having special qualities and characteristics to meet man's special needs. Those qualities and characteristics include such things as size, shape, height, strength, stamina, endurance, hardiness, speed, agility, temperament, colour, beauty, and so on.

In all there are about 200 breeds and 300 types of domestic horse in existence today. They are categorised as follows:

CATEGORY	APPROXIMATE No.
Heavy	45
Heavy/Light	5
Light	250
Light/Pony	15
Pony	185
	500

Section 4.3
The Heavy Horse

The heavy or draught breeds, being suited to pull loads, were once the workhorses of the world and a very important factor in the economies of many countries. They became redundant in the early part of the twentieth century. However, a few farmers still use them as workhorses, a few breweries use them for publicity purposes, and in at least one country they have until recently been bred for meat. Generally they are now bred for hobby or pleasure purposes.

Most of the heavy breeds are known as "cold bloods". They are delineated from light horses by size, their conformation being for strength as opposed to speed. Some breeds can be categorised as either heavy horse or light horse.

Section 4.4
The Light Horse

Most of today's horse breeds are light horses and are referred to as saddle or harness breeds. They are known as "hot bloods", or, as the case may be, "warm bloods". Some breeds can be known as either light horse or pony.

Section 4.5
The Pony

Horses and ponies are members of the same species, *Equus caballus*, but most breed authorities impose an artificial height distinction, classing equines standing 147cm (14.2 hands) or under at the withers as ponies and those standing in excess of that height as horses.

Notwithstanding the general height distinction, an Arab is always referred to as a horse, regardless of height, and an equine used for polo is always called a pony. A polo pony is a type, rather than a breed.

Some breeds that do not breed true may be classed as either horse or pony.

Section 4.6
Hot Bloods, Cold Bloods, Warm Bloods

These generic terms do not refer to the actual blood temperatures of horse breeds and types, but rather, for practical purposes, describe the temperament of such breeds and types.

The heavy horses that are stolid with calm, even, temperaments are called the "cold bloods".

The light horses, such as the Arab and the thoroughbred, that exhibit a marked degree of vigour or adventure are called the "hot bloods".

The mix of light and light/heavy horses, including the majority of riding horses and performance horses (the hunters, the showjumpers, and the eventers), are called "warm bloods".

In some countries, but not all, the terms in question are used to signify the amount of Arab or thoroughbred blood in the immediate ancestry of particular breeds or types.

The overlaps between the groups of hot bloods, cold bloods, and warm bloods, is fine and largely a matter of personal opinion.

PART 3
USE OF THE HORSE

Chapter	5	Use of the Horse Before Mechanisation
Section	5.1	Domestication of the Horse
	5.2	Early Use of the Horse For Draught Purposes
	5.3	Early Use of the Horse For Riding Purposes
	5.4	First Use of the Horse In Warfare
	5.5	Early Principles of Training And Riding
	5.6	Invention of Saddle and Stirrup
	5.7	The Age of Chivalry
	5.8	The Renaissance Period
	5.9	Recodification of Principles of Training and Riding
	5.10	Horse Phased Out of Warfare
	5.11	Famous Chargers
Chapter	6	Use of the Horse in Australia
Section	6.1	Horses Not Indigenous to Australia
	6.2	Horses Imported to Meet Needs of Colony
	6.3	The Waler or Australian Stock Horse
	6.4	The Australian Pony
	6.5	Brumbies
Chapter	7	Use of the Horse in Modern Life
Section	7.1	Transition from Utilitarian Need to Recreational Use
	7.2	Hunts and Point-to-Point Racing
	7.3	Jump Racing in Britain and Ireland
	7.4	Jump Racing in Australia
	7.5	Harness Racing

CHAPTER 5 USE OF THE HORSE BEFORE MECHANISATION

Section 5.1
Domestication of the Horse

During the Old Stone Age, humans were mainly supplied with what was necessary to sustain life, by the animals they hunted and killed and by the plants they gathered. They lived a nomadic or semi-nomadic way of life following the animals as they travelled searching for suitable climate and vegetation.

During the New Stone Age, which followed the last Ice Age and covered the period from about 10 000 to 6000 years ago, men profoundly modified their way of life. They ceased being wandering hunters and gatherers and began living settled lives as herders and growers.

In the course of settlement men domesticated various animals, including sheep, goats, pigs, cattle, and horses. Some experts postulate that domestication of the horse took place in North-east Europe and Central Asia between 7000 to 5000 years ago when the horse would have been no more than a small shaggy pony somewhat like the Mongolian wild horse. How, when, or where such domestication actually occurred, however, is not precisely known.

Section 5.2
Early Use of the Horse for Draught Purposes

The first use of the horse as a working animal was for draught purposes, pulling various kinds of vehicles for the conveyance of man and his chattels. Early vehicles were mounted on runners such as sleds, sledges, and sleighs, but after the invention of the wheel some 4000 years ago, various vehicles mounted on wheels were developed.

Chariots, drawn by horses wearing a light breast-girth, were used in warfare some centuries before chariot racing became a popular sport in Rome about 2000 years ago. Chariot races may well have been more dangerous than war itself, and were made even more hazardous at the early Olympiads by the introduction of many distractions designed to frighten horses.

The use of the horse for draught purposes was revolutionised by the development of the simple horsecollar about 1000 years ago.

Throughout the horse era, the harnessed horse pulled or hauled all sorts of implements and vehicles for all kinds of purposes — for agriculture, commerce, trade, travel, warfare, and so on.

Section 5.3
Early Use of the Horse for Riding Purposes

The first pictorial record of man riding a horse was found in the tomb of Horemheb, an Egyptian pharaoh who died about 3300 years ago.

After the Egyptians, the next recorded horsemen were the Assyrians, and records dated about 2800 years ago indicate that they rode the horse by sitting in the centre of its back. Other notable early horsemen were the Persians, Scythians, and the Greeks.

Section 5.4
First Use of the Horse in Warfare

There is evidence that the horse was used from very early times in providing fighting man with transport and communication. This subsidiary role eventually changed to one of cavalry dominance, the first such dominant use being thought to have been by Hannibal, a Carthaginian general 2200 years ago.

Section 5.5
Early Principles of Training and Riding

We are told that cuneiform tablets of the Hittites, dated about 3500 years ago, recorded principles established by Kikkulis, horsemaster to their kings, about the feeding and training of horses. Kikkulis counselled the use of kindness, rather than force.

We are also told that the first available documentation on the art of equitation (training and riding the horse) are two manuals (called "Hippike" and "Hippaarchikos") written by a Greek general named Xenophon about 2400 years ago. In his manuals, Xenophon quoted from earlier equitation manuals written by Simon of Athens and Plinius, but those documents have been lost to antiquity.

The training methods of the ancient Greeks were based on such things as intuition, psychology, patience, understanding, and kindness.

After the fall of the Greek Empire the kind and intuitive training methods of the ancient Greeks were generally replaced by cruel methods under which the training process was looked upon as a contest of strength between man and horse. In most cases man overpowered and outwitted the horse and broke its spirit: the horse was "broken-in".

Section 5.6
Invention of Saddle and Stirrup

At the time Xenophon compiled his manuals the horse rider had a great disadvantage in that the saddle had not been invented: man rode the horse bareback or used only a cloth or pad for protection from sweat or chafing. It was not until about 1600 years ago that the saddle came into use. It was first used by mercenary Nubian soldiers from the Nile Valley and was made of cured skin, built high at both pommel and canticle to form a seat, and was held in position by a girth strap.

About 1000 years ago came the invention of the stirrup and its first known use was by the Huns of Mongolia.

The saddle and stirrup made it much easier to ride the horse and following their inventions the use of the horse by man accelerated.

Section 5.7
The Age of Chivalry

During the medieval period (that is, the time in European history between classical antiquity and the Italian Renaissance) about 1500 to 500 years ago, the system of knighthood was instituted and observed. This was indeed the age of the horse.

At first, when knights wore comparatively light chainmail armour and their horses wore only head protection, the light, aristocratic and speedy horse was in demand for jousts, tourneys and battle. This position continued until the Battle of Crecy (1346) when English use of the bow and arrow cut down the French troops.

Thereafter, as a protective measure, knights encased themselves almost completely in heavy, jointed metal plates. This increase in the weight of armour caused a demand for larger, heavier, and stronger horses to replace the light and speedy horse. Indeed, in England, laws were enacted forbidding the breeding of small, light horses.

The days of the slow-moving heavily-armoured knights came to an end at the Battle of Pavia (1525) following the development and introduction of gunpowder and firearms into warfare.

The new warfare led to men discarding cumbersome armour and the heavy horse was replaced with the light, manoeuvrable, and speedy horse.

Section 5.8
The Renaissance Period

The Renaissance period of between 500 to 400 years ago witnessed the development and recognition of more advanced equitation by, and for, royalty, the aristocracy, and the military.

From the Renaissance period onwards, riding schools sprang up all over Europe. These schools were mainly sponsored by the royal courts and were intended to provide training in the art of mounted warfare.

Section 5.9
Recodification of Principles of Training and Riding

Since Xenophon's time there continued to be great dedication to the art of equitation and about 300 years ago a Frenchman named Francios Robichon de la Gueriniere recodified the principles of classical equitation in his manual, *l'Ecole de Cavalarie*. That work became the basis of teaching of the great European riding schools, particularly of the Spanish Riding School in Vienna, which is still in existence.

Section 5.10
Horse Phased Out of Warfare

For more than 2000 years the horse played a significant role in the conduct of wars. As the circumstances and instruments of war changed from time to time during that period so did the needs of national armies change for suitable types of horses capable of meeting those circumstances. At one stage the heavy horses were required, at another, the light horses.

Eventually modern technology made horses redundant for war purposes and they were last used in the 1914 to 1918 World War.

Section 5.11
Famous Chargers

Famous chargers that were immortalised by their famous owners include Alexander the Great's "Bucephalus", which is the first warhorse known by name to history; Napoleon's "Marengo", a small grey Arab; and the Duke of Wellington's "Copenhagen", a chestnut thoroughbred.

CHAPTER 6 USE OF THE HORSE IN AUSTRALIA

Section 6.1
Horses Not Indigenous to Australia

There is no evidence that any members of fossil genus, *Equus*, the first true horse, or any of its descendants ever travelled to the Australasian zoogeographical region. No equine fossils have been found in the region. Indeed there were no horses in Australia when the first fleet of settlers arrived in 1788.

Section 6.2
Horses Imported to Meet Needs of Colony

Governor Phillip's fleet brought into Australia (or rather the Colony of New South Wales as it was then known) six horses of mixed breed that had been taken on board at the Cape of Good Hope. During the next few decades, some horses of similar breeding were imported from the same source while better-quality stock were imported from Great Britain, Persia, and India. The small numbers of imported stock thrived on the rich pastureland and warm climate and by the year 1820 had increased to some 5000 head.

Of the 400-odd stallions of all breeds imported in the first 100 years of the colony, most were thoroughbreds. Although the thoroughbreds were originally imported to improve the quality of the early stock of mixed breed, they were later imported solely for racing which soon became a regular and expanding sport.

Other imports over the years have included Arabs, Clydesdales, Percherons, Cleveland Bays, British Ponies, American Quarter Horses, American Trotters (Standardbreds), Appaloosas, and so on. The Clydesdales were imported from Great Britain to replace bullocks in meeting the needs of the expanding primary industries while Cleveland Bays were imported from the same source to improve the size and type of the carriage horses.

In Australia, as in many other countries, the horse became an essential part of man's activities in various fields - industry, warfare, sport and recreation. After the 1914 to 1918 World War, however, mechanisation replaced the horse for war purposes and, to a marked extent, in industry. Nevertheless, the horse is still an essential part of everyday life on pastoral properties and enjoys a prestigious position in the fields of sport and recreation.

Section 6.3
The Waler or Australian Stock Horse

From the mixed breeding lines of the stock that were imported in the early decades of the Colony of New South Wales there developed a good type of saddle horse. This horse was in demand, both in the colony as a stock horse and also as a cavalry remount for the British Army in India. It was called the "Waler" after the name of the colony.

Noted for its courage and endurance, some 120,000 Walers were exported to various countries for use by the allied armies during the 1914 to 1918 World War.

The name "Waler" was after some time replaced by the new name "Australian Stock Horse" and a separate breed was established under that name. Horses of that breed (the result of crossing hack mares with Arab, thoroughbred, or Anglo-Arab stallions) have many of the characteristics of the thoroughbred. They are good general-purpose saddle horses, however, their physique and height may vary considerably.

Section 6.4
The Australian Pony

A good type of pony, having intelligence, gameness, and endurance, and standing at 12 hands to 14 hands was developed in Australia. It stemmed mainly from imported Welsh Mountain and Arab stock with infusions of other bloods, including the thoroughbred.

Section 6.5
Brumbies

The brumby is a wild horse descended from domestic horses that escaped captivity or that were turned loose as unwanted during the mid-nineteenth century gold rush and, much later, early in the twentieth century as a consequence of the introduction of mechanisation. They thrived numerically and in time became pestilent, causing damage to pastures, fences, and water holes. Consequently, graziers took various steps to destroy them. As a result, there are few brumbies left today.

The origin of the term "brumby" is not known, but it is generally thought to have derived from one of three sources: the name of a pioneer horsebreeder, James Brumby; the name of a station and creek in Queensland, Baramba; or the Queensland Aboriginal word, *baroomby*, meaning "wild".

CHAPTER 7 USE OF THE HORSE IN MODERN LIFE

Section 7.1
Transition from Utilitarian Need to Recreational Use

With the gradual introduction of technological changes — mainly the advent of the steam and gasoline engines — man's dependence upon the horse as a workhorse disappeared. Man's love of the horse and its behavioural characteristics, and man's need of the horse for companionship, affection, recreation, sporting, and pleasure purposes, however, ensured that the horse as a leisurehorse was here to stay. As such, the horse now enjoys an important and popular position in modern life.

Man's contemporary use of the horse for sport at competitive, or non-competitive, level includes the following activities: flat racing (the main subject of this book); hunts and point-to-point racing; jump racing; harness racing; dressage; eventing; endurance racing; combined driving; show jumping; show hacking; show stud events; polo; polocrosse; rodeos; campdrafting; western riding; pony clubs; riding schools; mounted police patrols; and so on.

Because some Australian race clubs program mixed race meetings (flat races and jump races) we have a close, but brief, look at jump racing.

Section 7.2
Hunts and Point-To-Point Racing

Long ago man hunted wild animals out of sheer necessity — in order to live. When man changed his lifestyle from hunter to farmer, hunting ceased to be a necessity, but man continued to hunt a variety of game, simply for sport or profit.

Organised equestrian hunting, that is to say, the chase of game by mounted horsemen pursuing a pack of hounds, originated in Great Britain and, in time, spread to other countries.

Nowadays live quarry has been replaced by the drag for the purposes of the chase. A material with aniseed, or some other aromatic substance, is dragged over a course to leave an artificial scent for the hounds to follow.

In Australia, hunting clubs and fraternities are mainly located in the southern States.

Some recognised hunt clubs conduct point-to-point steeplechase meetings in a rural atmosphere over cross-country courses during the winter season. The term "steeplechase" is derived from the name given in eighteenth century Britain to match races from a starting point to the distant steeple of the village church.

Any horse trained and used for hunting may be called "a hunter". Various types having the required conformation, weight-carrying and jumping ability, and other essential qualities have been developed. The thoroughbred, or certain thoroughbred crosses, are usually suitable.

Section 7.3
Jump Racing in Britain and Ireland

Jump racing over hurdles or fences on public racecourses developed in Britain during the first-half of the nineteenth century directly from the sport of hunting. Today, in that country, national hunt racing, as it is called, is conducted during the winter months and attracts almost as large a following as flat racing does. While Newmarket remains exclusively a centre for flat racing, Cheltenham is its jumping counterpart. Some clubs, however, promote both codes of racing and hold mixed meetings during the spring and autumn.

The world's greatest steeplechase, first run in 1839, is the Grand National Steeplechase which is run over 4.5 miles (7.2 km) at the unique course at Aintree, near Liverpool, in England.

While jump racing (national hunt racing) thrives in Britain and Ireland, it has never really caught on in other countries although some countries provide limited opportunities for the jumpers.

Section 7.4
Jump Racing in Australia

Some race clubs in Victoria, South Australia, and Tasmania, conduct mixed meetings, comprising one or two jumping races and five or so flat races, during the wet autumn and winter months. The jumping races may be programmed for open, or restricted, class jumpers according to conditions set forth in the approved programs.

In hurdle races the obstacles are wooden frame hurdles, one metre in height. These races are run over distances varying from a minimum of 2800m up to, and sometimes in excess of, 5000m.

In steeplechases the obstacles are brush fences, not less than 1.15 metres in height. These races are run over distances varying from a minimum of 3200m up to, and sometimes in excess of, 5000m.

In hurdle and steeplechase handicap races the minimum top weight is 67kg and the bottom limit weight 60kg, except in races for more than a prescribed amount of prize money, in which case the bottom limit weight is 57kg.

Horses competing in hurdle races and steeplechases are thoroughbreds, usually six years or older which do not possess the speed or the pace necessarily required for flat races, but which are suited by their high weights, slow running, and the long distances of such events.

The main jumping races are the Grand National Hurdle Race and the Grand National Steeplechase run at Flemington, Melbourne, in mid-winter.

Section 7.5
Harness Racing

Trotting and pacing races are contested by Standardbred horses harnessed to a special light two-wheeled sulky from which the driver exercises control. The distinction between trotting and pacing is that a trotter moves its legs in diagonal pairs whereas the pacer moves its legs in lateral pairs.

Standardbreds, a term derived from the standard that was used to test their ability before registration, were developed as a breed in North America during the eighteenth century. The foundation sire of the breed was "Messenger", an imported English thoroughbred which was a descendant of "Darley Arabian". Standardbreds have had a great influence on trotting strains world wide.

Harness racing clubs conduct day or night meetings all year-round. The sport is very popular.

PART 4
EARLY HISTORY OF THE THOROUGHBRED

Chapter	8	Development of the Thoroughbred
Section	8.1	The Thoroughbred's Progenitor — The Arab
	8.2	Foundation Sires
	8.3	Foundation Dams
	8.4	The First General Stud Book
	8.5	Spread of the Thoroughbred
	8.6	Derivation of Term "Thoroughbred"
	8.7	Terms "Thoroughbred" and "Racehorse" Synonymous
	8.8	Use of Thoroughbred Other Than for Racing
	8.9	Use of Thoroughbred for Improving Other Breeds

PART 4 EARLY HISTORY OF THE THOROUGHBRED

CHAPTER 8 DEVELOPMENT OF THE THOROUGHBRED

Section 8.1
The Thoroughbred's Progenitor — The Arab

Origins of the Arab are unknown, but cave drawings in Egypt and China indicate that it existed some 7000 years ago.

The Arab was established as a breed centuries before any other. It is native to Arabia and is allied with, or closely related to, the Barb breed of the Barbary Coast and the Turk breed of Turkey. The Arab, Barb and Turk breeds are referred to as the "Ancient Eastern Breeds".

Conformation of the Arab is unique and symmetrical. Indeed, quality is everywhere in evidence in the Arab.

Records indicate that the Eastern breeds were imported into Britain early in the thirteenth century, during the reign of King John, and at various times during subsequent centuries, particularly during the reigns of James I and Charles II, in the seventeenth century.

The importation of the Eastern horses into Britain at various times was because of the changing nature of warfare, the needs of royalty and the aristocracy, the delights of hunting and racing, and so on.

The Arab breed has proven prepotency and the ability to "nick" with almost all other breeds. Having the gift of absolute breeding dominance, it has been most influential in light horse breeding. Most breeds of light horse were either originally based on, or improved directly or indirectly by, Arab blood. It is best known for its creation of the thoroughbred.

Section 8.2
Foundation Sires

Eastern stallions that were imported into Britain and contributed to the making of the thoroughbred breed included the following:

- "Byerley Turk"
- "Darley Arabian"
- "Godolphin Arabian"
- "Helnsley Turk"
- "Lister Turk"
- "Leedes Arabian"
- "Darcy White Turk"
- "Darcy Yellow Turk"
- "Alcock Arabian" (from which every grey thoroughbred has descended).

While those and other stallions imported to Britain from the East played a part in the development of the thoroughbred, the greatest contribution in that regard was made by the "Byerley Turk", the "Darley Arabian", and the "Godolphin Arabian". Those three stallions are referred to as the founding fathers because all thoroughbreds in the world today trace their ancestry in direct male line back to them.

The "Byerley Turk" arrived in Britain in 1689. This charger had been captured from the Turks at the Battle of Buda by Captain (later Colonel) Byerley who, on his retirement from the army, put him to stud. The Byerley Turk was the great-great-grandsire of "Herod" (or properly "King Herod") the horse that was an immensely successful racehorse and sire. One of Herod's sons, "Highflyer", was just as successful as his sire. (His owner, Richard Tattersall, was the founder of a famous British firm of bloodstock auctioneers.)

The "Darley Arabian" was imported to Britain in 1704 by Thomas Darley who at that time held the office of British Consul in Aleppo. The "Darley Arabian" was successful with his first-generation progeny, siring "Flying Childers" who was the first truly great racehorse. Through "Bartletts' Childers" (brother of "Flying Childers") the "Darley Arabian" became the great-great-grandsire of "Eclipse", famous racehorse and sire.

The "Godolphin Arabian", sometimes called the "Godolphin Barb", was foaled in Syria. He was imported by Edward Coke from France in 1729 and later sold to Lord Godolphin who had a stud at Cambridge. This stallion became the grandsire of the famous "Matchem".

In turn, "Herod", "Eclipse", and "Matchem" (descendant stallions of the three foundation sires, the "Byerley Turk", the "Darley Turk", and the "Godolphin Arabian") dominated the development of the thoroughbred and established outstanding male lines that are of paramount importance in thoroughbred breeding.

Section 8.3
Foundation Dams

Before the three founding stallions were imported there already existed fine galloping horses in Britain — some of them having Eastern or part-Eastern blood. From such fine horses mares having high qualities were selected for service by the great sires.

While there is no precise information on the breeding of the selected mares, the quality of their progeny is proof enough of their high breeding.

Section 8.4
The First General Stud Book

Development of the thoroughbred continued at an outstanding rate, and by the end of the eighteenth century it had been established as an independent breed. Records had not been kept systematically, however, and a properly kept stud book was necessary. At the direction of the British Jockey Club, the first General Stud Book was prepared by James Weatherby who was also the Keeper of the Match Book and publisher of the

Racing Calendar on behalf of the Club. Since then the book has been kept up to date by the family firm of Weatherby.

Section 8.5
Spread of the Thoroughbred

Conjointly with the development and racing of the thoroughbred in England, there developed throughout the world a growing interest in, and demand for, the breed. Bloodstock auction sales held in England began to attract international buyers and, for the next 50 years, Britain did an enormous trade in thoroughbred exports to almost every country in the world.

In many countries having the required equable, temperate climate, breeding has been very successful. To meet the special demands of the local markets, breeders in those countries have developed different characteristics in the breed.

The standard of performances accordingly varies from country to country.

Section 8.6
Derivation of Term "Thoroughbred"

While considerable Arab blood was bred into the line at first, thoroughbreds are now exclusively bred with one another.

The word "thoroughbred" derives from the literal translation of the Arabic *Kehilan* which is a generic term for the Arabian breed and means "pure-bred all through".

Section 8.7
Terms "Thoroughbred" and "Racehorse" Synonymous

Worldwide many breeds and types of horses are raced against each other in widely diverse contests of speed or endurance, and indeed have been so raced for thousands of years. Any horse bred and kept for racing in any form thus comes within the meaning of the word "racehorse". The designation truly belongs to the thoroughbred, the fastest horse in the world, however, and today the terms "thoroughbred" and "racehorse" are used synonymously.

Section 8.8
Use of Thoroughbred Other Than For Racing

The thoroughbred was primarily bred as a racehorse and indeed is the fastest horse in the world. As indicated elsewhere in this book, however, the majority of thoroughbreds foaled each year are not suitable (for one reason or another) for highly competitive racing. Nevertheless, being a fine riding horse and possessing such characteristics as versatility, courage, and stamina, the thoroughbred excels at most forms of equestrian sport or activity. Many are, therefore, sold as potential hacks, hunters, polo ponies, and so on. Because of their temperament they are generally not suitable for classical dressage or for hobby horses for novices.

Section 8.9
Use of Thoroughbred for Improving Other Breeds

Thoroughbreds have been widely used throughout the world as foundation stock or to improve native breeds. In this regard it is second only to its progenitor, the Arab. Nearly all strains of sporting horse have been infused with thoroughbred quality.

PART 5

BLOODSTOCK (THOROUGHBRED) BREEDERS

Chapter	9	Breeders
Section	9.1	Categories of Breeders
	9.2	Productivity Efficiency
	9.3	Ownership of Stud Stallions
	9.4	Financial Viability of Breeders
	9.5	Annual Auction Sales of Yearlings
	9.6	Mixed Auction Sales
	9.7	Bloodhorse Breeders' Association of Australia
	9.8	Bonus or Incentive Schemes
Chapter	10	Stud Farms
Section	10.1	Simple Breeding in the Wild
	10.2	Complex Breeding on the Stud Farm
	10.3	Management of Mares and Foals
	10.4	Stud Farm Personnel

PART 5 BLOODSTOCK (THOROUGHBRED) BREEDERS

CHAPTER 9 BREEDERS

Section 9.1
Categories of Breeders

Bloodstock (ie. thoroughbred) breeders may be categorised under three general headings: full-time professional breeders; part-time or semi-professional breeders; and non-commercial, casual, or hobby breeders.

Full-time professional breeders are those who own a stud and whose business is solely or predominantly the production of yearlings for sale at the annual yearling sales and the provision of stallion and care services to mares not owned by the stud.

The category, part-time or semi-professional breeders, includes those who own a property and a limited number of stud stock and who conduct a breeding business in conjunction with an agricultural, pastoral, or other business. Such breeders may own a stallion or put their mares to outside stallions.

The third category, non-commercial, casual, or hobby breeders, includes those who own one or two broodmares, agist them on a property, pay for stallion services, and breed one or two foals each year for their own racing enjoyment, sale, or leasing out.

Section 9.2
Productivity Efficiency

Reproduction is the ongoing natural process of biological events whereby individuals generate new individuals and perpetuate the species. Reproductive efficiency is said by veterinarians to be lower in the equine than other species of farm animals, and lower in the thoroughbred than other breeds of equines.

Productivity in the thoroughbred breeding industry may be measured by a number of indicators. From an efficiency viewpoint an acceptable measure, however, is the percentage of live foals produced annually and the soundness of such foals for the purpose for which they were bred.

Published results about research findings relative to past breeding seasons indicate that of all mares covered in a season, about 35 per cent failed to produce live foals, 35 per cent produced foals that, for one reason or another, were not introduced into racing, and only 30 per cent produced foals that were later introduced into racing and actually raced.

Section 9.3
Ownership of Stud Stallions

A stud stallion may be owned by a person in his own right or a group or association of persons. Indeed most highly valued stallions are owned by an association of persons called a "syndicate" under conditions set forth in the syndicate agreement.

An important source of income of breeders who own and stand stallions is the service fee charged to the owners of outside broodmares. Fees vary according to the quality and popularity of the stallion, and also to the locality where the stallion is standing. Leading sires command very high service fees and only selected high quality mares are accepted for service. Stallions which are highly in demand could be expected to serve about 50 mares in a season.

Section 9.4
Financial Viability of Breeders

Income of the professional breeder mainly comprises: the aggregate return from the annual sale of yearlings produced by the stud's own herd of mares; receipts from bonus or incentive schemes of the Bloodhorse Breeders' Association of Australia; fees for stallion services to outside mares; and care and agistment of outside mares.

Capital and operating costs are high and depend on such things as: location of the stud property; number and quality of stud stock; number and quality of staff; quality of soil and grass pasture; climatic conditions; rainfall; water supply; state of buildings, fences, plant and equipment, and so on.

Being in a professional breeding business requires large monetary outlays for the acquiring and maintaining of assets, including livestock. It also requires specialised knowledge, skill, understanding, patience, and certain other high qualifications. In some cases it may have significant rewards in money and achievement. In others, monetary rewards may be small, if any.

Section 9.5
Annual Auction Sales of Yearlings

Auction sales of yearlings are conducted by bloodstock agents early each calendar year. At time of sale the youngsters are about sixteen to eighteen months old. Particulars of stock being offered for sale are set forth in the auctioneer's catalogue which lists the yearlings by lot numbers. Potential buyers may, before auction date, inspect the lots in which they may be interested at the vendors' studs or at the auctioneer's stables.

Selling prices of the draft of yearlings offered at auction depend upon the demand by buyers, that is to say, the desire of buyers to purchase and possess, coupled with their purchasing power at time of auction. Factors affecting such market demand include: the assessed quality of the stock in terms of bloodlines, soundness, and potential; and general influences such as the general economic situation, prize money and other incentives, and prevailing climatic conditions. Demand goes up and down with the economic cycle.

Section 9.6
Mixed Auction Sales

While most of the yearlings sold in Australia in any year pass through the annual yearling sales ring between late December and Easter, some are offered for sale at mixed auction sales up until June. Other stock offered at mixed auction sales held throughout the year may include weanlings, two-year-olds, all-aged stock, broodmares, tried racehorses, or untried stock.

Section 9.7
Bloodhorse Breeders' Association of Australia

The Bloodhorse Breeders' Association of Australia is an Australia-wide organisation with a division in each State and a Federal Council.

The BBAA is the official organisation of breeders. It provides a unified approach by its members in the protection and promotion of their interests in all facets of the breeding industry. It is recognised by Federal and State governments and all sections of the racing industry.

Section 9.8
Bonus or Incentive Schemes

Some State bonus or incentive schemes have been established and maintained by the respective governments, Principal Clubs or divisions of Bloodhorse Breeders' Associations of those States for any one or more of the following purposes:

(a) to promote the State breeding industry generally;

(b) to benefit breeders by increasing demand for their stallions and the progeny of those stallions;

(c) to provide financial reward to breeders and stallion owners whose produce are successful in their racing careers;

(d) to benefit owners by the provision of added prize money for specified races; and so on.

These schemes provide broadly for the establishment and maintenance of a fund; registration by participating breeders and owners of stallions of their produce of weanlings; the payment into the fund by such breeders and owners, of weanling registration fees; grants to the fund by the State Government from racing revenue; and in cases where horses registered under a particular scheme win specified races, payments out of the fund to the racehorse owner, breeder, or stallion owner as the case might be.

Yearlings registered under any such scheme are indicated in annual yearling sales catalogues.

PART 5 BLOODSTOCK (THOROUGHBRED) BREEDERS

CHAPTER 10 **STUD FARMS**

Section 10.1
Simple Breeding in the Wild

In the wild and natural way of equine living, the stallion and his harem of mares maintained close social bonds throughout their lives. Under the influence of evolutionary forces, mares became sexually ripe only in spring and summer so that foals were born some eleven months later during a season that provided optimal chances of survival. The stallion determined when one of his mares was sexually ripe by observing her oestrous straddle, smelling her heat odour, and finally confirming her sexual state by taste. Mating took place only when the stallion was satisfied that the mare was in a conducive state.

Section 10.2
Complex Breeding on the Stud Farm

A stud farm is any property where thoroughbreds are bred and raised.

Stud farm mating procedure bears little resemblance to the natural mating of the wild horses. For many reasons, on a thoroughbred stud farm, the stallion is isolated from his mares, confined to a special paddock, housed in a special stable, and given a special diet. He may be taken out of his confined area for the purpose of being exercised by being led or ridden around the stud farm. The mares run in temporary, arbitrarily selected groups — the barren; the pregnant; and the mothers with foals at foot. Weanlings or yearlings run in groups according to sex, colts in one group and fillies in another.

As a result of necessity, breeders have altered the environment. Such interference with natural conditions entails the use of unnatural procedures such as hormonal treatment and teasing mares in an attempt to bring them to a state conducive to mating.

Section 10.3
Management of Mares and Foals

The temperate climate of Australian breeding areas allows horses to be bred and reared in the open for most of the year. That condition of living may be referred to as "grass-kept" or "pasture-kept", but such terms do not accurately describe the position because mares and foals kept on pasture are usually provided regularly with supplemental food to meet their specific requirements and to meet any deficiency that may exist in pasture herbage. They are usually kept in suitable, properly fenced fields; provided with a constant supply of clean water, shelter sheds, and suitable facilities for extra feeding; and inspected regularly to ensure that all are present and sound. Conditions vary according to district and latitude, and there are times when the mares and foals are necessarily stabled or rugged. Rugs are usually waterproofed, warmly lined, and carefully fitted.

The free-ranging open-air system is greatly advantageous when compared with the stable-confinement system. The open-air system allows for greater freedom and a more natural herd existence in which social bonds are less seriously interrupted. Confinement to stables for long periods is unnatural, unhealthy, and expensive, involving capital and recurrent costs.

Section 10.4
Stud Farm Personnel

The professional manager of a stud farm, that is, the studmaster, needs to be highly qualified in the many subjects associated with bloodhorse breeding, marketing, and racing; and with farm, business and personnel management. It is also important that this person be of good fame and repute in racing industry circles.

The studmaster cannot be expected to know and do all things. Consequently, assistance of specialised services, from a studman, foreman, farmer, farrier, trainer, and other supporting staff is required.

Stud farms also need the services of an equine veterinary surgeon. In this regard they may employ a veterinarian as a permanent member of the staff; have a veterinarian in residence full-time only during the busy breeding and foaling season; or may arrange for visits from a local practitioner. Much of the veterinarian's work is of a routine, preventive nature.

PART 6

BLOODSTOCK (THOROUGHBRED) BREEDING

Chapter	11	Breeding Methods
Section	11.1	Introduction
	11.2	Selective Breeding
	11.3	Inbreeding
	11.4	Linebreeding
	11.5	Outbreeding
	11.6	Breeding Nicks
Chapter	12	Basic Genetic Concepts
Section	12.1	Introduction
	12.2	Composition of Horse's Body
	12.3	Body Cells
	12.4	Chromosomes
	12.5	Genes
	12.6	Transmission of Heredity
	12.7	Heredity and Environment
	12.8	Estimating Heredity and Environmental Factors
Chapter	13	Improvement Through Genetics
Section	13.1	Chance Supersedes Science in Breeding
	13.2	Herd Improvement Through Genetics
	13.3	Locating Superior Individuals
	13.4	Pedigrees
	13.5	Genetic Importance of Ancestors
	13.6	Relative Importance of Sire and Dam
	13.7	Relationship of Offspring

CHAPTER 11 BREEDING METHODS

Section 11.1
Introduction

In the early years of horse breeding the general principle followed by horse breeders was that as like tends to beget like, the best must be bred to the best to produce superior stock.

For that reason, during the seventeenth century, outstanding horses were imported into England from the East and mated with outstanding native horses. This method of breeding proved quite effective. Later, during the period of development of the English thoroughbred, outstanding animals were produced by improved breeding procedures.

Today the simply stated principle "breed the best to the best" is still valid. Unfortunately, in practice, many breeders breed the best they have to the best they have or can afford. Methods used by breeders to improve herds include: selective breeding; inbreeding; linebreeding; and outbreeding.

Section 11.2
Selective breeding

Natural selection is the breeding method of nature whereby, in the struggle for existence, the unfit are eliminated and the fittest are singled out for reproduction and perpetuation resulting in the adaptation of types within a species to a specific environment. In its selection process, nature seeks to breed the most vigorous individuals.

Artificial selection is the breeding method practised by man whereby man seeks to concentrate desirable genes in a population for his specific purposes (such as speed, movement, or colour). This he does by the selection of superior animals possessing the desirable traits for the breeding purpose and eliminating the inferior.

Section 11.3
Inbreeding

Inbreeding is the production of offspring by the mating of closely related horses. The closer the relationship of the parents then the higher is the degree of inbreeding in the offspring. Severe inbreeding is usually referred to as "closebreeding".

The purpose of inbreeding is to develop a genetically superior line by concentrating desirable genes in a herd and then, by selective mating, greatly increasing the frequency of pairs of genes that are identical. Inbreeding increases breeding purity and, accompanied by selective mating, consistently produces similar offspring.

Unfortunately, inbreeding can be a very dangerous and costly practice because often undesirable genes are increased rather than the desirable genes and this causes the accentuation of genetic defects, rather than the sought-after high quality traits. In such

A full-time thoroughbred breeder conducts a breeding business primarily or solely for the production of yearlings. On the other hand a part-time breeder conducts a breeding business in conjunction with a pastoral, agricultural, or other business. Stud properties therefore vary and are part of the rural scene. The above scene is of Wild Oak Farm, The Oaks, NSW.   (Refer to Section 9.1)   Photo courtesy of Steve Hart Photographics.

Some stud properties are showplaces where visitors and tourists are welcome. The above tranquil scene is the central area of Wild Oak Farm, The Oaks, NSW.   (Refer to Section 9.1)   Photo courtesy of Steve Hart Photographics.

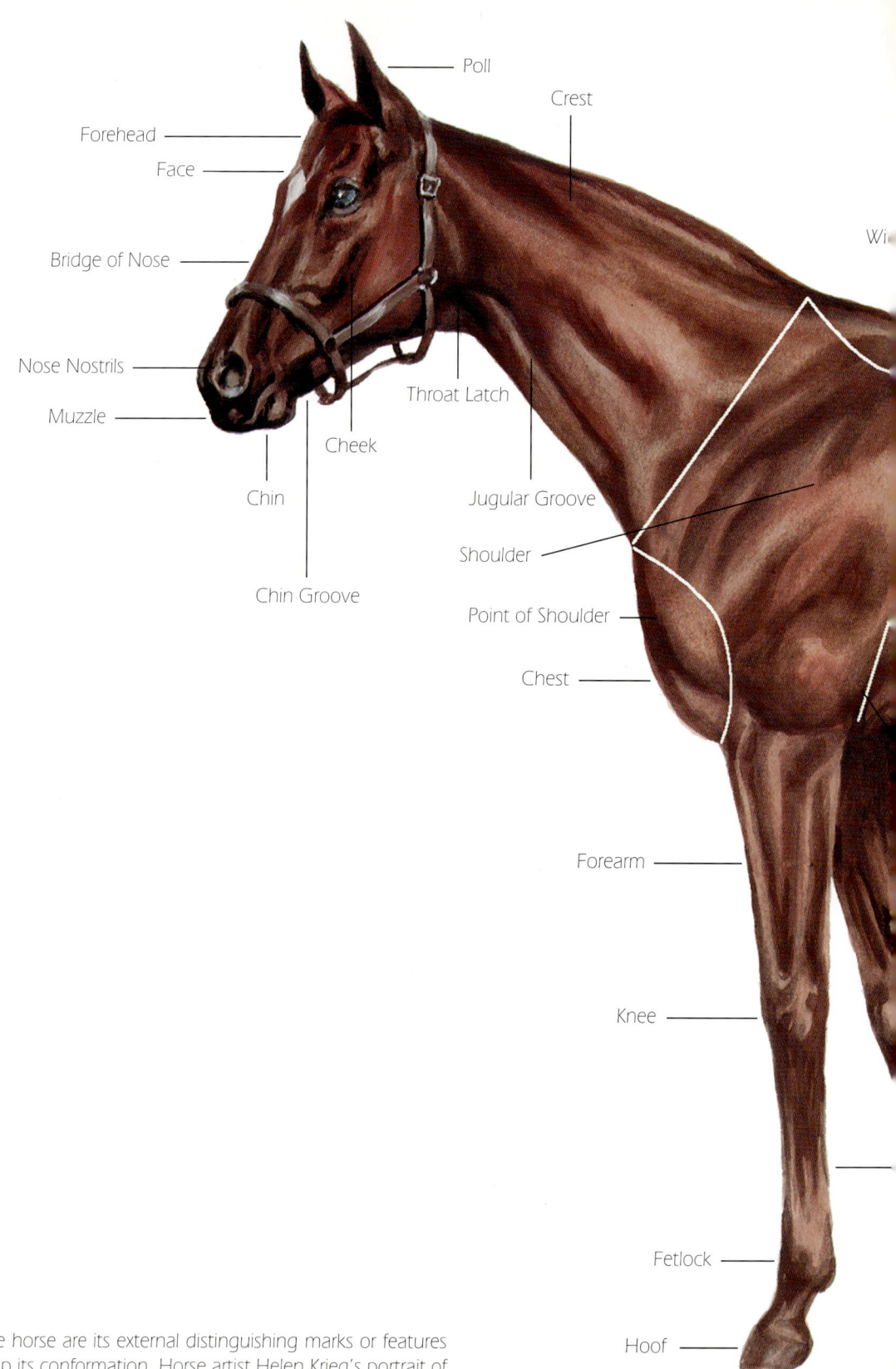

Points of the horse are its external distinguishing marks or features that make up its conformation. Horse artist Helen Krieg's portrait of Todman has been used to provide the above model.

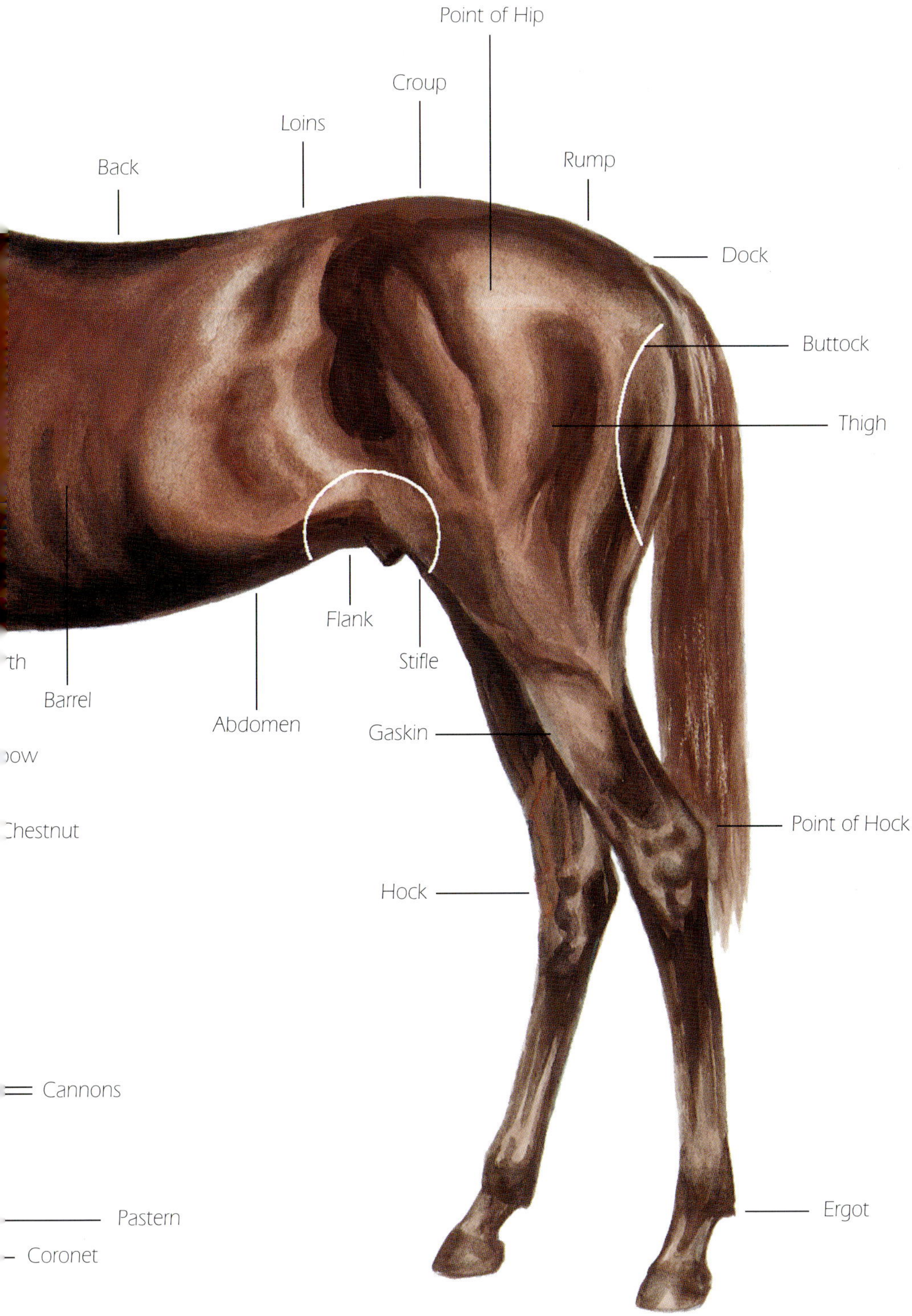

Point of Hip
Croup
Loins
Back
Rump
Dock
Buttock
Thigh
Flank
Stifle
th
Barrel
Abdomen
Gaskin
oow
Point of Hock
Chestnut
Hock
Cannons
Ergot
Pastern
Coronet

The temperate climate of Australian breeding areas allows horses to be bred and reared for most of the year under conditions called "grass-kept" or "pasture-kept". They spend most of the time in the open paddock but at times are provided with supplementary food, shelter and rugs. (Refer to Section 10.3.)   Photo courtesy Alan Peach Photography.

Thoroughbred foals are usually weaned at 5 to 6 months. However provided the mare maintains good condition, the longer the foal suckles the mother's milk the better. The foal will grow to five times its birth-weight in one year (Refer to Section 14.22)   Photo courtesy of Steve Hart Photographics.

a case, the breeder must eliminate the defective animals from the herd. Inbreeding also causes a decline in traits related to physical fitness, particularly vigour.

Thoroughbred breeders do not generally practise inbreeding, but rather employ a special form of mild inbreeding, called linebreeding, to develop lines that can be crossed with a reasonable amount of success.

Section 11.4
Linebreeding

Linebreeding is a special or controlled form of inbreeding of individuals of a herd which have pedigrees tracing back to a common ancestor. To be successful, not only must the ancestor have been a genetically superior horse, but each individual in the particular linebreeding process must also have been a high quality animal. The objective of this breeding process is to concentrate the genes of the admired ancestor in the line. This is not attempted when using inbreeding.

The percentage of inbreeding in the linebreeding process is not nearly as high as in the inbreeding method. For this reason, the linebreeding process of eliminating undesirable genes is much slower than under inbreeding. On the other hand, vigour does not decline as sharply in linebreeding.

Breeders of thoroughbreds employ linebreeding, rather than inbreeding because they consider it a more feasible, less hazardous, and less expensive method of herd improvement.

Section 11.5
Outbreeding

Outbreeding (or outcrossing) is the production of offspring by the mating of horses, usually of genetic superiority, that are not closely related within the last three or four generations.

Outbreeding is used by breeders seeking more vigorous, healthier, stronger animals, or to conceal genetic weaknesses. For example the crossing of two or more superior lines developed by inbreeding or linebreeding usually produces offspring that are of superior quality to their parents.

Section 11.6
Breeding Nicks

A "nick" is a breeding term meaning a combination or crossing of racing bloodlines which have an affinity for each other, each line contributing qualities that the other lacks. In other words, the qualities of the sire and the dam (or rather the sire of the dam) supplement each other.

Good nicks can only be established by trial and error, that is, by performance, rather than by theory. They thus take some time to be recognised. Once established, however, good nicks can be put to good use in the selection of parents.

CHAPTER 12 BASIC GENETIC CONCEPTS

Section 12.1
Introduction

Genetics is the science dealing with the structure and action of hereditary material of organisms (chromosomes and their genes), the transmission of such material from ancestors to descendants, and the resemblances and differences of such descendent organisms flowing from the interaction of their genes and the environment.

Genetic principles properly applied in thoroughbred breeding enhance the probability of producing good racehorses consistently. Equine genetics is, therefore, a matter of vital importance for the thoroughbred breeder.

Experts say that while much genetic research has been carried out, the science is comparatively new, and much remains to be done.

What are hereditary structures and how do they function? In this chapter we take a broad look at the structure of the horse, the units of which that structure is composed, the manner in which structural units are transmitted by parents to progeny, and the effects that such transmitted hereditary material have upon the characteristics of the progeny. In other words, a broad brush is taken to present an overview of the fundamental concepts and principles involved in genetics and of their application in horse breeding.

Section 12.2
Composition of Horse's Body

The body of the horse, like that of other mammalian species, is composed of four basic kinds of tissue, namely: connective tissue; muscle tissue; nerve tissue; and covering or lining tissue called "epithelium".

Each definite kind of tissue is composed of countless numbers of body cells of the same general type and products of those cells.

Section 12.3
Body Cells

Each body cell is a microscopic, complex entity consisting of a semi-permeable membrane or wall surrounding a mass of jelly-like cytoplasm. Suspended in the cytoplasm are specialised structures including the nucleus and ribosomes which synthesise proteins.

The nucleus is the largest of those specialised structures. It is an essential element in the growth metabolism and reproduction of the cell. It contains the chromosomes and their genes.

Section 12.4
Chromosomes

Each nucleus of each body cell of the horse contains 64 chromosomes (microscopic, threadlike structures) arranged in 32 pairs. Pairs are homologous, that is to say, they correspond in type of structure and in origin, but not necessarily in function because they may carry different genes.

One of each chromosome pair is received from the sire and the other from the dam. Chromosomes are the carriers of the genes.

Section 12.5
Genes

Genes are units of inheritance. They are carried on chromosomes and are thus transmitted from parents to progeny in which they develop into hereditary character as they react with other genes and the environment.

Genes determine particular features, qualities or characteristics of the horse. For example, they determine such things as colour of the hair, skin, and eyes; height; body structure; speed; movements; and so on. This function is performed by their origination and control of the synthesis of proteins in the cytoplasm of the body cells.

Proteins, of which there are thousands of types, form the whole or part of the many tissues of the horse's body and are produced by 20 different substances called "amino acids".

Codes or directions for the structure of a certain protein are issued by genes to bodies in the cytoplasm called "ribosomes" and through their action the amino acids are produced to form the protein required. A specific code is issued for each such protein.

Thus, through the operation of the code referred to above, called the "genetic code", genes are responsible for the biochemical reactions that significantly affect the many different tissues and biological functions of the horse's body.

As explained later, the body processes of the horse may also be affected by non-genetic factors called "environmental factors" (see Sections 12.7 and 12.8).

Section 12.6
Transmission of Heredity

Certain of the horse's body cells called "gametocytes" produce the sex or reproductive cells called "gametes". The male sex cells, spermatozoa, are produced in the testicles of the stallion and the female sex cells, ova are produced in the ovaries of the broodmare.

During gamete production called "meiosis" the members of the chromosome pairs in the gametocytes segregate (the paternal from the maternal) and only one member of each pair enters the nucleus of a gamete. A gamete thus contains only 32 chromosomes which are arranged individually and not in pairs. (This compares with 64 chromosomes arranged in pairs in the normal body cell.) Which chromosomes enter a gamete is purely a matter of chance.

When after coitus between stallion and broodmare, a spermatozoon finds, penetrates, and fertilises the ovum, the two such gametes become as one and the chromosomes of the male gamete pair with the chromosomes of the female gamete. Thus, the standard of 64 chromosomes arranged in 32 pairs is restored in the new organism with one member of each pair coming from the sire and the other from the dam.

All the hereditary characteristics that the foal can inherit are thus transmitted to it by its parents at that moment of conception.

Later the impregnated ovum commences the process of cell division and the new organism, the embryo, develops in the uterus of the mare.

Section 12.7
Heredity and Environment

Individual horses within a population vary in form, appearance, and function. Those observable variations can be measured in various ways by applying genetic principles. They are caused by heredity, environment, or the joint action of heredity and environment.

Non-genetic factors that influence the processes of the horse's body are all the various things that the horse experiences from the beginning of its life as a one-cell organism. These are referred to as "environmental factors". They may be internal or external and include such things as nutrition, disease, accidents, sunlight, temperature, experiences with man and animal, and so on.

In summary, both genetic factors and environmental factors, working independently or together, play an important role in determining the structure, appearance, and behaviour of every horse.

Section 12.8
Estimating Heredity and Environmental Factors

While both genetic and environmental factors affect an individual's traits, by applying principles of genetics, geneticists can estimate the degree to which variations or characteristics in individuals are caused by heredity or environment.

The established estimating method in this regard may be used by geneticists in ascertaining and advising breeders of the cause of superiority in horses being considered for mating. The only superiority that is transmittable from parent to offspring is superiority due to heredity. Superiority due to environment is not so transmittable. Indeed, borne out by experience, horses having genetic superiority produce superior offspring while horses having environmental superiority produce mediocre offspring.

The estimating method may also be used in herd improvement. Where the estimate indicates that an adverse characteristic is due to deficient environment, remedial action may be taken to improve the environmental factors involved. On the other hand, where the estimate indicates that a bad trait is due to heredity, remedial action can only be taken by improving the breeding plan.

CHAPTER 13 IMPROVEMENT THROUGH GENETICS

Section 13.1
Chance Supersedes Science in Breeding

The ultimate objective in thoroughbred breeding is, in genetic terms, to produce horses possessing only desirable genes. This is unattainable. Even where genetic principles are applied in herd improvement, chance still supersedes science. It is purely a matter of chance:

- how the pairs of chromosomes of the parents' gametocytes segregate during the development of their gametes (sex cells) and act independently in those gametes;
- which male gamete unites with the ovum in the uterus of the mare and forms the initial body cell of the new organism (embryo foal);
- how the chromosomes (and their innumerable genes) combine in pairs in that new cell; and
- how the genes and the environment, working independently or together, express themselves in, or influence, the characteristics of the new individual.

Predictions about products of matings are thus impossible. The most carefully planned mating may well produce a show champion lacking competitive racing ability.

This is the basis of the wonder, the fascination, the excitement, and the interest in thoroughbred breeding.

Section 13.2
Herd Improvement Through Genetics

While chance does, in fact, supersede science in breeding, the application of genetic principles through breeding provides for increasing the chances of success by increasing the frequency of desirable genes and the homozygosity of gene pairs in a herd, thus making traits highly inheritable.

A horse is "homozygous" when its chromosomes contain identical gene pairs for any given pair of hereditary characteristics and hence breeds true for those characteristics. A horse is "heterozygous" when its chromosomes contain genes for two unlike characteristics and does not breed true to type.

A breeder may seek to improve his herd and develop superior stock by:

- acquiring horses that possess much superior heredity (desirable genes) and introducing those horses into an existing herd of good quality horses;
- concentrating those desirable genes at as high a frequency and in as large a proportion of the herd as practicable, by selection and inbreeding over the course of years;

- ascertaining, through genetic estimating methods, the horses possessing the desirable genes and then preparing a breeding plan for such superior stock, breeding the best to the best; and
- supplying the proper environment for the development of the genetic potential of the offspring.

The practical application of the simply stated procedures for herd improvement through breeding involves many things, including knowledge of genetic and breeding principles, time, patience, dedication and, of course, plenty of money. An application of genetic principles does not remove the chance factor in breeding, but it does greatly enhance the probability of producing good racehorses consistently.

Section 13.3
Locating Superior Individuals

In carrying out the task of selecting, locating, and acquiring genetically superior breeding stock, the breeder is basically seeking superior individuals that are members of superior families and that have highly heritable traits.

In ascertaining the genetic superiority or otherwise of an individual, it is necessary to examine the individual and its traits and performance and also the records, including performances, of its close ancestors, progeny if any, and close collateral relatives. Any such comparison of the individual with its close relatives should be with all such relatives and not only with those with superior traits and performances.

Section 13.4
Pedigrees

A pedigree of a thoroughbred is a table or chart indicating its line of descent (parents, grandparents and further back to a chosen number of generations) as recorded in the stud book. The usual layout of a pedigree is as follows:

"URANUS" (AUS) CH. C. 1990

Sire*	Grand Sire*	GGS*	et al
		GGD*	et al
	Grand Dam*	GGS*	et al
		GGD*	et al
Dam*	Grand Sire*	GGS*	et al
		GGD*	et al
	Grand Dam*	GGS*	et al
		GGD*	et al

*Country of breeding and year of birth are also shown.

A pedigree is far more use in its full form, that is to say, when supported by subsidiary records containing particulars of the horse in question as follows:

- Summary of its race performance.
- Summary of its stud record.
- Race performances, stud performances, and progeny of recent ancestors.

The appraisal of a horse through its pedigree depends on the skill, knowledge, and understanding of the appraiser.

Section 13.5
Genetic Importance of Ancestors

The importance of ancestors as indicated in the genealogical chart or pedigree of a horse can be calculated as below.

In a case where no inbreeding is involved in the ancestral line, a horse receives 50 per cent of its hereditary material from each parent; or 25 per cent from each grandparent; or 12.5 per cent from each great-grandparent. In a case where inbreeding is involved, however, the percentage of hereditary material received from its ancestors depends upon the number of times any such ancestor appears in the pedigree.

A study of the quality of the horses on both the paternal and the maternal sides of the pedigree will indicate the nature of the ancestral genes transmitted to the foal and which are likely to influence its makeup. If its ancestors on both sides were mostly top quality individuals, it is highly probable that its genes will be mostly good. On the other hand, the greater the number of mediocre or poor quality individuals in ancestral lines of either side, the more undesirable genes the foal is likely to possess.

Section 13.6
Relative Importance of Sire and Dam

When written pedigrees of equines were first established, prominence was given in the breeding system to the female line of descent. For example, breeders of Arabian horses bred within lines that traced back to famous mares. Today, however, the importance of the sire's side of the pedigrees is often stressed rather than the dam's side.

It is not surprising that the question is often raised among turf patrons as to the relative importance of the sire or dam in transmitting quality to a foal.

The relationship between the factors, racecourse performance and selection for stud, is much greater in stallions than in mares. A small percentage of entires that race are selected for stud use and one of the selection criteria is an excellent racing record. On the other hand, a large percentage of mares that race are later used for breeding — and many, perhaps most, of the mares retired for breeding purposes are so retired because of poor racecourse performance.

It has been demonstrated by some experts that the ability of a racehorse is due to about 33 per cent genetic effects and 66 per cent environmental effects. In this regard it is stressed that the environmental influence of the dam on the makeup of the progeny is very great because she conceives and carries the foal in her uterus for about a year and then delivers, nourishes, and cares for the foal until weaning. The stallion's environmental influence on the progeny is nil.

As indicated in Section 13.2, and as borne out by past experience, superior horses are produced by superior sires and dams: mediocre or poor quality horses are usually produced by mediocre or poor quality sires and dams. To breed genetically superior horses, the best stallions must be bred to the best mares — superiority cannot come from one parent only.

Section 13.7
Relationship of Offspring

According to breeding standards and usage, horses are:

(a) brothers and sisters if they are out of the same dam and by the same sire;

(b) half-brothers and half-sisters if they are out of the same dam, but by different sires;

(c) no relation to each other if they are out of different dams, but by the same sire.

The reason underpinning that usage centres on the sire that may be bred to numerous mares in the one year. But for the standard there would be confusion. With so many half-brothers and half-sisters, the relationship would be meaningless.

Full brothers and sisters are usually very different in quality and performance. One may be a champion and the other a plugger. The same cross of bloodlines rarely repeats itself.

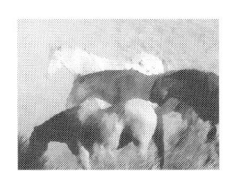

PART 7
THE BREEDING PROCESS

Chapter	14	The Breeding Process
Section	14.1	The Covering Season
	14.2	Definitions: Breeding Season, Breeding Cycle
	14.3	The Stallion
	14.4	Sex Drive of the Stallion
	14.5	Semen Quality
	14.6	Overuse of Stallion
	14.7	Stallion Subfertility
	14.8	Artificial Insemination Prohibited
	14.9	Broodmares
	14.10	Mares Serviced at Stud
	14.11	Veterinary Services to Mares
	14.12	The Oestrous Cycle
	14.13	Teasing Mares
	14.14	Optimum Time for Coitus
	14.15	Mating
	14.16	Conception
	14.17	Twin Conceptions
	14.18	Pregnancy Diagnosis
	14.19	Gestation
	14.20	Foaling
	14.21	Covering at Foal Heat
	14.22	Rearing the Foal

PART 7 THE BREEDING PROCESS

CHAPTER 14 THE BREEDING PROCESS

Section 14.1
The Covering Season

Horses have an inherent sexual rhythm and breeding pattern.

Sexual activity in mares is at its highest in the late spring and in summer. During the seasons of autumn, winter, and early spring, mares do not naturally experience their oestrous cycles and are then said to be in a state of anoestrus. The natural constraint was to ensure the last stage of pregnancy, the delivery of foals, and the after-foaling sexual activity occurred when climatic conditions were favourable and food plentiful.

By artificial and veterinary interference with nature, man may influence mares to experience oestrous cycles outside their natural season and at a time required by breeders. Aids in this regard include: stabling; artificial lighting; hand-feeding; and hormonal treatment.

Having regard to the foregoing and the practicalities of the breeding and racing industries, thoroughbred broodmares in Australia (and other countries in the Southern Hemisphere) are mainly covered between 1 September and 30 November with some late coverings during December.

The practical considerations referred to above include such things as: the limitation of a stallion's services; the period of gestation of a mare — eleven months; the common artificial birthday of thoroughbreds, 1 August; and the need for foals to be born as soon as practicable after that date.

Most foals are born between 1 August and 30 November with some late foals in December.

Section 14.2
Definitions: Breeding Season, Breeding Cycle

In the official records of the *Australian Stud Book (ASB)*, terms have the meanings assigned to them as follows:

Breeding Season: means a twelve-month period that begins on 1 August of one calendar year and ends on 31 July of the next calendar year. (The *ASB* points out that the terms "covering season" and "foaling season" are more descriptive of a season than the term "breeding season". Nevertheless, the *ASB* definition has the covering season and the foaling season each extending over a twelve-month period regardless of the practical periods of those seasons.)

Breeding Cycle: means a 24-month period which consists of a covering season followed by a foaling season — that is to say, two complete consecutive breeding seasons. (Breeding cycles overlap one another because any single breeding season is, at the same time, the foaling season of one breeding cycle and the covering season of the following breeding cycle.)

Covering: means the natural act of a stallion mating with a mare by the system of "hand covering" or "paddock covering".

Section 14.3
The Stallion

Qualities of a thoroughbred stallion include such things as: near-perfect conformation and action; soundness; good constitution and temperament; an outstanding pedigree; an excellent racing record; high quality semen; and a good fertility record.

During his racing career the potential stallion is isolated from physical and sexual conduct with other horses. On arrival at the stud his sexual drive may be low, and his semen quality poor.

At the stud he is kept in isolation, having sexual contact with the mares only at time of planned mating. He is provided with a loose box and exercise paddock; kept in a good state of fitness; fed an appropriate high protein diet for maximum fertility during the breeding season; and allowed to romp in a paddock during the out-of-season months.

The art of serving or covering mares is acquired by the stallion working under the control of an experienced handler. In his first season a young stallion may cover a very limited number of mares, preferably beginning with placid, flaccid, and co-operating matrons. After that, the number is increased to 40 to 60 mares a season.

Section 14.4
Sex Drive of the Stallion

Libido, or strength of the sexual drive of stallions, varies among individuals and may be affected by such things as the season, the service demands made upon them, the ageing process, or physical problems.

A stallion may remain active well into his twenties although the number of mares he is able to cover in a season reduces with age. With the ageing process, degenerative changes occur which reduce the quality of the semen.

Section 14.5
Semen Quality

There is need from time to time to evaluate the fertility of stallions for quality of semen from their ejaculations.

Indicators used in evaluating the quality of semen include the volume of ejaculation, the number of sperm in the ejaculation, sperm form and structure (morphology), sperm motility, the length of time sperm survive under certain conditions, and the composition and quality of the seminal plasma.

Section 14.6
Overuse of Stallion

Some stallions can be used once, some twice, and some even thrice a day while maintaining semen quality sufficient for maximum fertility. Some stallions may become subfertile or even sterile after about six weeks, however, if used daily, and accordingly can only be used two or three times a week.

Section 14.7
Stallion Subfertility

A fertile stallion is one that delivers semen of the highest quality and is least affected by certain variables such as season, frequency of ejaculations, and mating with subfertile or difficult mares. On the other hand, a subfertile stallion is one that delivers semen of poor quality and is seriously affected by the above variables. He has a less than average ability to obtain conception.

Section 14.8
Artificial Insemination Prohibited

Use of the technique of artificial insemination in thoroughbred breeding is prohibited by the stud book authorities.

Artificial insemination is used in the breeding of other breeds of equines, cattle and other farm animals. It provides for the artificial collection of an ejaculation of semen from a selected male animal; splitting the ejaculation into several portions; storage of such splits until required; and introduction of splits into the genital tracts of female animals by hand or syringe inseminator.

Section 14.9
Broodmares

A sire and a dam each contribute half the genes of their offspring. In addition, the mare provides the environment for foetal and foal development.

Prerequisites of a good broodmare include: a suitable pedigree that fits in with the breeding program; preferably linebreeding; femininity; fertility; fecundity; strong mothering ability; excellence of conformation and action; soundness; and good constitution and temperament.

The natural breeding age of mares is from three to twenty years, but extremes are avoided. A filly may well have oestrus from about fifteen months of age, but is infertile until reaching sexual maturity at three years.

Section 14.10
Mares Serviced at Stud

The mares to be serviced at a stud comprise: the mares owned by the stud; mares owned by persons other than the stud, but permanently agisted and cared for at the stud; visiting mares sent to the stud for service and that leave the stud when they are certified as being pregnant; and visiting mares, called "walk-in mares" that are brought to the stud, served, and taken home almost immediately.

Each mare is prepared for breeding by ensuring that she is in a suitable condition and fitness. In most cases, veterinary inspection and certification are required to ensure that the mare is free of disease and that there is nothing to debar her from such services.

Section 14.11
Veterinary Services to Mares

When an owner enters into contract with a studmaster for the supply of stud services for the impregnation of his broodmare, such owner is liable for all the costs involved for stallion services, routine and special veterinary examination and treatment, and feed and general care of the mare.

The veterinary services involved are necessary to prevent or to treat disease, to ensure the mare conceives as soon as practicable, and to minimise the number of stallion services.

Section 14.12
The Oestrous Cycle

"Oestrus" is the period during which the ovum (egg) is shed from the ovary of the mare and passed into the fallopian tube where it is available for fertilisation by the stallion's sperm.

The recurring period in which the relative series of physiological changes in sexual organs and glands repeat themselves, is called the "oestrous cycle". On average, oestrus lasts for five days and dioestrus for fifteen days so that the typical oestrous cycle lasts 20 days in all. The cycle may vary quite markedly, according to the individual and the season.

When a mare is in oestrus she is said, in horseman's language, to be "in season", "on heat", "horsing", "on" or "showing". During the period in between oestrus, the mare will not accept the stallion and at that time she is said to be in "dioestrus", "out of season", "out of heat", "off", or "not showing".

It is important for breeding managerial purposes that the oestrous cycle of each mare to be serviced is properly established and synchronised.

Section 14.13
Teasing Mares

Teasing a mare is an attempt to cause her to show signs of her sexual state, that is to say, to show by her behaviour whether she is in an oestrous or dioestrous condition. A wide variety of teasing methods may be used.

Mares awaiting stallion service are teased daily and thereafter observed for signs of oestrus.

After receiving the reports of the teasing supervisor and veterinarian, the studmaster prepares the programs for his stallions for the ensuing days. Timing of stallion services is vital.

Section 14.14
Optimum Time for Coitus

Once the egg is shed from the ovary and passed into the fallopian tube, it is capable of being fertilised by the stallion's sperm for a period up to 24 hours. After that time if it is not fertilised, it dies. There is, thus, an optimum time for coitus to ensure that sperm are present in the tube at the time of ovulation. The mare should be served by the stallion before, and not after, ovulation. This ensures that sperm are present at the site of fertilisation when the egg arrives in the oviduct.

Section 14.15
Mating

When the mare is considered to be in a state of readiness she is led to the covering area where her buttocks and perineum are washed and she is specially dressed for the occasion.

The stallion, after being washed, is led to a position a few lengths behind and slightly to the nearside of the mare so that they can see and smell each other. He is then led alongside her and allowed to nuzzle her neck and head. After that he is allowed to explore her genital area.

The act of coitus lasts only a few minutes. In most cases the service is carried out smoothly and as quickly as practicable.

After the sexual union the stallion and mare are quickly separated. The stallion is washed and returned to his box while the mare is led around for some minutes to prevent her staling. She is later turned out with other mares and kept under observation.

Section 14.16
Conception

After the courtship and physiological copulation between stallion and mare, the sperm deposited in the vagina swim through the cervix and uterus into the fallopian tube in search of the ovum. If the ovum is present, ripe, and located, only one spermatozoon (male gamete) enters and fertilises it. Conception has occurred. The two cells have become as one. The development of a new life has begun.

Some hours later the fertilised ovum divides into two cells. Cell division continues and the tiny developing mass of life attaches itself to the wall of the uterus and draws nourishment from it. As time goes by membranes form around the embryo and it is cushioned in a bag of waters or amnion. A structure called the placenta grows on the wall of the uterus and the developing organism is connected to it by the umbilical cord.

The term "embryo" means the new organism as it develops into horse-like form in the mother's womb up to the end of about the ninth week. Thereafter, until parturition, the developing organism is called a foetus. (For the purposes of this book the terms are interchangeable.)

Section 14.17
Twin Conceptions

In about 98 per cent of cases, thoroughbred mares have single conceptions while the remaining 2 per cent are reported as being twin conceptions.

All twin conceptions end disastrously. The reason why a mare is incapable of carrying twins to full term or of producing healthy twins is that the placenta membrane of the thoroughbred is designed as a singleton to cover the whole of the uterine wall surface, but in the case of twin conceptions two placentas have to share that surface. In the resultant struggle, one foetus becomes dominant at the expense of the other. Usually both are lost as one dies and the other is expelled with it from the uterus in a process known as "slipping twins".

Section 14.18
Pregnancy Diagnosis

Because oestrus is frequently erratic in mares, the sexual behaviour of mares after stallion service cannot be entirely relied upon as an indication of pregnancy or otherwise. Various clinical and biological methods, however, are available for diagnosing pregnancy, including rectal palpation, blood serum testing, urine testing, and ultrasound scanning.

"Pregnancy" is defined in the *Thoroughbred Breeders' Guide to The Australian Stud Book* as the state of a female horse that does not show oestrus for a period of 60 days after being served and:

(i) gives a positive reaction to a recognised biological test for conception applied after the 45th day from the last service, or

(ii) positive signs of conception are found by a veterinary surgeon on rectal and vaginal examinations carried out at least 45 days after the last service or on ultrasound examination carried out at least 25 days after the last service.

While pregnancy in a mare may be established as early as 14 days after service, because of the incidence of abortion (slipping) in early stages of pregnancy, it is customary not to make final veterinary confirmation and certification until the 45th day after service or later.

Section 14.19
Gestation

The period of gestation, averaging about 340 days or eleven months, is usually normal and uneventful and the mare's requirements are modest — suitable feeding with mineral additives, water, exercise, company, and, where necessary, shelter.

When a mare is nearing the end of her pregnancy and is observed to be getting close to foaling, she is placed under closer observation.

Section 14.20
Foaling

Signs of approaching foaling include a large and swollen udder; beestings (a wax-like substance) on the teats; running milk; sagging quarters on either side of the croup; distension of the vulva; general restlessness; and so on.

The mare has the ability to control the time of foaling (parturition) and this usually takes place at about 2.00 am.

In normal presentation, the forefeet of the foal emerge first, followed by the foal's head lying on its forelegs, then the shoulders, and thereafter the rest of the foal slides out comparatively easily.

After delivery, the foal gradually becomes functional and takes its first feed. The mare's "first milk" is not milk, but colostrum.

Section 14.21
Covering at Foal Heat

A mare usually comes on heat about 6 to 10 days after foaling and this is called her "foal heat". Where foaling has been normal and trouble-free, the mare, particularly one that is bred regularly, may be served during foal heat for another foal the following year and she is most likely to conceive from such covering. Some breeders and equine veterinary surgeons, however, are opposed to a mare being covered during her foal heat, particularly if she has been subject to undue stress at foaling.

Section 14.22
Rearing the Foal

Having regard to the weather, the mare and newly-born foal can be put out in a paddock with a suitable shelter box available.

In the natural state the mare suckles her foal for about six to eight months. During that time the foal grows increasingly independent of the dam and the weaning process takes place co-operatively. Because of economic and managerial considerations, however, stud farm management does not wait for natural weaning and thoroughbred foals are usually weaned at five to six months.

Youngsters of both sexes are called "foals" until age of weaning; then "weanlings" until their first official birthday on 1 August; then "yearlings" until their second official birthday.

Colt weanlings and yearlings are paddocked together. Filly weanlings and yearlings have their own paddock.

Stud farm management provides for routine handling education, veterinary inspection and medication, and farriery treatment of the youngsters.

Rory's Jester (by Crown Jester from Rory's Rocket and foaled in 1982) has been a successful Australian sire during the late 1980s and 1990s.   (Refer to Sections 13.6 and 14.3)   Photo courtesy Martin King Sportpix.

Danehill (by Danzig from Razyana and foaled in 1986) has dominated Australian thoroughbred breeding during the 1990s. Owned by Coolmore Stud, Ireland operating through Collingrove Stud (a partnership of Robert Sangster and Colin Hayes) Danehill is one of a range of world class "shuttle sires" that travel to Australia each year during the southern hemisphere covering season. Those superior international stallions have greatly improved Australian bloodlines.
(Refer to Section 14.8)   Photo courtesy of Martin King Sportpix.

Colt weanlings and yearlings are paddocked separately from filly weanlings and yearlings. Full of the joy of life, the colts frolic, fight and race as they share their early life and paddock. The fillies are more demure.
(Refer to Section 14.22)   Photo courtesy Martin King Sportpix.

A youngster enjoys the freedom of the paddock.   (Refer to Section 14.22)   Photo courtesy of Steve Hart Photographics.

PART 8
BEHAVIOUR OF THE RACEHORSE

Chapter	15	Behaviour of the Racehorse
Section	15.1	Equine Intelligence
	15.2	Factors Influencing Equine Behaviour
	15.3	Horse a Reflex Animal
	15.4	Herding Instinct
	15.5	Horse is Non-Aggressive
	15.6	Horse — A Creature of Instinct
	15.7	Peculiar Equine Senses
	15.8	Individuality of Horses

CHAPTER 15 BEHAVIOUR OF THE RACEHORSE

Section 15.1
Equine Intelligence

Opinions expressed by horsemen indicate two schools of thought: (1) the horse is intelligent and reason can be used in its education; and (2) the horse is a dumb brute which must be broken to obedience.

Equine experts say that, in their opinion, reference by the horsemen to the intelligence of the horse is not reference to intelligence as such, but rather reference to the standard of its behaviour or the degree of its ability to perform as required.

In other words the horse is not a creature of reason.

Section 15.2
Factors Influencing Equine Behaviour

Hereditary factors and environmental factors, acting jointly or severally, influence the behaviour of the horse.

During the evolution of the horse each genera has passed on to succeeding genera many characteristics which determine the behaviour of the horse.

Underlying many aspects of its behaviour today are certain basic characteristics on which its survival in the wild depended. The horse was, and still remains, primarily a reflex animal; in its psychology there is a dominant natural herding instinct; and it is by nature non-aggressive and instinctively runs from trouble.

Section 15.3
Horse a Reflex Animal

The nervous system of a horse is composed of the central nervous system consisting of the brain (which is very small in relation to the size of the horse) and the spinal cord, and the peripheral nervous system. Operation of the nervous system depends upon two distinct systems called the "sensory system" and the "motor system".

In the wild state the horse responded to the stimuli from the sensory system by appropriate reflex or voluntary action. It must be remembered that the horse remains primarily a reflex animal.

Section 15.4
Herding Instinct

Much of the behavioural pattern of all types and breeds of present-day domestic horse, *equus caballus*, is instinctive and is inherited from its ancestors.

Those ancestors lived in herds that were social, non-territorial organisations that functioned smoothly. They were based on selective and orderly reproduction and protection of every individual of the herd.

The social unit of the herd was the family group which consisted of the stallion, up to six mares, and their offspring. Within each group there existed a social strata with the stallion as leader and members of the group subservient to the stallion in varying degrees.

Offspring were weaned at about eleven months and then remained part of the family group until they were about two or three years of age when, after a process of delicate rejection by their elders, they left of their own volition.

The young horses so ejected from the family groups after coming of age joined bachelor or spinster groups, the numbers of which fluctuated as horses joined or left to form new family groups or join existing family groups.

When danger was imminent, several family groups in the danger area would band together usually in flight. When the danger had passed, each family group would reassemble and resume normal life.

The groups did not have territorial claims and were not restricted to areas that might become arid and devoid of food and water. They travelled — sometimes over long distances and under treacherous conditions — searching for food or a warmer climate.

Section 15.5
Horse is Non-Aggressive

The horse, being herbivorous, has always been non-aggressive; a pacifist by nature; always remaining entirely on the defensive; the hunted, but never the hunter.

Section 15.6
Horse — A Creature of Instinct

Long since gone are the herds of wild horses. The natural dominant herding instinct has been suppressed.

Breeding and growth of the modern horse is achieved in controlled small groups. Many, particularly the thoroughbred, are kept closely confined in stables, an environment that is artificial and stressful. They have become lonely and demanding individuals, almost entirely dependent upon man.

Today, even though in the domestic state the original stimuli have long been absent, the behaviour of the horse is still strongly influenced by hereditary stimuli. It is still a creature of instinct, rather than of reason, its mentality being based on instincts developed in the wild.

Section 15.7
Peculiar Equine Senses

Each of the senses by which horses perceive external objects and their own bodily changes (that is, the senses of sight, hearing, smell, taste, and touch) are integral to their personality and relevant to behavioural pattern. The senses of the horse are developed in accordance with basic instincts, but the equine sense of sight is peculiar to the species.

The location of the eyes and the width between them do not allow both eyes to be focused directly to the front. By tilting the whole head to one side, however, the horse is able to see in front with one eye only.

The ears are located forward and can be erected and directed at will towards a sound. Pricked and alert ears evince signs of response and attention. Horses memorise the pitch or tone of human vocal commands.

Horses do not use the sense of smell to a marked extent — they nuzzle other horses, rather than sniff or smell them. The smell of fear given off by a fearful or nervous handler, however, is without doubt perceived by the horse which reacts accordingly.

Section 15.8
Individuality of Horses

While horses have much in common (for example, under the same set of circumstances they act in an instinctive manner) each horse is an individual and has individual needs.

There is a great variety in the behaviour of horses ranging from very good to very bad.

Some horses obey only grudgingly and only after the exercise of discipline by their handlers. Some obey, but only when asked. Some obey instantly even trying to anticipate their handler's wishes.

For racehorses, in particular, notice may well be taken of Banjo Paterson's poem "Do they know?", that is to say, do they know what racing is all about? His reply was a retort, "Do you think they don't know?"

A racegoer may observe that a good racehorse may appear to, and probably does, run its own race without the need for any direction from its rider; may during a race indicate resentment of the rider's use of the whip or spurs by unexpected behaviour such as running in or running out; may revel in applause after winning a race; and so on.

PART 9

THE BODY OF THE RACEHORSE

Chapter	16		Conformation Generally
Section	16.1		Bones, Joints and Muscles
	16.2		Points
	16.3		Conformation Important, but not an End in Itself
	16.4		Presence
	16.5		Size and Proportional Compatibility
	16.6		Measurement of Height
	16.7		Balance
	16.8		Nearside/Offside
	16.9		Variation in Conformation of Sprinters and Stayers
Chapter	17		Detailed Conformation
Section	17.1		Ideal Marks of Quality of Racehorse
	17.2		Comment on above by a Renowned Horseman
Chapter	18		The Foot and the Farrier
Section	18.1		The Foot
	18.2		The Farrier
	18.3		Farriery Care
	18.4		Shoeing
Chapter	19		Gaits of the Horse
Section	19.1		Gaits
	19.2		Evaluating Horse's Action
Chapter	20		Colours and Markings
Section	20.1		Skin and Coat
	20.2		Evolution of Colours
	20.3		Instability of Early Colour
	20.4		Colour of the Thoroughbreds
	20.5		Horsemen's Colour Preference
	20.6		Markings

CHAPTER 16 **CONFORMATION GENERALLY**

Section 16.1
Bones, Joints and Muscles

More than 200 individual bones are fitted together to form the skeleton of the horse. Functions of the bones include the protection of internal organs, support for the body, and the provision of mobility. The chemical structure of bones (of which the basis is calcium phosphate) makes them strong, resilient, and light.

Bones are connected to one another by joints that are capped with cartilage. This material is resilient and smooth and any wear at the surface is immediately repaired. Tough cords of connective tissue called "ligaments" bind bones together and strengthen the joints. Joint surfaces are lubricated by bursae which are oil-producing (synovia) sacs.

Movement and activity of the animal body are produced by voluntary muscles. These muscles are masses of contractible fibres connected to bone or other part by cords of tough, inelastic tissue called "tendons" or "sinews". (The other type of muscles, called "involuntary muscles", carry on activities with little or no conscious control by the brain, for example, the contraction of the heart, the propulsion of food along the intestines, and so on.)

Section 16.2
Points

Points may be defined as the distinguishing marks of a horse used as a standard in breeding. A well-conformed horse of any breed will not only have the good points of its breed, but will have those points balanced and in proportion relative to one another.

Because every horse has the same basic bone structure, the individual parts or points of the body of any horse, irrespective of its type or breed, are identified by the same names.

Section 16.3
Conformation Important, but Not an End in Itself

Although the "heart" is the most vital cog in the thoroughbred's machinery, the horse must also have the proper physical build for its "heart" to function at its most desirable level. The better the design, the better the machine. All the moving parts of the machine must be balanced, of proportionate size, and work in harmony so that the machine operates efficiently and effectively at all speeds.

While selectively bred to run and to strive to win, to be successful a thoroughbred racehorse must have the necessary ability, courage, stamina, and soundness to win. The types of individuals possessing those qualities, however, are hard to distinguish.

History records that the conformation of many horses that were high quality performers left much to be desired. They had, of course, the qualities necessary to win. Hence the saying that good conformation is important, but not an end in itself.

Section 16.4
Presence

In assessing a horse, the horseman will first stand back a short distance and view the horse as a whole, having regard to its size, balance, general conformation, and so on.

A good horse by its whole makeup should attract and impress the "eye" of the horseman. Indeed it is the horse's "presence" and good action or movement that selects it above others for a more detailed examination.

Section 16.5
Size and Proportional Compatibility

As indicated in the following table, height of the breed when fully grown ranges from 14.2 to 17.3 hands, according to the purposes for which they are bred.

TYPE	USUAL RANGE IN HANDS
Hacks	14.2 to 15.3
Racehorses — Sprinters	15.1 to 16.1
Stayers	15.2 to 16.3
Steeplechasers	15.2 to 16.3
Hunters	15.1 to 17.3

A large-sized racehorse may have some advantages such as greater driving power, greater stride, and so on. Many horsemen, however, are prejudiced against large horses. They are of the opinion that a big horse is more likely to be unsound in its wind than a smaller horse and point out that the bigger horse is more easily thrown off balance during a race. Perhaps the medium-sized horse is preferred.

Section 16.6
Measurement of Height

The height of a horse is measured with a "T" measuring stick from the highest part of the withers straight to the ground while the horse is standing on even ground with its head and neck held in a straight line from its back.

Under the imperial linear system, height is measured and expressed in terms of "hands", a hand being the equivalent of 4 inches. A fractional measurement of say 65 inches, which is 16 hands plus 1 inch, is expressed in writing as 16-1hh.

The term "hand" derives from the original custom of measuring horses in clenched fists. With the introduction of the imperial system of linear measurement, the hand became a measure of 4 inches which is the average measurement of the clenched fist.

In Australia and New Zealand, height is officially measured and expressed under the metric system. The measurement referred to above (65 inches or 16-1hh) is expressed in metric terms as 165.1 cm. The metric equivalent of the hand is 101.6mm or 10.16cm.

Section 16.7
Balance

It is vital that a horse be well balanced and carry itself well, that is to say, the weight should be evenly distributed on its legs and there should be a steady equilibrium or smoothness in its action or movement.

Section 16.8
Nearside/Offside

A horse is always handled and mounted from the left side. Accordingly it has been customary for horsemen, when referring to the left side of a horse to use the term "nearside", and when referring to the right side to use the term "offside". Parts of the horse's body have thus been identified by those terms, for example, the near foreleg or the off hindleg. The veterinary profession have for some time, however, discontinued use of the terms "nearside" and "offside" and, as a standard practice, now identify the lateral parts of a horse's body simply as left or right.

Section 16.9
Variation in Conformation of Sprinters and Stayers

The distance over which a horse will have the most competency in performance depends upon its conformation with that of a sprinter usually markedly different from that of a stayer.

Sprinters, that is, horses that excel in races up to 1600m, are usually shorter coupled with heavier and shorter bone structure and musculature than stayers. Their overall robust or chunky conformation provides for a quick and powerful action.

Types of sprinters vary more than do types of stayers. Indeed, some sprinters are of somewhat similar conformation to that of stayers and this type often have the ability to excel in races of beyond 1600m.

Stayers usually have an overall elegant conformation providing for a long striding action. They are usually of lankier or rangier build with longer unobtrusive musculature and flat-boned structure than the muscular type sprinters. Middle-distance performers usually feature combinations and modifications of characteristics of both the sprinter and the stayer.

PART 9 THE BODY OF THE RACEHORSE

CHAPTER 17 DETAILED CONFORMATION

Section 17.1
Ideal Marks of Quality of Racehorse

For the purpose of considering conformation, the horse may be divided into three parts by two vertical lines, one extending through the withers and the other through the loins.

The first or front part is called the "forehand" and consists of the head, neck, withers, shoulders, and forelegs.

The second or middle part is called the "body" or "mid-piece" and consists of the back, loins, chest, belly, and flanks.

The third or hind part is called the "hindquarters" and consists of the hindquarters proper, tail, and hindlegs.

Subject to what has been said about the marked difference that may exist in conformation between sprinters and stayers, some of the most commonly accepted ideal marks of quality in the structure of a racehorse are dealt with below.

Head and Neck

Vital factors affecting a horse's galloping ability include the following:

(a) Size and weight of the head: in proportion to the size of the neck, the head of the muscular-type sprinter should be short whereas the head of the rangy stayer should be average to long. It should be seen to be light to carry.

In general, the head should be neat, refined, well-balanced, and well modelled, with bone structure, veins, and muscles showing through fine skin. It should indicate breeding, intelligence, quality, honesty, and courage.

(b) Angle at which the head and neck meet: the angle should allow the horse to bend its neck at the poll in a pleasing curve.

(c) Length, strength and flexibility of the neck: the neck of the muscular-type sprinter is deep, muscular, short, and stoutly joined to the head. On the other hand, the neck of the rangy stayer is lean, comparatively long, and lightly muscled.

(d) Angle at which the neck and body meet: in general, the neck should be well set on at a right angle to the body, and well-shaped, tapering to the head, slightly convex on top, concaving nicely underneath to the chest and shoulders.

Forehead: The area between the eyes, arch of the nose, and poll should be wide, full, and flat, tapering to a fine but not too fine muzzle.

Face: The area between the tip of the nose and the forehead (called the "face", or the "arch" or "bridge of the nose") should generally be long, narrow, and flat. The face line from the side view should be straight.

Muzzle: This term includes the nostrils, lips, gums, and teeth.

Nostrils: Ideally these should be large, full, and flaring but not dilated. Small or narrow nostrils restrict breathing.

Lips: These should be thin and fine. Both upper and lower lips are very sensitive.

Jaws and Teeth: Teeth should be sound and regular. The bite should be good, that is, top and bottom teeth should meet evenly. Deformities of the lower jaw affect grazing and make mastication difficult.

Chin and Chin Groove: The chin is the protuberance below the lower lip on the underside of the lower jaw. The marked depression behind the chin is called the "chin groove".

Cheeks: The area below the eyes and above the jaw should be moderately broad and flat with powerful muscles beneath to operate the lower jaw. Cheeks should curve up to a well-defined throat.

Eyes: Eyes should be matching (that is, of the same size, colour, and appearance), set equally and wide apart, large, prominent, bright, clear, intelligent, and bold, showing fire and courage.

Ears: The ears are very sensitive and mobile. They should be small to medium in size, set wide apart, finely formed, pointed at the top, active, cocked, and alert.

Poll: This area, above the forehead and immediately behind the ears, is the anterior point of the neck.

Forelock: This is the continuation of the mane that hangs forward between the ears over the forehead, covering the poll.

Mane: Hair of the mane should be fine. It may be left flowing free but for racing purposes is usually trimmed.

Crest: This is the upper side of the neck from which the mane grows. It should be well muscled, slightly convex but not too pronounced.

Throat: Lying at the junction of the head and the neck, the throat contains the gullet and the windpipe. It should be well defined.

Jugular Groove: This marked furrow or groove along the lower side of the neck contains the jugular vein.

Withers: These should be well shaped, starting at the base of the crest, being highest at the top of the shoulder and gradually sloping well back. They should also be well covered with muscle at the sides. A horse with good withers usually has a good shoulder.

Shoulders: Shoulders extend from below the withers to the upper arm. They should be in proportion to good withers, narrow on top, long, deep set, well muscled, with a marked slope from withers to the breast.

Chest: The chest is that part of the body between the neck and the abdomen, containing the cavity enclosed by the ribs, and so on, in which the heart, lungs, and so on, are situated.

The breast, or front part of the chest, should be big, deep, wide (but not too bosomy), full, and well developed.

The curve of the ribs forms what is known as the "ribcage" or "barrel". The circumference thereof, immediately behind the forelegs, is called the "girth".

The barrel should be deep and of great girth. This gives plenty of room for lung expansion and heart function.

Ribs should be long, convex, well sprung, and spaced well back, with the posterior ribs close to the point of the hip.

Belly and flanks: The belly, containing the digestive organs, is situated behind the rib cage and below the loins. The belly should be proportionate to the size of the horse and relative to the fitness of the horse for racing. At peak of fitness, the belly will be light and taper gradually towards the flanks which should be strong and well formed.

Underline: The underline or lower line of the body should be parallel to the ground along the barrel and gently slope up to the flanks.

Where a horse is slack, undeveloped or cut away too much behind the girth or where the body joins the hindquarters, it is said to be "tucked-up".

Top-line: The top-line is the line from the ears, along the neck and the back to the tail. It should be a flowing line with a hint of angularity, indicating strength.

Back: The region between the withers and the loins should be nicely curved (not too flat, and not too hollow), well muscled, and strong. Some length of back is important for speed.

Most stayers have long, straight, and strong backs, but lightly framed hindquarters.

Loins: That part of the top-line immediately behind the saddle should be as short as practicable, broad, well arched, very strong, and well muscled. The loins of the stayer are comparatively fine.

Hindquarters: The hindquarters comprise that part between the rear of the flank and the dock or root of the tail, and extend down to the gaskin. The points of the hindquarters include the croup, point of the hip, buttocks, and stifle.

A horse should be wider at the hindquarters than in front. It has better use of its front legs if its weight is well balanced further back.

The large and powerful muscles of the hind limbs (quarters, thighs, and gaskins) provide the propulsive force of the horse. Anything that assists in that action is good. Anything that hinders propulsion is a serious fault, for example, weak quarters, front heavy, and so on.

Croup: The croup is that part of the top-line from the loins to the root of the tail. It should be high and well muscled.

The croup-line should slope only very gently. Where the rump slopes sharply downwards from the point of croup or point of hip to the dock, the fault is referred to as a "goose rump".

Point of the Hip: The hip is the external bony protuberance of the pelvis on either side of a horse just behind the posterior rib.

Points of the hips should be even with proportionate breadth between them.

Buttocks: The buttocks are that part of the hindquarters below the dock and root of the tail, and behind the thighs. They should be large, long, well-developed muscularly, well rounded, and pear-shaped.

Thighs: These should be long, deep, thick, muscular, well developed and well let down.

Stifle: This is the junction of the tibia and the patella (that is, it corresponds with the junction of the human shinbone and kneecap). Stifles should be clear and wide. The point of the stifle is the forward part which should be prominent.

Sheath: The sheath of the entire or gelding is the fold of loose skin protecting the forward end of its penis. It should be large and well formed.

Vulva: The external female genitalia, comprising the two pairs of labia and the cleft between them, should be well developed.

Tail: The tail should be well set (but not too low) strong, muscular, and covered with fine hair. The tail and the root of the tail (called the "dock") should be carried well away from the body.

Legs: All legs should be true, straight, squarely under the body, refined, clean, hard, strong, with proper quality, length, and density of bone, and be set at proper angles, so that there is no undue stress on any part of the leg. Tendons and ligaments should be well defined, that is, pencil-like.

Upper Arm: The upper arm should slope back from the point of the shoulder to the point of the elbow, forming a right angle with the slope of the shoulder.

Elbows: The elbow joint on each foreleg is located between the upper arm and the forearm.

Elbows should be large, well-developed muscularly, and well defined. They should also be well separated from the body to allow freedom of movement and good ground coverage.

Forearms: The forearm extends from the elbow to the knee on each foreleg. They should be long, wide, and well developed.

Knees: The knee joint is located on each foreleg between the forearm and the cannon.

Knees should be clean, bony, strong, well developed, flat in front, and as large as practicable for the size of the horse. They should also face the front and be a matching pair. The trapezium bone should be well defined.

Gaskin: The gaskin or second thigh lies between the stifle and the hock joint on each hindleg. Gaskins should be well defined, strong, and well developed.

Hock: This is the joint on each hindleg between the gaskin and the cannon. Hocks should be set fairly high, clean, wide, deep, sturdy, well defined, well developed, proportionately large, with a well-marked point of hock, and well supported beneath.

Cannons: The cannon is (a) on each foreleg, the bone extending from the knee to the fetlock, that is, the "shin bone"; and (b) on each hindleg, the bone extending from the hock to the fetlock, that is, the "shank bone".

Cannons should have plenty of good, clean, bone, and should be short, strong, sound, flat (not rounded), and parallel. The tendons should be well defined.

Chestnuts: These horny outgrowths are located (a) in the forelegs, on the inside of the forearm above the knee and (b) in the hindlegs, on the inside of the cannon below the hock.

Fetlocks: The fetlock is the joint between the cannon and the pastern on each leg. Fetlocks of the forelegs should be a matching pair, as should fetlocks of the hindlegs. All should be refined, well developed, strong, broad, and free of blemishes.

Ergots: These rough pads of flesh or horny growth are located at the back of each fetlock joint. They are the vestigial remains of footpads.

Pasterns: The pastern of each of the four legs is that part between the fetlock joint and the coronet.

Pasterns of the forelegs should be a matching pair, as should those of the hindlegs. They should be of medium length, free of lumps, and set at the same angle as the foot. The angle of the fore pair should be about 45 degrees and the angle of the hind pair a little steeper.

Coronets: The coronet of each of the four legs is that part of the pastern immediately adjoining the hoof.

Feet or Hooves: These should be of medium size; angled to the ground (from side view) at same angle as pasterns; point to the front; well-shaped; smooth preferably dark horn; with each pair matching although the front pair may be a little larger and rounder, and the back pair a little more oval.

On the underside of the foot, "heels" should be strong and deep with a good width between heels, and a definite space between heels and frog; "frog" should be well developed, tough and elastic and touch the ground; and the "sole" should be concave and firmly attached to the wall by the "white line".

Section 17.2
Comment on Above by a Renowned Horseman

After reading the preceding ideal marks of quality of a racehorse, renowned horseman Jack O'Hagan looked wistful and said: "I have known many good gallopers that were of bad appearance. They were like Mulligan's Mare: 'Bad 'uns to look at, good 'uns to go' (A. B. Paterson). There are no fixed patterns of conformation. Their real test is their ability to gallop at racing speeds over racing distances. Qualities are not always displayed externally — the important ones come from inside. Thoroughbreds are bred and trained to gallop, not to compete in the show ring." So history records, and Jack O'Hagan recalls, that the conformation of many horses that were good performers left much to be desired. Hence it is repeated that comformation is important but not an end in itself. Horsemen still look first and longest at the eye!

CHAPTER 18 THE FOOT AND THE FARRIER

Section 18.1
The Foot

The feet are the foundations that support all the upper structure. Each foot or hoof is a very intricate organised structure designed to serve as a shock absorber. Weight is borne primarily on the bottom or undersurface of the horny wall, the bars, the adjacent part of the horny sole, and the horny frog.

Section 18.2
The Farrier

The farrier or shoeing smith is a person who has the training and skill for making and putting on horseshoes and also has special training and skill in minor veterinary matters, particularly those associated with the feet. The farrier is trained to observe foot problems and, where necessary, to take remedial action with respect to faults in the construction of the foot so far as the skill of the farrier allows.

Section 18.3
Farriery Care

Young horses start to develop permanent hooves when they are about three months old. Professional farriery care needs to start at about that time and to continue on a regular basis. Such care includes procedures for manicuring (trimming and rasping of hooves) and also, where necessary, the procedures for correcting any deviation from proper foot conformation and growth.

Hoof trimming is not a simple matter. It determines the angle of inclination of the feet to the ground — which should be the same as that of the pasterns.

Feet, whether shod, or not, need to be inspected, cleaned, and oiled regularly. The cleaning process is necessary to remove accumulated debris and small stones from the frog cleft. The process also enables close inspection for any early indications of disease. Indeed, the foot is subject to many diseases and injuries.

Section 18.4
Shoeing

Wear and damage to the feet are caused by such factors as friction, concussion, moisture, and so on. The purpose of shoeing is to prevent excessive wear. The shoe is the metal or plastic plate attached to the hoof to protect it.

A horse is not permitted to start in a race unless it is fully shod with approved plates or tips at the time of leaving the Mounting Yard. In exceptional circumstances, however, the stewards may permit a horse to run barefooted or partly shod.

Horses that are to start in a race may only be attended by a licensed farrier or registered employees of a licensed farrier and every such horse is required to be inspected before starting in the race by the farrier's supervisor.

All plates and tips must be made of approved material that can be forged or moulded into shape. The maximum weight of plates and tips must not exceed 120g for all sizes up to a 28cm foot and 140g for all larger sizes.

There are various types of plates and tips. Those that vary from the standard approved aluminium nail-on patterns can only be used in accordance with Local Rules and subject to such Rules, with approval and monitoring by stewards.

Farriers have a responsibility imposed upon them to ensure that plates and tips which they use conform in all respects with the Rules of Racing.

Any mishap to a plate or tip during a race must be reported promptly to the stewards by the trainer of the horse concerned.

Colourful Gai Waterhouse. Gai took over the Randwick stables of her legendary father T. J. Smith in 1992 and bounded away to become an immediate success. She has now established herself as a horsewoman and trainer in her own right. Gai commands personal admiration and respect. (Refer to Section 30.3) Photo courtesy Alan Peach Photography.

The 1997 QTC Stradbroke Handicap run at Eagle Farm over 1 400 metres was won by the three-year old filly Dane Ripper (Danehill ex Red Express) from Quick Flick and Celestial Choir. The winner was ridden by Chris Munce and prepared by ace trainer Bart Cummings.

Peter Gallagher, QTC Chairman, has indicated that the Stradbroke is his Club's "signature" event. It is certainly one of the top races in Australia. (Refer to Section 43.11)   Photo courtesy Alan Peach Photography.

After a feature race is over and correct weight is declared, attaching trophies are presented to the connections of the winning horse and they are honoured for their achievements. In the above photo the jubilant connections of Dane Ripper hold aloft the trophy presented to them after Dane Ripper won the 1997 QTC Stradbroke Handicap. Host Club Chairman Peter Gallagher and Queensland Racing Minister Russell Cooper made the presentation.

Refer to section 50.7)   Photo courtesy Alan Peach Photography.

CHAPTER 19 GAITS OF THE HORSE

Section 19.1
Gaits

The four basic gaits are the walk, trot, canter, and gallop, and in each of these the horse moves on the diagonal in different time, but in rhythm. Movements other than those basic gaits include pacing and ambling.

The gallop of the gallopers is a natural fast four-beat gait in which the horse moves at its fastest pace by leaps. In the course of each leap all four feet are off the ground in momentary suspension. The feet then touch the ground in the following sequence: near hind, off hind, near fore, off fore, or as the case may be, off hind, near hind, off fore, near fore.

In order to negotiate a turn quickly and safely, either at the canter or gallop, a horse should make the turn with the legs leading on the side to which it is turning. So the racehorse is trained to start with the appropriate leading legs depending whether it is required to run in a clockwise or an anti-clockwise direction.

(One of the general rules of punting is not to back a horse that is running clockwise or anti-clockwise for the first time.)

Section 19.2
Evaluating Horse's Action

The "action" of a horse means the ease, or otherwise, at which the horse moves forward. Such movement should be free and even, equal on all limbs, straight, and without any inward or outward twisting.

If a horse walks correctly it is likely that all its other forward movements will also be good. Steps should be straight from the shoulder, true, even, long, low, free, sweeping, and overtracking, with extension of the toe. The feet should be picked up freely and cleanly without any dragging of the hind toes or stumbling.

Where the horse puts its feet when walking is termed "tracking". It is said to be "tracking true" when the hind foot is placed in the print left by the forefoot on the same side respectively without any deviation in the raising and lowering of the foot from the line of the feet and the point of the shoulder. Where there is deviation from that line and (a) the hind feet are placed outside that line, the fault is termed "tracking out"; (b) the hind feet are placed inside that line with perhaps swing of the body, the fault is termed "plaiting"; (c) one hind foot is placed outside that line and one inside, the fault is termed "tracking false".

Where, in the walking action, the hind foot is placed in front of the print made by the forefoot, the action is called "overtracking" and conversely, where it is placed behind such print, it is called "undertracking". A good horse overtracks. When cantering or galloping the horse should be well balanced whether running straight or turning.

A horse that is sound, well conformed, and well educated and managed, will invariably be a "free mover", that is to say, its action will be free, smooth, efficient, and effective. Conversely, a horse that is unsound, badly conformed, or poorly educated or managed, will have faulty, inefficient action, and will be prone to strain and injury.

CHAPTER 20 COLOURS AND MARKINGS

Section 20.1
Skin and Coat

The skin of the horse is composed of three layers: the epidermis or outer layer of dead cells that are constantly being shed; the dermis or true skin in which are located sweat glands, hair follicles, nerve endings, and so on; and the sub-dermis which binds the true skin to the underlying bone or muscle. The skin is soft and flexible to degrees that vary with its position on the body. Colour of the skin is due to the blood tinge that shows through translucent tissue and to various pigments, particularly melanin.

The thoroughbred has a fine coat with short hairs allowing small veins and muscles to show through, especially after work. Rugging or stabling are necessary for health care during cold weather.

A horse in good health and condition has a coat that is smooth and dry (depending upon air humidity) with a natural bloom or sheen to it. On the other hand, a horse that is ill, stale, or unfit, has a coat that is dull or patchy, or that unnaturally stands out from the skin.

Section 20.2
Evolution of Colours

Nature in its wonder provided the horse in the wild with coat colourings that assisted in its protection from predators by camouflage. After domestication many coat colours emerged for a number of reasons, including specialised breeding for colour.

Today there is a wide range of body colours and infinite variations in head, leg, and body markings.

Section 20.3
Instability of Early Colour

The colour of the foal at birth is usually a temporary colour only. The colour of its muzzle and eyelids will often reveal what its second or adult colour will be. Because of this instability of early colour and in order to prevent discrepancies in descriptions, the permanent or adult colour is not ascertained for registration purposes until the foal coat has been shed and the permanent coat colour established. This happens when the horse is nine or more months old.

Section 20.4
Colour of the Thoroughbreds

The *ASB* accepts for a thoroughbred —

(a) six descriptions of colour, namely: bay, black, brown, chestnut, grey, and white; and

(b) six descriptions of combined colours, namely: bay or brown, brown or black, grey-chestnut, grey-bay, grey-brown and grey-black.

The Australian Non Stud Book Register accepts horses with five additional coat colours, namely: appaloosa, cream, dun, pied and roan.

Black, brown, chestnut, and white horses are described according to the basic hair colour in their body coat. Bay and grey horses are described according to the patterns formed by two or more of these four basic hair colours in their coat. (White hairs present as solid markings, or ticking or flecking do not affect the description of the colour and must be described separately.)

Black — Black hairs are general throughout the body coat, limbs, mane and tail. Hairs of other colours are not present, but white hairs may be present as markings, flecking or ticking.

Brown — Black and brown hairs are general throughout the body coat; black hairs appear on the limbs, mane and tail; and brown hairs are present on the muzzle, the eyelids and often on the flanks. The descriptions "bay or brown" and "brown or black" are acceptable for horses which may be difficult to describe precisely.

Chestnut — The colour of the body coat and limbs may vary from a light washy yellow, through golden and reddish shades to a dark liver. The mane and tail may be darker or lighter than the body coat while the lighter coloured chestnuts can have a flaxen mane and tail.

White — This colour is not well defined in the thoroughbred and is very rare. The foals are born white, or predominantly white. Coloured hairs may be present on the poll, ears, or the tail. Tufts or patches of coloured hair may be present on the body. Some white horses have blue eyes.

Bay — The colour of the body coat may vary from a dull red brown to a yellow brown, approaching chestnut. The mane and tail are always black, as are the points, that is the lower parts of the legs, the muzzle and the tips of the ears.

Grey — The body coat consists of an uneven mixture of chestnut or brown or black hairs and white hairs. The horse's coat does not contain grey hair. The foal has coloured hair at birth, but with increasing age white hairs replace the coloured hairs to produce an appearance of grey. The white hairs usually appear first on the face and eventually the whole coat can appear white. The transitional stages between the coloured coat and the white coat can be described as grey-chestnut, grey-bay, grey-brown or grey-black. The mane, tail and points of a young grey horse contain a higher proportion of coloured hairs than the body coat.

The Keeper of the Stud Book accepts into official records only:
- chestnut progeny from the mating of a chestnut to a chestnut except where the progeny shows evidence of a white diluting gene;
- a grey horse if it has at least one grey parent;
- grey progeny sired by a stallion which has been identified, by an analysis of its stud record, as being a homozygous grey;

- non-chestnut progeny by a stallion which has been identified, by an analysis of its stud record, as being homozygous for a coat colour dominant to chestnut.

Section 20.5
Horsemen's Colour Preference

Horsemen are generally of the opinion that a thoroughbred should be of a good, solid, whole colour and preferably dark, often prefering a dark bay with black points. They do not like light bay, a washed-out chestnut, or too much white. Nor do they like a white sock or stocking probably because it indicates a light-coloured hoof which, they claim, does not have the toughness of a dark or blue hoof.

Section 20.6
Markings

The variations in head, leg, and body markings of horses are infinite and cannot be accurately described by a limited number of terms without certain arbitrary groupings. In some cases a combination of terms must be employed. All certificates of registration must conform with the standard terms as prescribed and be accompanied by a diagram on which the markings are indicated accurately.

Head markings are described by such terms as "star", "blaze", "snip", "stripe", and so on. Limb markings, in colloquially used terms not officially recognised, include white stocking, white sock, white fetlock, white pastern, white coronet, white heel, and so on.

Markings grow in size with the growth of a horse but never change in shape.

PART 10

FOOD AND HEALTH OF THE RACEHORSE

Chapter	21	Food and Nutrition
Section	21.1	Feeding — A Balance of Art and Science
	21.2	The Equine Digestive System
	21.3	Food Classifications
	21.4	Bulk Foods
	21.5	Energy Foods
	21.6	Vitamins and Minerals
	21.7	Daily Feed Intake
	21.8	Feeding Requirements of Thoroughbred Stock
	21.9	Feeding the Racehorse
	21.10	Stable Visitors' Titbits
	21.11	Unhygienic and Faulty Feeding
	21.12	Poisonous Plants
	21.13	Watering — An Important Part of Feeding
Chapter	22	Health and Medicine
Section	22.1	Health and Its Signs
	22.2	Veterinary Medicine
	22.3	"Horse Doctors"
	22.4	Disease and Its Signs
	22.5	Disease-producing Organisms
	22.6	Disease-producing Parasites
	22.7	Control of Parasites
	22.8	Preventive Medicine or Hygiene
	22.9	Duty of Trainer and Handler to Sick Horses
	22.10	Bleeders
	22.11	Care of the Sick Horse
	22.12	Temperature, Respiration and Pulse
	22.13	Weight
	22.14	Death or Destruction of Racehorse
Chapter	23	Life Span
Section	23.1	Uniformity of Age of Thoroughbreds
	23.2	Dental Age Chart
	23.3	Age Comparison — Equine and Human

CHAPTER 21 FOOD AND NUTRITION

Section 21.1
Feeding — A Balance of Art and Science

The essential feature of nutrition is that it must be considered for the individual horse. Guidelines have been prepared and issued on nutrition by veterinary surgeons and nutritionists, but there are no inflexible rules, nor could there be. Horses are individuals with different tastes and needs. Some are good doers while others are faddish and pickers. Some are naturally lean no matter what they eat while others become gross almost from looking at food.

In the feeding of a horse, therefore, there must be proper balance between theory on one hand, and practical experience on the other. In other words there must be a balance between science and art about what to feed and when to feed each individual horse, so that through such feeding and associated exercise it will attain and will maintain good health and condition in all respects.

Section 21.2
The Equine Digestive System

Proper feeding management requires some knowledge and understanding of the means by which a horse ingests and digests its food and absorbs nutrients into its bloodstream and lymph.

The horse is a non-ruminant herbivore, that is, it is adapted by nature to live by grazing on grass or herbage most of the day without regurgitation and cud-chewing like the ruminant herbivores (cattle, sheep, and so on).

The function of the horse's digestive system is to break ingested complex food material, such as grass, hay, and corn, into simple and safe substances (such as carbohydrates, proteins [amino acids], fatty acids, and so on) in a soluble form that permits ready absorption through the tissues of the intestines into the bloodstream and lymph to provide the body with the following essentials: energy; body repair materials; growth materials (through the period of active growth); vitamins, and other substances.

The amount of food that can be eaten by a horse at any one time is restricted by its comparatively small stomach. Food passes fairly quickly through the stomach and when empty its muscular contractions give the sensation of hunger. So the horse, in its natural state, eats little and often with small quantities of food passing almost continuously through its digestive and excretory systems.

Section 21.3
Food Classifications

Food of the horse may be simply classified as bulk foods (roughage), energy foods (carbohydrates, proteins, and fats), and supplementary foods (vitamins, mineral salts and trace elements).

Section 21.4
Bulk Foods

The staple diet of the fully pastured horse comprises natural grasses and other herbage of which there are many varieties of different food value. The partly pastured horse may also be given access, at times, to cultivated green crops and may be fed some oats. Grass and other green feeds are succulent and have a high water content, but low carbohydrate content.

On the other hand, the roughage foods of the fully stabled horse are non-succulent hays or chaffs. These foods do not yield much nutriment, but contain a significant percentage of crude fibre.

Root vegetables, particularly carrots which are rich in vitamin A, are valuable supplements to the ration of the stabled horse, adding variety and succulence.

Section 21.5
Energy Foods

Energy foods (called the "short", "hard" or "concentrated" foods) of the stabled horse include grains such as oats, barley, and corn (also called "maize"); beans and peas: oilseeds, particularly linseed; bran in small quantities; sugar in liquid form, particularly molasses; and manufactured cubes. These palatable foods comprise the following:

- Carbohydrate concentrates: these provide the main source of energy, sugar glucose, but if the energy is not immediately needed the carbohydrates are stored in the liver as glycogen for later use. Any excess that cannot be handled by the liver is converted into body fat.
- Protein concentrates: these build new tissue, repair damaged tissue, make hormones and enzymes, keep the acid-alkaline blood content balanced, and so on. As protein is digested it is broken down into smaller compounds, called amino acids, which, when they reach the body cells, are formed into protein again.
- Fat concentrates: these are a major source of energy and are necessary for the proper functioning of all tissues.

Section 21.6
Vitamins and Minerals

Essential food substances such as vitamins and minerals are only required by the equine body in comparatively small quantities but, without them, proper metabolism cannot take place. Indeed, the equine body can be endangered by a single vitamin or mineral deficiency.

The most important vitamins are A, B complex, C, D, and E. Vitamin D (sunshine vitamin) is plentiful in Australia while minute quantities of other vitamins are found in their natural state in a balanced ration.

In addition to vitamins the body requires salt (sodium chloride), iron and other mineral substances. Nature provides for these in balanced diets.

Under some circumstances it is considered necessary to supplement a horse's ration with vitamins and minerals and for this purpose there are various proprietary preparations.

Section 21.7
Daily Feed Intake

The type and quantity of food required by a horse depends upon such factors as the following: the purpose for which it is being used; its associated workload; its age and sex; its size and weight; whether it is fully stabled, partly stabled, or fully pastured; and the prevailing climate and season.

Section 21.8
Feeding Requirements of Thoroughbred Stock

The diet of the racehorse undergoing training and racing needs to be very high in energy while the energy intake of a horse when idle must necessarily be reduced to conform to the needs of its idle state. Special diets may be necessary for breeding stock (stallions, broodmares, and foals) and for sick or convalescing animals.

Section 21.9
Feeding the Racehorse

The thoroughbred needs a great amount of energy for the performance of muscular effort during the intensive work of racing. The efficiency with which it performs that work depends upon its production of the necessary energy when required during a race by:

(a) having stored in its muscles and liver sufficient glycogen and other substances; and

(b) being capable of supplying its muscles with large amounts of oxygen speedily and efficiently by having developed, through proper training, good respiratory and circulatory systems.

The trainer decides, having been advised by a veterinary surgeon or nutritionist, the feeding tables, or resorting to horse sense, as to the total amount of the daily ration, the components of that ration, and the number of feeds for each horse.

A highly stressed racehorse needs a special ration rich in energy, low in fibre, and fortified with vitamins and minerals to maintain proper nutrient balance.

It is impracticable to prescribe or to classify rations for racehorses. Substantial variations of rations may occur as between horses of the one trainer and as between trainers.

Indeed the skill and judgment of the trainer are vital in feeding. Some trainers may, through feeding and handling, have their horses in good condition in all respects while others lacking such skill and judgment will have horses poor in condition in many respects.

Section 21.10
Stable Visitors' Titbits

Trainers do not approve of owners or visitors giving titbits to the stabled racehorse. Titbits such as sugar lumps, bread, apples, and so on, may interfere with the horse's digestion. If anything, horse cubes should be substituted.

Section 21.11
Unhygienic and Faulty Feeding

Good management should provide for good quality feed to be bought in the first instance and it should be properly stored, handled, and regularly inspected. Stale and spoiled fodder becomes heavily contaminated, with such things as harmful bacteria, vermin, parasites and their eggs, dust, dirt, animal faeces, mould, fungal spores, fungal poison, and so on.

Section 21.12
Poisonous Plants

There are many plants poisonous to horses. Horses have an instinctive sense for these, however, and will not eat them if they are at pasture and have the right of selection. Unfortunately where hay containing poisonous plants is included in a horse's fodder, the horse, in the unnatural circumstances, may eat such plants and become poisoned.

Section 21.13
Watering — An Important Part of Feeding

The horse, like other animals, is mostly made up of water and there is constant need to replenish losses incurred through excretion. Water keeps all bodily processes functioning and regulates the body temperature. Therefore, the horse should be allowed to drink freely at any time except, of course, it should never be allowed to drink quickly or excessively when hot. For this purpose an ample supply of fresh clean water should always be available to the horse.

CHAPTER 22 HEALTH AND MEDICINE

Section 22.1
Health and its Signs

A horse's health depends upon certain essentials, namely, proper surroundings, sufficient and suitable food, and the maintenance of vital activity of the whole organism.

Signs of a healthy horse include such things as: alertness; brightness of manner; normal easy posture; cocked and mobile ears; clear eyes; pink and moist membranes of the eyes, nose, and mouth; clean nose; good body condition; supple and elastic skin; glossy coat and appendages; healthy hooves; good appetite; normal respiration, pulse, and temperature; regular and proper functioning of the organs of digestion, secretion, and excretion; normal gait at all paces; enjoyment of work; and so on.

Section 22.2
Veterinary Medicine

"Veterinary medicine" is that branch of medicine about the study, prevention, diagnosis and treatment of animal diseases.

Some veterinary surgeons who specialise in the prevention, diagnosis and treatment of horse diseases are called "equine veterinary surgeons". There is an Australian Equine Veterinarian Association and only those specialists who are approved by the proprietors of the *ASB* may issue horse identification certificates, take blood samples, or perform certain other services as are required by the Keeper of the Stud Book.

Section 22.3
Horse Doctors

There are many persons unqualified in veterinary science who are ready to advise owners about the treatment of their horses. Those people may possess knowledge handed down by word-of-mouth of customary or traditional treatments of horse diseases (that is, folklore). They may be well intentioned and may, in cases, obtain some success.

A person who pretends to have knowledge, skill, or qualifications that he or she does not possess, or who offers advice not based on the principles of veterinary medicine is practising "equine quackery" and is commonly referred to as a "horse doctor".

In these times any owner or person responsible for the health care of a horse is simply foolhardy to seek other than the services of an equine veterinarian.

Section 22.4
Disease and its Signs

Disease, defined simply, is any departure from normal health or, strictly, any condition where body structure or function is abnormally altered.

Disease can be inherited, congenital, or acquired; general or local; structural or functional; contagious or non-contagious.

Many horses may have a predisposition to disease which may cause the body or any of its parts to be less resistant to the action of an exciting cause (see below). Predisposing causes include: age, sex, temperament, colour (grey horses are more subject to melanotic tumours than horses of any other colour), individual susceptibility including allergies, heredity, predisposition from certain diseases to others, debility, deficiency of essential food components, and so on.

Exciting causes, or the agents responsible for disease, include: disease-producing organisms; mechanical causes, being injuries, over-exertion, pressure, friction, impaction by ingesta, foreign bodies, or calculi; chemical, thermal, or electrical causes; and causes through neglect. Included under the heading, neglect, are failure to observe basic preventive measures, failure to carry out sound husbandry procedures, and failure to take preventive veterinary treatment measures.

For any disease the veterinary surgeon's responsibilities are to determine the nature and circumstances of the disease (diagnose); forecast the probable course and termination of the disease (prognose); and decide upon the treatment (prescribe).

Section 22.5
Disease-Producing Organisms

Infective diseases are caused by organisms, called "germs" or "microbes", of which there are five types, namely: bacteria, protozoa, viruses, parasites, and fungi. Most of such organisms are microscopic, although viruses are ultramicroscopic and some parasites are macroscopic.

Fortunately, most bacteria are more helpful to man and beast than harmful. Some, however, are disease-producing.

Section 22.6
Disease-Producing Parasites

A parasite is an organism that lives in, or on, another organism, called the "host", at whose expense the parasite obtains nourishment. Parasites, or their larvae, or the toxins from tissue damaged by such parasites or larvae, are responsible for a great variety of diseases in the horse.

External parasites which include lice, mange mites, and ticks, may be commonly found on neglected animals, but rarely on the well-groomed, well-cared-for thoroughbred.

Internal parasites of most common concern to the health of the horse are various types of worms and their larvae, and the larvae of various types of flies. Symptoms of internal parasite infestation differ according to the type of parasite, but may include such things as: digestive disorders such as colic or diarrhoea; dropped abdomen; loss of appetite; loss of condition; coughing; listlessness; weakness; anaemia; blood clotting; gastric ulcers; intestinal blockages; dry staring coat; and so on. Complications may include ruptured intestines, pneumonia, and so on.

Section 22.7
Control of Parasites

Complete control of parasites is impossible, although, much can be done to reduce the dangers and losses from heavy parasitical infestation. The correct approach is prevention rather than curing. Management measures for effective control include the preparation and rigid enforcement of a sanitation program for the place or establishment where horses are kept and an inspection and treatment program for every horse.

Section 22.8
Preventive Medicine or Hygiene

Preventive, or prophylactic, medicine is that branch of medicine which attempts to maintain the balance of health when disease is imminent. It is, therefore, closely allied to hygiene, which is concerned with the maintenance of health and prevention of diseases generally.

If a horse is to function efficiently and to attain or maintain usefulness for the service expected of it, it must be kept in good health, that is, free from disease. The primary responsibility for this lies with the manager of any place or establishment where horses are kept. The manager must be in consultation with a veterinary surgeon, and knowing the nature of diseases and the causes, prepare programs providing for their control, detection, and treatment.

Planned daily exercise of the confined horse is necessary for good circulation, muscle tone, digestion, and prevention of constipation and colic. Horses that are not exercised adequately may become bored, nervous, develop behavioural vices, and contract diseases through bad circulation.

Section 22.9
Duty of Trainer and Handler to Sick Horses

It is not the duty of the trainer to diagnose a disease, but to know from experience and constant observation when something is wrong with a horse. The trainer will know of the troubles to which racehorses are prone and will personally attend to ailments of a minor nature. For comparatively severe disease, however, the trainer should have an understanding and knowledge to apply first aid, assess the need and urgency for a visit by the veterinary surgeon, and co-operate with the veterinarian in managing and nursing the sick horse.

Section 22.10
Bleeders

Nose bleeding (epistaxis) from one nostril of a horse after a training gallop or race is common in racehorses. The origin of such bleeding is invariably from the mucous membrane of the nasal chamber. A horse may suffer recurring attacks without injury and ultimately become quite normal.

Where, however, a horse under the control of a trainer suffers an attack of bleeding from both nostrils at any time then, in accordance with the Rules of Racing, that trainer must, as soon as practicable, report such bleeding to the stewards.

In such event the horse in question without the permission of stewards: (a) cannot be trained or galloped on any racecourse for a period of two months; (b) cannot be started in any race for a period of three months and then only after a satisfactory gallop of at least 1000m in the presence of a steward.

Further, the Australian Rules of Racing provide that if a horse suffers more than one attack of bleeding from both nostrils, it is ineligible to start in any race.

Section 22.11
Care of the Sick Horse

In a well-managed stable when signs of comparatively serious sickness are observed in a horse, it and its clothing and gear are isolated, its bedding removed, its stable disinfected, and the veterinarian called.

It takes good nursing and time for the horse to recover. As it gradually recovers, its diet and exercise are gradually altered.

Section 22.12
Temperature, Respiration, and Pulse

When nursing a sick horse its temperature, respiration, and pulse, must be taken regularly and must be recorded.

Temperature is taken by inserting the bulbous, clinical thermometer gently into the anus. After about three minutes the thermometer is removed and read. Normal temperature reading for a mature horse is about 38°C or 100.5°F. Fluctuations of more than about 1°C or 2°F indicate some abnormality.

Respiration rate is ascertained by watching the rise and fall of the rib cage. Normal rate for a mature horse in a state of rest is between 10 and 15 respirations per minute.

Pulse rate is taken by feeling with the first two fingers at the back of the jaw, at the inside of the elbow, or immediately above the fetlock. The usual rate for a mature horse fluctuates between 35 and 40 beats per minute.

The frequency and force of respiration and pulse are affected by disease, exercise, or emotion.

Section 22.13
Weight

The weight of a horse in racing condition generally varies between 535kg and 585kg, although some are of lighter weight and some of heavier weight.

A good horseman can "fairly closely" estimate the weight of a horse merely by visual inspection.

Section 22.14
Death or Destruction of Racehorse

The death of a registered racehorse, and the cause of death, if known, are required to be reported to the Principal Club in the case of a horse in training by the trainer, or by the owner when death occurs at any other time.

In the event of any horse being injured on a racecourse and in the opinion of the stewards or an approved veterinary surgeon, destruction of such horse is advisable to save unnecessary suffering, the stewards or veterinary surgeon may order the horse to be destroyed and appoint a person to perform that task.

A horse may be destroyed by injection of a drug, clubbing, or shooting. Shooting is the best method, provided the animal is shot in the right place and that is the point of intersection of diagonal lines drawn from the base of the ear to the centre of the eye of the opposite side.

The manner of disposal of the carcass of a dead horse (that is, by burning, burial, or disposal to a rendering firm) depends upon the cause of death and this needs to be known or determined by a veterinary surgeon.

PART 10 FOOD AND HEALTH OF THE RACEHORSE

CHAPTER 23 LIFE SPAN

Section 23.1
Uniformity of Age of Thoroughbreds

The breeding season in Australia (as in all other countries in the Southern Hemisphere) is in spring which officially starts on 1 September. Allowing for the gestation period of about eleven months, foaling takes place between August and December of the following year. In accordance with the Rules of Racing the age of a horse is reckoned from 1 August in the year in which it is foaled if it is foaled on or after that date. If foaled before that date, however, its age is reckoned from the 1 August of the previous year.

In the Northern Hemisphere the age of horses is reckoned from 1 January in similar manner to that explained above.

Section 23.2
Dental Age Chart

Although the age of a thoroughbred is documented and readily determined, there are times when a veterinarian or horseman may need to assess a horse's age. To do this they may use either the Infundibulum Theory or the Dental Age Chart.

The Infundibulum Theory, although disproved scientifically, is still used for ordinary practical purposes of estimating a horse's age. Under the theory, the disappearance of the infundibulum or marked depression in the table of the crown of the incisor teeth, was thought to occur constantly at definite periods during the life of a horse.

As the result of research a Dental Age Chart has been developed indicating the most consistent times at which various teeth appear, grow, shape, colour, wear, groove, and erupt. Although the times of any such happenings may vary because of the habits and uses of a horse, the nature of its food, and so on, the examination of the teeth and their dentition is one of the main methods used to determine the age of a horse.

The upper and lower sets of teeth of the adult horse are identical in that each set comprises three pairs of incisors or biting teeth (the centrals, laterals, and corners) in front; if a male horse, a tush, canine, or bridle tooth on each side behind the corner incisor; and after a gap called the "bars of the mouth", six molars or grinders on each side.

Foals cut their two central incisors when they are about 10 days old and these are followed within six weeks by the lateral incisors, and within nine weeks by the corner incisors. Those white milk teeth are gradually replaced from the age of three by yellow permanent teeth starting with the central incisors. The lateral incisors are replaced at four, and the corner incisors at five. The tushes or bridle teeth have also usually grown by that time.

Section 23.3
Age Comparison — Equine and Human

Officially, a horse is described as "aged" when it is more than seven years old. This custom arose in the past when the age of the horse could be measured up to that age with some accuracy. Thereafter measurement was guesswork.

There is no standard formula for corresponding equine years and human years. However, veterinary estimations relative to corresponding equine and human ages are somewhat as indicated in the following table:

EQUINE AGE YEARS	HUMAN AGE YEARS
1	1–7
2	8–11
3	12–15
4	16–19
5	20–23
6	24–27
7	28–31
8	32–35
9	36–39
10	40+
15	50+
20	60+
25	70+
30	80+

Generally a horse is not fully matured until it attains five years of age at which time it is considered to have attained its full height.

At about fifteen years of age the usefulness of a horse of either sex is usually well on the decline, although some, at that time, are full of life and vigour. On a mean average horses live to about eighteen but, of course, the exceptional and fit ones may live on well past that age.

PART 11

REGISTRATION OF THOROUGHBRED PEDIGREES AND RACEHORSES

Chapter	24	Registration of Pedigrees
Section	24.1	Development of the Thoroughbred in Australia
	24.2	The Australian Stud Book (ASB)
	24.3	Eligibility for Admission to the ASB
	24.4	Bases of Entries in ASB or Non-Stud Book Register
	24.5	Broodmare Records
	24.6	Female Families
	24.7	Foal Identification
	24.8	Freeze-branding
	24.9	Blood-typing
Chapter	25	Registration of Racehorses
Section	25.1	The Registrar of Racehorses
	25.2	Registration Prerequisite to Racing
	25.3	Naming of Horse
	25.4	Certificate of Registration
	25.5	Document of Description
	25.6	Transfer of Ownership

CHAPTER 24 REGISTRATION OF PEDIGREES

Section 24.1
Development of the Thoroughbred in Australia

Early thoroughbred imports into Australia included "Rockingham" (UK) in 1799 and "Northumberland" (UK) and "Washington" (USA) in 1802. Some notable Arab stallions were also imported in the early years.

Up until about 1830 imports were mainly from India, but after that time the quality and quantity of thoroughbred imports improved significantly with an influx of stallions and mares from England and Ireland. Some of those imports included winners of England's classic or prestigious races, such as; "The Hermit", "Fisherman", "Pitsford", "The Marquis", "Marchioness" and "Hawthornden". Although Arab blood was vital in the early years, the thoroughbred breed has been refined to a stage where every full thoroughbred in Australia can be traced back in parentage for at least 100 years in the *Australian Stud Book (ASB)* and has a minimum of 18 generations of pure blood.

Section 24.2
The Australian Stud Book (ASB)

The term "Australian Stud Book" means the official records as kept and published for thoroughbred bloodlines in Australia.

The joint proprietors of the *ASB* are the Australian Jockey Club and the Victoria Racing Club. Those proprietors have appointed an official called "The Keeper of the Australian Stud Book" and charged him with the function and duty of keeping and ensuring the accuracy, quality, and integrity of *ASB* records. The Keeper and the organisation which assists him in the performance of his responsibility (hence referred to as the *KASB*) are located in offices of the Australian Jockey Club at Royal Randwick Racecourse.

Objectives of the KASB are, among other things:

- To ensure the true parentage, accurate description, and identification of all thoroughbreds born in Australia. This is achieved by requiring various returns to be furnished by breeders and owners about breeding stock and their offspring and by establishing identification benchmarks.
- To record and publish the breeding lines of the thoroughbred in Australia. The *ASB* established and maintained in this regard has been approved by the International Stud Book Committee.
- To provide a recording service about breeding lines of horses of predominantly *thoroughbred* bloodlines that are ineligible for inclusion in the *ASB*. The Australian *Non-Stud Book Register* is maintained in this regard.
- To ensure the accuracy of pedigrees and descriptions of all imported thoroughbreds.
- To provide documentation about exported thoroughbreds for overseas stud authorities; and so on.

Section 24.3
Eligibility for Admission to the ASB

For a horse or mare to be eligible for admission to the *ASB* it must have been recorded previously in:

(a) the *ASB* (as a foaling record under its dam); or

(b) a foreign Stud Book recognised by the joint proprietors of the *ASB* and be the product of a mating between a sire and dam both registered before 1 January 1980 in a Stud Book approved by the International Stud Book Committee, or trace in all lines of its pedigree to horses so registered; or

(c) the Australian *Non-Stud Book Register* and been promoted to Stud Book status by the joint proprietors of the *ASB* supported by the unanimous agreement of the International Stud Book Committee.

Alternatively it must be satisfactorily proven that the horse or mare has eight recorded crosses consecutively with horses qualified as in categories (b) and (c) above, including the cross of which it is the progeny.

Section 24.4
Bases of Entries in ASB or Non-Stud Book Register

Entries in the *ASB* or the *Non-Stud Book Register* are based on four types of documents (recording the activities of sires and dams) which are required to be lodged by breeders with the *KASB*. Those documents are as follows:

(1) *Stallion Return Forms* which are required to be lodged by persons responsible for stallions before the start of each season for each stallion intended to be used to cover mares during that season.

(2) *Service Date Declaration Reports* whereby persons in charge of stallions furnish particulars of all coverings of mares by their stallions during that season.

(3) *Covering Certificates* prepared by persons in charge of stallions and furnished by breeders responsible for the broodmares covered.

(4) *Mare Return Forms* lodged by people concerned with broodmares for which they are responsible, declaring the outcome of stallion coverings or, as the case may be, advising of decisions not to have mares covered.

Section 24.5
Broodmare Records

The *KASB* record of broodmares comprises two broad categories namely (1) mares with open records for which Mare Return Forms can be accepted and (2) mares with closed records for which Mare Return Forms cannot be accepted.

Mares with open records are further categorised as active broodmares and potential broodmares.

Active broodmares are those for which a Mare Return Form has been lodged in at least one of the past two seasons and also those listed for the first time on a Stallion Service Date Declaration Report.

Potential broodmares are those less than ten years old that have never been listed on a Service Date Declaration Report and for which a Mare Return Form has never been lodged. (These mares may be racemares or used for some non-racing or non-thoroughbred purpose.) When a potential broodmare is covered for the first time, as indicated on a Service Date Declaration Report, she is assigned to the active broodmare category and a Mare Return Form must be lodged for her.

Mares with closed records are categorised by their fate: dead; pensioned-off; unofficially exported; dropped out; shipped out; or not bred.

Changes between categories of mares may, in some cases, be routine while in others the process may only be permitted under extenuating circumstances.

Section 24.6
Female Families

The *KASB* records "Family Tables" which detail the female line of descent from:

(a) an imported taproot mare (which has a foaling reference in a recognised stud book) whose descendants have established a recognised female family line in Australia or New Zealand; or

(b) a colonial taproot mare (whose origin is not traceable to a mare in the *English Stud Book* or in any other recognised stud book) whose descendants have established a recognised female colonial family line in Australia or New Zealand.

There are 19 families with colonial taproots that are accepted by the KASB.

Section 24.7
Foal Identification

Every foal must be accurately identified before acceptance into the *KASB* official records. The benchmarks of the identification process are the description of the natural features of the horse (see Chapter 20 for colours and markings), the freeze-brand, and the blood type.

For this purpose a veterinarian (appointed or approved by the *KASB*) attends every foal or weanling at a time after 31 March each year for the purpose of compiling a description of the animal and taking a blood sample for blood-typing.

When a yearling or weanling has been identified, blood-typed, and parentage validated, the KASB issues to the breeder/owner an Identification Certificate and a Parentage Validation Advice which together form the "Identification Document for an Unnamed Racehorse". This document must accompany the horse at all times until it is registered by the Registrar of Racehorses.

Section 24.8
Freeze-branding

Foals and weanlings are required to be freeze-branded (firebranding, acid branding, and alkali branding are not accepted) in sufficient time for their brands to be discernible by 31 March of their first year of life. This is required so that at the time of examination by a veterinarian the brands are present as white hair markings. This takes about six weeks from the time of application of the brand.

The brand comprises:

(a) a stud, station, owner, or agent's distinguishing brand consisting of letters or symbols;

(b) an identification brand consisting of two numbers, one above the other, the top number indicating the foal drop number and the bottom number indicating the last figure of the year or deemed year of foaling.

Brands must be placed on the near or off-shoulders and must comply in all respects with the law of the State or Territory where the horse is bred.

Section 24.9
Blood-Typing

Every horse must be "parentage validated" before it is eligible for acceptance into the *KASB* official records. The term "parentage validated" means that the horse's blood type has been tested against the blood-types of its nominated sire and dam and the horse cannot be excluded as being the progeny of those two animals.

Blood samples are collected from horses at required times by veterinarians appointed or approved by the *KASB* and delivered for blood-typing to the Australian Bloodtyping Research Laboratory at the St Lucia campus of the University of Queensland. That laboratory was developed for the *KASB* and is approved by the International Stud Book Committee.

In the blood-typing process of a horse's blood sample, blood groups and blood proteins are demonstrated in a way to enable them to be tested against another horse's blood-type. Where blood-typing cannot produce a solution (for example, in a double mating of two closely related stallions) the laboratory has a range of DNA tests for use as a definitive back-up to routine blood-typing. (DNA typing means the application of DNA technology to demonstrate variations in the DNA structure of genes.)

Results of blood-typing by the laboratory are recorded in a computerised data bank of blood profiles.

PART 11 REGISTRATION OF THOROUGHBRED PEDIGREES AND RACEHORSES

CHAPTER 25 REGISTRATION OF RACEHORSES

Section 25.1
The Registrar of Racehorses

Registration of racehorses was introduced in all States of Australia in 1911, among other things, to overcome the problems that had been experienced as a result of a number of horses (particularly well performed horses named after some champion) having the same name.

While Principal Clubs have the primary responsibility for the registration of galloping horses the function of registering all racehorses in Australia is performed on their behalf by the Registrar of Racehorses. The Registrar is appointed by the Australian Jockey Club and a Deputy Registrar by some Principal Clubs.

Section 25.2
Registration Prerequisite to Racing

The Australian Rules of Racing provide that no horse may be entered for, or run in, any race or barrier trial unless it has been registered by the Registrar of Racehorses. There are certain provisions to cover horses registered abroad and unregistered yearlings.

An application to register a horse must give particulars on a standard form about the following matters: breeder; owner; age; sex; colour; any brands or distinguishing marks; pedigree; six proposed names of the horse in order of preference; and other such information as the Registrar may consider necessary.

Under the Rules a horse cannot be registered for racing unless it has been accepted for inclusion as a foal in:

- the *ASB*;
- the Australian Non-Stud Book Register;
- the stud book of a recognised turf authority overseas; or
- the non-stud book register of a recognised authority overseas.

Section 25.3
Naming of Horse

The Registrar may refuse to register any name which, for any reason, he may consider undesirable. Except with the approval of the Registrar, a horse may not be registered with the same name as any other horse previously registered in Australia until 15 years after the date of the previous registration of the name.

The Registrar may approve a change of name of a registered horse, but in such a case the horse is not permitted to run in a race under the new name until the Document of Description in that name has been issued by the Registrar. The old name as well as the new name must be given in every entry form (and race book) until the horse has run in six races in the territory of one Principal Club or in two races within its metropolitan area or suburban radius.

In the case of a thoroughbred born overseas and imported into Australia a suffix indicating its country of origin is an integral part of such horse's name.

Section 25.4
Certificate of Registration

Upon allowing an application for registration of a horse the Registrar issues a Certificate of Registration to the owner.

Section 25.5
Document of Description

This term means a document bearing that name that has been issued by the Registrar of Racehorses about the identity of a racehorse described therein. The term includes a Certificate of Registration.

The certificate sets forth particulars of the age, sex, colour, markings, brand, pedigree, owners, and so on of that horse.

The certificate authenticates the identity of a horse and must necessarily accompany it wherever it goes. It is for practical purposes its passport.

No horse is permitted to start in a race or barrier trial conducted by any race club unless the Document of Description of the horse is produced, if required, to the stewards or their authorised representative before that race or trial.

Section 25.6
Transfer of Ownership

Every transfer of ownership after registration must be advised by the transferee to the Registrar for registration of such transfer. Upon allowing an application for transfer of ownership the Registrar makes an appropriate endorsement upon the Document of Description.

PART 12
OWNERS AND OWNERSHIP

Chapter	26	Owners and Lessees
Section	26.1	Who May Own or Lease
	26.2	Partnerships
	26.3	Syndicates
	26.4	Promoters
	26.5	Leases
	26.6	Assumed Names of Owners and Lessees
	26.7	Racing Colours
	26.8	Racehorse Owners' Association
Chapter	27	Financial Viability of Ownership
Section	27.1	Ownership Costs
	27.2	Ownership Income
	27.3	Ownership not Financially Viable
	27.4	Owners — The Keystone of the Racing Industry
	27.5	Auxiliary Ownership Purposes
Chapter	28	Buying and Selling a Racehorse
Section	28.1	Contract of Sale
	28.2	Sale with Engagements
	28.3	Insurance
Chapter	29	Soundness of Horse for Racing
Section	29.1	Soundness
	29.2	Examination as to Soundness

CHAPTER 26 OWNERS AND LESSEES

Section 26.1
Who May Own or Lease

The owner or lessee of a racehorse may be:

(a) a person;

(b) a partnership of not fewer than two nor more than six persons;

(c) a syndicate being —

- a combination of not fewer than seven nor more than 20 people;
- a firm being a person or any number of people not exceeding twenty, registered and carrying on business;
- a company incorporated and carrying on business;
- a stud being a person, partnership, firm, or company engaged in the breeding of horses for racing.

Section 26.2
Partnerships

While a partnership may consist of from two to six people, only one of those people may be empowered to manage the horse concerned. The person vested with that right of management is the person named first on the Document of Description or the Lease Agreement unless the partners appoint one of the other partners to act as manager.

Section 26.3
Syndicates

Every body or association of people that wishes to own, lease, or race a horse as a syndicate must apply to the Principal Club for registration.

An application to register a syndicate must be accompanied by the Syndicate Agreement and Trust Deed duly completed in the prescribed form.

Section 26.4
Promoters

The term "promoter" means any person or group or association of persons who, for valuable consideration, offers or invites any other person or group or association of persons to subscribe for shares or participate in any manner or scheme, the objects of which include the breeding or racing of a thoroughbred horse or horses.

Every promoter is required to hold a dealer's licence issued by the Australian Securities Commission and be recorded on the Register of Promoters held by the Principal Club and the Registrar of Racehorses. Promoters must obtain approval from the Principal Club for each Promoter's Disclosure Statement before an offer is made.

Section 26.5
Leases

The owner of a racehorse who wishes to retain ownership for breeding purposes after its racing career is finished, or for any other purpose, may lease the horse to a person, partnership, or syndicate under conditions set forth in the Lease Agreement.

The Agreement is required to be in the prescribed form and furnished to the Principal Club for registration. If the lease is determined before the due date, notice thereof is required to be lodged with the Principal Club before the horse in question is thereafter nominated for a race.

Financial arrangements usually provide for the lessee to meet all training and racing costs and to receive all prizemoney won, save a stipulated percentage (usually one-third) of such prizemoney which is payable to the lessor. The lessor of course is responsible for the original cost of breeding or purchase of the horse in question, and for insurance during the term of the lease if considered necessary.

Section 26.6
Assumed Names of Owners and Lessees

If an owner or lessee wishes to avoid publicity, notice, or formal attentions, such person may, with appropriate approval, conceal his or her identity by the use of an assumed name.

In the first instance such person must apply to the Registrar of Racehorses for approval and entry of appropriate particulars in a Register of Assumed Names. If such approval is granted, the Principal Club may register and annually renew that assumed name.

Section 26.7
Racing Colours

Every owner or lessee of a racehorse is required to apply to the Principal Club for approval and registration of racing colours selected by such person. Provided that the proposed colours are in accordance with guidelines issued under the Rules and are not registered in the name of any other person, the Principal Club may approve and register those colours for the exclusive use of the applicant. Where the person has two or more horses starting in the one race, all but one of such horses is required to carry some distinguishing mark as ordered by the stewards.

Section 26.8
Racehorse Owners' Association

Membership of the Racehorse Owners' Association is open to any person being the owner or part-owner or lessee of a horse registered in accordance with the Australian Rules of Racing. The objects of the Association are stated as being: to foster the sport of horseracing; to protect and improve the rights, privileges and conditions of horse owners by direct or indirect negotiation with relevant parties; to deal with all or any matter or matters conducive to the advancement of racing generally; and to negotiate competitive insurance rates for racehorses.

PART 12 OWNERS AND OWNERSHIP

CHAPTER 27 FINANCIAL VIABILITY OF OWNERSHIP

Section 27.1
Ownership Costs

Costs of ownership include the initial capital cost of purchase of the racehorse and the recurrent costs that are incurred while the horse is being trained, raced, or spelled.

The main recurrent cost is the training fee which is a matter for agreement between owner and trainer although fees to be charged by trainers are recommended from time to time by the Trainers' Association.

In addition to the training fee, the trainer will pass on to the owner costs incurred for such things as: veterinary services; farriery services; vitamin and mineral feed supplements; track and trial fees; saddlery, clothing, and bandages supplied; and transport.

Racing costs borne by the owner include nomination and acceptance fees; farrier's plating service; riding fees; and transport. Some clubs allow rebates to owners for some racing expenses as an inducement to race their horses at meetings conducted by such clubs. Spelling costs and insurance are also borne by the owner.

Section 27.2
Ownership Income

On the other hand, there is the amount of prize money won by the horse in question for the year.

From prize money won, payments are made by way of direct deduction by the Race Club at prescribed percentage rates of 10 per cent and 5 per cent to the trainer and jockey respectively.

In addition, the connections may elect to make gifts to the trainer and jockey and any other person, such as the strapper, closely associated with the horse.

Section 27.3
Ownership Not Financially Viable

The comparison for any year of average prize money earned against ownership costs (see Appendix to Section 69.7) indicates that on average a racehorse earns far less prize money than the recurrent costs met by the owner in training, racing, and caring for it. There is no recovery of capital cost from prize money. Of course, on completion of its racing career, a mare may have a residual value as a broodmare and a stallion may have a residual value as a sire.

The average method of comparison indicates that racehorse ownership is not a viable investment proposition. That finding is confirmed by an analysis of prize money distributions to owners and trainers which indicates quite clearly that the overwhelming proportion of the total amount of prize money distributed each year goes to a small group of owners and trainers. Most horses earn little, if any, prize money and their owners incur substantial losses.

As indicated in Section 43.7, about 40 per cent of racehorses fail to win a race during their careers, 20 per cent win only one race, 10 per cent win only two races, and 30 per cent win three or more races.

Section 27.4
Owners — The Keystone of the Racing Industry

Owners and punters are the keystone of the racing industry. Without them there would not be an industry; they indeed are necessary for the existence, continuance and financial wellbeing of the industry.

The huge sums of money paid by owners for the purchase and upkeep of racehorses provides income or employment to other participants in the industry, particularly the breeders and the trainers.

Section 27.5
Auxiliary Ownership Purposes

Most owners incur substantial losses. The question may well be raised that if the probability of owners getting any return from their substantial outlays is very low, that is to say, if ownership is seldom a rational pursuit, why are there so many owners and so many persons aspiring to be owners?

Ownership has been said to be a form of long odds gambling in which the possibility of leading in a classic winner is equivalent to winning a major lottery. All owners would naturally hope that the horse they purchase has the potential to win races and hence prize money and bets. People have other reasons for becoming and, despite heavy costs, continuing to be owners of racehorses -

- Some hope through ownership to cultivate the friendship of trainers, jockeys, other owners and racing people and so have access to "inside knowledge" for betting purposes.
- Some, being business people, seek the opportunity through ownership to foster business relationships.
- Some are prepared to pay for participation through ownership in the racing sport, entertainment, or society which gives them so much pleasure.
- Some develop a strong emotional attachment to their horses and could no more part with their horses than with their children.
- And so on.

CHAPTER 28 BUYING AND SELLING A RACEHORSE

Section 28.1
Contract of Sale

A contract for the purchase or sale of a racehorse may be entered into at an auction sale conducted by a bloodstock agent, or privately in response to advertisement or other contact.

Underpinning the contract is the common law principle "caveat emptor" or "let the buyer beware", and unless proper precautions are taken before entering into the contract, the buyer could have made a poor purchase. Firstly, it is vital that the intending buyer examine the horse and its identification papers before purchase. Other precautions which the buyer may take include the following:

(a) commissioning an equine veterinary surgeon to examine and report on the soundness of the horse in question for the purpose of racing or, as the case may be, breeding;

(b) questioning the vendor about the soundness, qualities, and suitability of the horse for the purposes required and also about the temperament of the horse and whether it is free from vices or bad habits;

(c) obtaining from other pertinent sources, all relevant information about the horse;

(d) seeking the benefit of advice from a horseman preferably an independent professional having the relative knowledge, experience and "eye for a horse";

(e) ensuring that the contract document is properly drawn up.

Conditions and warranties concerning the contract of sale should be expressed in writing in the contract document. If not so expressed, certain matters which are vital to a contract are generally required by law to be implied.

For a sale by auction, certain responsibilities are imposed upon the auctioneer by law. Consequently, the conditions of sale are specified in the auction catalogue.

Broadly, the law provides that if any "condition" of the contract is not met, the contract may be rescinded by the party suffering damage who may sue for damages. If the conditions of the contract are met but a "warranty" is not, the contract stands, but the buyer may sue for damages.

In the event of a dispute between buyer and vendor after a contract for sale has been entered into, the legal aspects become very technical. The conditions and warranties set forth in the contract document, or implied by law, become vital considerations.

Section 28.2
Sale with Engagements

In the absence of any agreement to the contrary, horses are taken to be sold with their engagements. Such sale is required to be registered in accordance with the Rules, and the transfer of the engagements is required to be submitted to the committee of the club concerned or the stewards for approval.

Section 28.3
Insurance

A prudent owner should, as from the time of acquiring an insurable interest in a racehorse or breeding stock, insure and keep that interest insured against mortality and other risks, including third party risks.

CHAPTER 29 SOUNDNESS OF HORSE FOR RACING

Section 29.1
Soundness

A horse is sound if it has good, natural health and body formation and is not impeded by any disease, the effects of any disease or accident, any vice or other thing, from being naturally useful.

A horse is unsound if there is any departure from good, natural health and body formation caused by disease, accident, or otherwise, which departure diminishes or is likely to diminish the natural usefulness of the horse for the purposes for which it is used or proposed to be used.

The question of soundness is primarily one of usefulness. If the horse in question has a disease the nature of which impedes the usefulness of the horse for the purpose for which it is used or to be used then the horse is unsound, but if the disease does not impede its usefulness for such purpose it may be considered sound.

Further, the question relates to the soundness at a particular time, that is to say, at the time of inspection or time of sale.

Section 29.2
Examination as to Soundness

The only people qualified to examine a horse and express opinion as to its soundness or unsoundness are equine veterinary surgeons. These professional persons have the necessary skill, ability, up-to-date knowledge, and experience in that field and the necessary specialised equipment and facilities.

Any person who has the need and authority to ascertain or be informed as to the soundness of a horse, should engage the services of an equine veterinary surgeon. The scope and cost of any such inspection is a matter for discussion and agreement between the veterinarian and the client. Normally, the veterinarian would carry out standard inspection procedures laid down by the Equine Veterinary Surgeons' Association and which have been developed having regard, among other things, to the risks of litigation arising from such inspections and reports thereon. The standard procedures are limited in that they may not provide for certain tests to be carried out as a matter of routine. Those tests or special techniques to ascertain, for example, if drugs were administered before inspection to conceal symptoms that may otherwise have been revealed, may include X-rays, electrocardiographs, laryngoscopy, laboratory tests of blood, skin, urine, or saliva, and so on. If the client wishes any test or examination not included in the routine inspection procedure to be carried out, it is a matter for discussion and agreement before the inspection is made.

On completion of an examination the veterinarian prepares a report on that examination in which he indicates his findings and expresses an opinion as to the soundness or unsoundness of the horse at the time of such examination. If the examination is for a purchase the veterinarian may also express opinion as to the suitability of the horse for the purpose for which the horse is being so purchased. If the examination is for insurance, the veterinarian will make a recommendation as to whether or not in his opinion the horse is an acceptable insurance risk.

PART 13
TRAINERS AND TRAINING

Chapter	30	Trainers
Section	30.1	Licensing of Trainers
	30.2	Services Provided by Trainers
	30.3	Skill and Competence of Trainers
	30.4	Trainers' Association
	30.5	Stablehands
	30.6	Stable Returns
	30.7	Prohibited Substances
	30.8	Sampling and Testing for Prohibited Substances
	30.9	Use of Batteries
Chapter	31	Financial Viability of Training
Section	31.1	Income of Trainers
	31.2	Expenses of Trainers
	31.3	Average Cost of Training a Horse
	31.4	Financial Viability of Trainers
Chapter	32	Training
Section	32.1	Early Education of Youngsters
	32.2	Early Racetrack Training
	32.3	Training Programs
	32.4	Conditioning of Horses Resuming from Spelling
	32.5	Trackwork
	32.6	Barrier Trials
	32.7	Conditioning Runs
	32.8	First-Uppers
	32.9	Races Won by Fit Horses
	32.10	Horses on the Decline
	32.11	Letting-Down
	32.12	Spells
	32.13	Length of Spell
	32.14	Let-Ups

CHAPTER 30 **TRAINERS**

Section 30.1
Licensing of Trainers

Unless a horse is trained by a person holding a licence or permit to train, it cannot be entered for, or run in, any race at a registered race meeting or in any organised trial.

A person wishing to train horses may apply for a licence or permit to a licensing authority being a Principal Club or an Association having jurisdiction in the area in which the person proposes to train.

The licensing authority may, at its discretion, grant an application and issue a general (or open) authorisation or a provisional (or restricted) authorisation to train.

Restrictions may provide that the authorised person may only train horses owned or leased by him or her solely or in partnership with family members (that is, an owner-trainer's authority); for races in a provincial or country area; for picnic races; or as the case may be in some States for jumping races.

Application for renewal of the licence or permit is required to be made annually.

Where a trainer wishes to visit and race horses in an area other than the area covered by licence or permit, he or she may, under certain circumstances, be permitted to do so by the appropriate licensing authority.

Section 30.2
Services Provided by Trainers

Trainers provide owners or lessees of racehorses with the service of caring for, training and racing their horses for agreed-upon periods and remuneration.

The responsibilities of a trainer in carrying out that service are complex and demanding.

There is much more to a trainer's responsibilities than looking after horses. Ancillary to that main service, the trainer is required, among other things:

- To observe the Rules of Racing in all respects.
- To have regular consultations with the owners or lessees of the horses entrusted to the trainer.
- To provide advice to clients or potential clients about the quality of yearlings being offered for sale. Accordingly the trainer must study sale catalogues, visit studs to inspect yearlings, and attend sales.
- To ensure race day procedures are properly carried out for his or her horses, and attend race meetings.
- To keep a watchful eye on horses under his or her care that may be spelling.

- To ensure that the administrative, secretarial, and accounting duties associated with his business are properly discharged. These duties include the following matters:
    - The employment, training, rostering (seven-day week), and supervision of stablehands, apprentices, and other staff.
    - The maintenance of personal work-related history, payroll and ancillary records for staff.
    - The maintenance of records for individual horses concerning ownership, training, nominations, acceptances, race performances, earnings, services rendered including veterinary and farriery services, medical treatments, and so on.
    - The regular submission of stable returns.
    - The engagement of jockeys to ride horses.
    - The arrangement of clearances, travel permits, use of stables, and so on, when horses and licensees are required to travel outside their area of licence.
    - The payment of wages and creditors' accounts; collection of training fees; recovery of expenditure met on behalf of clients; keeping of cash books, ledgers and supporting records.
    - The maintenance of office equipment; and so on.

Section 30.3
Skill and Competence of Trainers

Any trainer can train a horse to run in a race, but the ability of a trainer to train a horse efficiently and effectively and to extract from it its maximum potential in a race is a rare gift. Trainers generally can be measured by their recurring results.

It is not necessary that the trainer be academically qualified in the relative field, but he or she needs to have the proper technical and business skills and knowledge, including knowledge of the basic principles on which management of the racehorse is based.

As in any other profession, the skill and competence of trainers vary. While a trainer must possess the necessary training qualities, in order to become a good and eventually a top trainer, however, he or she needs to have some good horses that can be developed into winners of good races.

There are some top, or otherwise fortunate trainers who are in the happy position that they can afford to choose the owners they wish to have as clients. On the other hand, less fortunate trainers cannot pick and choose and must seek stable patronage.

Section 30.4
Trainers' Association

In some States trainers are required to join the Racehorse Trainers' Association and during the currency of their licences or permits remain financial members of that Association.

Section 30.5
Stablehands

Racehorse training is a labour-intensive business. In order to assist in that regard a trainer may employ stablehands and apprentice jockeys to work in or about the training establishment or to take part in the training, working, custody, or management of racehorses. Such employment is subject to registration by the licensing authority and also to the Rules of Racing, apprenticeship agreements, and relevant industrial law and awards, including maintenance of a workers' compensation policy and payment of support superannuation contributions to an appropriate fund.

All registered stablehands are issued with identity cards which are required to be worn at all times when carrying out duties at a stable, on a racecourse, or elsewhere.

The number of persons employed by the trainer depends upon the number of horses being trained, the extent of the involvement of family members, and the qualification, dependability, and experience of any such family members or employees.

Leading trainers with large establishments normally employ one full-time stablehand for every three horses while trainers with small establishments may train up to five horses without full-time assistance.

Stablehands are also referred to as "strappers".

Section 30.6
Stable Returns

Stable returns must be prepared by each trainer and lodged with the Principal Club or District Association having jurisdiction over the area where the training establishment is situated.

These returns set forth the names and particulars of every horse:
- that is stabled at the trainer's stables at the date of the return;
- that entered such stables since the date of the previous return;
- that left such stables since the date of the previous return (that is, where a horse was transferred to another trainer's stables, retired, exported, or died).

Amended returns must be prepared and submitted each time there is any change in the particulars previously submitted.

The purpose of stable returns is to reduce the amount of information that a trainer would otherwise be required to furnish when nominating a horse for a race or barrier trial.

Indeed, unless the name and particulars of a horse have been furnished by a trainer in a stable return to the relative racing control body, neither the trainer concerned nor any other person may nominate the horse for any race or barrier trial.

Section 30.7
Prohibited Substances

History relates numerous cases where known or unknown persons have administered a drug to a racehorse for the purpose of improving its performance or disabling it from performing according to its ability and fitness. Stringent racing rules and procedures are now in force in an attempt to prevent cheating.

A prohibited drug is now called, for the purposes of the Rules, a "prohibited substance". That term is defined as any substance having a direct or indirect action on the following systems of the horse:

- the central or peripheral nervous system;
- the cardiovascular system;
- the respiratory system;
- the alimentary digestive system;
- the musculo-skeletal system;
- the urogenital system; or
- the endocrine system.

Prohibited substances include analgesics, anti-histamines, anti-inflammatory agents, blood coagulants, diuretics, hormones and their synthetic counterparts, corticosteroids, anabolic steroids, local anaesthetics, muscle relaxants, tranquillisers, vitamins administered by injection and so on.

Onus is placed on trainers to bring their horses to a racecourse for the purpose of engaging in a race without any prohibited substance detectable in their bodies. Where a prohibited substance is detected in a horse, the Rules provide for punishment of the trainer and any other person who was in charge of the horse at any relevant time. Accordingly trainers must take proper precautions about the feeding and safeguarding of horses that are to race and ensure that only authorised persons have access to those horses.

In a case where a trainer or a person authorised by the trainer gives any treatment to a horse for any ailment in the period of seven days before a race in which it is intended to start such horse, the trainer is required to advise the stewards in writing of such treatment and ailment before paying-up time for such race.

Section 30.8
Sampling and Testing for Prohibited Substances

As indicated earlier, trainers have a responsibility to present their horses for competition free from any prohibited substances.

At the discretion of the stewards, horses may be sampled for the presence of prohibited substances from the time of arrival on course on race day until approval is given by the stewards for them to be removed from the course. Samples so taken are delivered to a Racing Science Centre for analysis.

Section 30.9
Use of Batteries

The racing fraternity well know that the horse is very susceptible to electricity in any degree! The battery is sometimes used in training and history records numerous cases of its use in races.

The Rules of Racing provide that it is an offence for any person to use or have in his or her possession any electric or electronic apparatus or any improper contrivance capable of affecting the performance of a horse in a race or training gallop.

PART 13 TRAINERS AND TRAINING

CHAPTER 31 FINANCIAL VIABILITY OF TRAINING

Section 31.1
Income of Trainers

The income of a trainer comes from several sources, namely:

- training fees charged to owners at the rate recommended from time to time by the Racehorse Trainers' Association or at such other rate as may be agreed upon;
- a percentage of prize money won by horses trained by him or her at the rate prescribed by the Rules of Racing;
- a percentage of the earnings (riding fees and percentage of prize money) of an apprentice jockey indentured to him or her at the rate agreed between the trainer and the parents or legal representative of the apprentice and as indicated in the indenture agreement;
- gifts from owners, winning bets and so on.

Trainers have a dilemma when setting their training fee. If the fee is set too high, an owner may seek another trainer or discontinue ownership participation in the industry. Many trainers, particularly those with comparatively low operating costs, charge a weekly training fee less than, and in some cases less than half, the fee recommended by the Racehorse Trainers' Association.

Section 31.2
Expenses of Trainers

Expenses of trainers would primarily depend upon such factors as: the type of licence held; whether a full-time trainer, a part-time trainer, or an owner-trainer; whether located in a metropolitan, provincial or country area; the number and quality of horses being trained; the number of employees; whether stables and housing are owned or rented; and so on.

Operating expenses of a trainer include such items as: rent; wages and ancillary wages costs; feed and bedding for horses; provision and maintenance of motor vehicle and horse float; telephones, fax machines, computer costs; and so on.

Expenditure on certain other items — such as breaking-in fees, insurance of horses, horse transport, swimming, spelling, nomination and acceptance fees, veterinary services, farriers' services, and supplementary (vitamin or mineral) feed — are usually met in the first instance by the trainer and recouped from the owner.

Section 31.3
Average Cost of Training a Horse

The average cost of training a horse is the aggregate of all non-recoverable operating costs referred to above apportioned equally over each horse in the training establishment in question. That is to say the average cost to train a racehorse is about the same whether a trainer has 10 or 50 horses in his or her establishment. Each horse requires a stable; the amount of produce or feed required by each is similar; and the time required to train and maintain each horse is also similar.

Section 31.4
Financial Viability of Trainers

From available facts and factors it is clear that many, if not most, trainers would not earn a satisfactory return to compensate them for the very long hours they put into the business of training and the capital outlaid.

The training fee would seem to be barely sufficient to meet training costs and, accordingly, many trainers would rely heavily on their percentage earnings from prize money.

CHAPTER 32 TRAINING

Section 32.1
Early Education of Youngsters

Ideally, the education of a young thoroughbred destined for the racetrack is not a battle of willpower between horse and handler, but a gradual process whereby the handler builds up confidence and ready response in the horse. A little head collar or halter is placed on the foal at an early age, and it is taught progressively —

- to be handled;
- to follow willingly when led;
- to raise each foot on command for inspection by a studgroom, or for maintenance or corrective treatment by the farrier;
- to enter a stable trailer, or horse van;
- to lunge, that is to circle round the handler at various paces, in either direction;
- to accept the bit, the bridle, and the saddle and, gradually, the tightening of the girth;
- to accept mounting of a rider;
- to walk, trot, and then canter with a rider up;
- to be obedient and responsive to the rider;
- to accept travel, traffic, unusual noises and sights, other animals, clipping, and shoeing.

Where the ideal pattern of gradual and constructive education is followed it is seen that the so-called "breaking-in" is just another step in the daily routine. Unfortunately, the ideal program as indicated above is time-consuming, labour-intensive, and thus costly and, in most cases, impracticable.

Where the ideal pattern of early training is not followed, a youngster needs to be given some dismounted preliminary training so that it can be produced as a mannered youngster in the Yearling Sale Ring. By that time it should be used to the loose box and stable routine, and accustomed to the head collar, leading in hand, and so on.

When about eighteen to twenty months, the youngster is delivered to a specialist horse-breaker who possesses the necessary skill and infinite patience to complete the breaking-in process.

The term "breaking-in" derives from the training method under which the horse-breaker, after a contest of strength, overpowers and outwits the horse and breaks its spirit. This cruel method is usually not employed in the training of a racehorse. On the contrary, the specialist racehorse-breaker usually gains control of a horse through psychology, patience, understanding, intuition, and kindness.

A horse with an unbroken spirit gives far more when asked for its best than does the broken-spirited horse. Bad handling and breaking-in can ruin a horse.

After the horse is "broken-in", its early training continues with the object of developing its muscles, making it supple, getting it balanced and used to carrying weight. Thus, with training and appropriate feeding and grooming it is made fit and brought to a condition where more serious training can begin.

Section 32.2
Early Racetrack Training

After the early training and breaking-in of youngsters, racetrack training begins under the care of trainers to whom they are entrusted by owners.

Some trainers like the challenge associated with receiving two-year-olds into their care because there is always the possibility and hope that they will develop into good, high quality, or even champion horses. Besides, they say, it is easier — or rather not so hard — to bring the best out of a two-year-old than an older horse.

The main objectives of the early racetrack training are as follows:
- The development and toughening of muscles and ligaments by weeks of training at the slower paces.
- Training to gallop with other horses smoothly and without swerving. This is done by pacework followed by gallops over 200m or 400m lengthening gradually to 800m.
- Slow and patient familiarisation with the starting stalls and starter's bell and training to jump out well.
- Quiet behaviour by familiarisation with the training track; the presence of many other horses against which it must compete; racecourse crowds; and the excitement of a race meeting.

The training schedule and the race program for youngsters are determined by the trainer having regard to such things as the following: Some youngsters are precocious and have speed early while others, which are slower in developing, may prove to be better horses; the breeding pattern of the youngsters, that is, whether they have sprinting or staying blood in their pedigrees; the indications of a strong competitive spirit.

Section 32.3
Training Programs

A training program is prepared concerning many pertinent factors: the age, quality, and characteristics of the horse; if returning from a spell the length of that spell; and whether it is to be prepared for sprinting or staying events. The program must provide for methodical, controlled, and very gradual improvement.

Broadly the process involves subjecting the horse to increasing amounts of physical effort and stress over a period of several weeks while correspondingly increasing the feed ration of protein for energy and reducing the ration of carbohydrates.

The objective of the program is to gradually improve the horse in all respects particularly its muscular-skeletal, cardiovascular, and respiratory systems and so bring it into racing condition or fitness and, as a general rule, after racing, to peak and winning form.

Section 32.4
Conditioning of Horses Resuming from Spelling

When the overweight and soft-muscled horse is returned to the trainer's stables from the spelling farm or paddock it is necessary for the veterinary surgeon and the farrier to examine it and to provide their respective services before the trainer begins the long and gradual conditioning process.

The conditioning process begins with slow pacework increasing in speed and length of time. This is followed by gallops over short distances up to 400m lengthening gradually to distances up to 1000m. Now and then the horse may be galloped against the clock, or against a well-conditioned stablemate, or against other horses in a track gallop or barrier trial. The results of the horse's efforts in such trackwork or trials together with other factors such as recovery time of pulse rate and respiration rate after the efforts and blood counts, provide the trainer with an indication of the horse's conditioning progress.

Trackwork and barrier trials are merely exercise routines and in themselves are generally insufficient for the trainer to assess accurately the degree of a horse's fitness. To do so the trainer needs to observe its performance under actual race competition and also observe how it recovers after such competition.

Section 32.5
Trackwork

Trackwork is an important part of the conditioning process of the racehorse.

Neither the times of training gallops nor the winners of such gallops are of any significance to anyone but the trainer because of a number of factors, including the following:

- There is no comparison between an unstressful track gallop, particularly over a short distance, and a race with all its pressures.
- The weight carried by a horse in a training gallop, both on its back and on its feet (shoes rather than racing plates) are unknown.
- A horse may be sensational in its morning workouts, but may be a flop under the stress of real race competition — a "morning glory".
- Sometimes a horse may gallop much faster in its final track work-out before a race than planned by its trainer and consequently may not run its true race. In such a case the horse is said to have "left its race on the track".
- Many horses are lazy in work-outs, but produce their best effort in a race.
- Most winners are, paradoxically, not horses that run fast track gallops.

- Track gallops may be run on a training track with woodchip, sand, dirt, cinders or grass surface. If run on the course proper, the false rail may be located well out from the normal running rail position.

To a person not connected with the horse, the real value of its trackwork is the knowledge that the horse is being brought into, or being kept in, condition; an indication of the distance of the race for which it is being prepared; and where the name of the rider in the trackwork is known, a help in determining the suitability or eligibility of the rider engaged for a future race.

Section 32.6
Barrier Trials

A "barrier trial" means an event held or organised for the purpose of testing or training horses, for which no prize money, trophy, or other reward, gratuity, or privilege of more than a nominal value is offered and on which betting is unlawful.

Trials are conducted at a licensed racing venue by a race club acting with the approval or direction of a Principal Club or District Racing Association. Trials are supervised by stipendary stewards.

Subject to restrictive or mandatory conditions for the particular trials being conducted, trainers exercise a discretionary power as to whether or not they nominate their horses.

Trials are run under general racing conditions except that weights carried by the competing horses are "catch weights", that is, weight of the rider plus riding equipment; and horses are not required to run on their merits nor to be fully ridden out.

While trials serve a valuable purpose in the training of horses, not much value can be placed on them by punters except that, together with trackwork they do give a guide to the level of fitness of horses, particularly those resuming their careers after spells or let-ups. In the case of the youngsters, they often point to horses that later develop into good gallopers.

Section 32.7
Conditioning Runs

Some horses are specially trained to be in top condition and to attempt to win at their first start in a race after a spell. In most cases, however, after trackwork and barrier trials, the preparation of a horse is continued by competing it against seasoned gallopers in races. These gallopers need a number of such conditioning runs and usually display progressive improvement until they reach top form. On the other hand, some horses for one reason or another fail to come "to hand".

The number of conditioning runs referred to above is dependent upon such factors as the age and quality of the horse and the distance range for which it is being trained. Young and good quality horses improve much quicker than the older and lower quality horses.

In some cases, a trainer may attempt to conceal the state of fitness of a horse by distorting the usual pattern of preparation, starting it in unsuitable races, and so on.

Generally it may be said that racehorses follow a similar pattern of improvement each preparation after a spell — they may improve quickly or, as the case may be, only gradually and once they reach top racing form they may retain that form for a relatively short period or, as the case may be, for a relatively long period. The individual form patterns of previous preparations are good guides to a horse's probable pattern in a coming preparation.

Section 32.8
First-Uppers

The early starts of a horse after a spell are usually conditioning runs. A small but significant number of gallopers (7 per cent), however, being high quality horses well forward in condition or horses specially trained in that regard, do win "first-up".

Indicators that a horse may win first-up include such things as: its trained appearance in the mounting yard; its training program on the track and in barrier trial runs; its record of good performances in its past first-up runs; its placing, weight, rider, and distance of the race; the track and condition of the track.

As a general rule a punter should not back a horse at its first-up run if it is (a) to run over a distance beyond 1400m; (b) to run on a rain-affected track; (c) to be ridden by an unfashionable jockey or apprentice; (d) to carry a heavy weight of 57kg or more. Exceptions to that general rule are notable first-up winners.

Section 32.9
Races Won by Fit Horses

The object of training is to bring a horse into top racing condition and retain it in that condition for as long as practicable. (In cases, it may be observed that, however, a trainer may set a horse for a particular race and bring it to peak condition just for that race day!)

The degree of fitness of a horse at any time is well known to the trainer and the veterinary adviser. A punter can only make an assessment by the revealed form of the horse in races or race trials; by familiarity with the usual training procedures of the stable; and by observing the horse in the mounting yard before a race — if the punter has the skill to recognise fitness by sight. Indeed, the ability to predict when a horse will reach winning condition in any preparation is the rare skill of the successful punter. Nevertheless, a punter must learn to identify the indicators of fitness because statistically, 95 per cent of races are won by horses at, or nearing, peak fitness. Horses on the decline are not punting propositions.

Races are not won by fitness alone: The matter of ability is also vital. A horse that is improving in condition, but of superior ability, will often defeat a horse in peak condition, but of inferior ability.

Section 32.10
Horses on the Decline

The horse retains its peak condition for a relatively short period (say, about 10 weeks) and then begins to deteriorate when its is said to be "over the peak", "trained off", or "stale". The exception is the "iron horse" that thrives on racing and may keep in winning form for a long period — even up to a year.

It is often difficult, even for a trainer, to determine just when a horse has passed its peak of a particular preparation and is on the decline. Horses on the decline are rarely knowingly raced by good trainers but are often raced by poorer trainers who have only a few horses in their stable. Some trainers may start declining horses in a few races before spelling them for the purpose of getting some weight advantage at the beginning of their next preparation.

The astute punter may perceive signs of deterioration in the condition of a horse that has been in training and racing for some time, by its appearance or unusual behaviour before, or during, a race.

Once a horse goes "over the peak" and its condition begins to decline, there is only one remedy and that is to spell the horse from racing for a few months. In that manner the horse's will to compete is rekindled. Where, however, the deterioration in condition accompanies old age, or is because of, or aggravated by, over-racing, too much early racing, or ill-treatment, the decline is irreversible.

Section 32.11
Letting-Down

The routine of the racehorse should not be changed abruptly from training and racing to spelling. It should be let-down and roughened off very gradually before being moved from the unnatural life of the training stable to the more natural life of the spelling paddock.

Short or concentrated feeds should be cut down in stages while, correspondingly, more grass is introduced into the diet.

Unfortunately, these ideal practices of the past are generally not observed now. The changeover from training and racing routines to spelling is now done rather abruptly.

Section 32.12
Spells

Spells are breaks from training and racing owing to such factors as: a decline in racing fitness; injury or disease including a bleeding attack; or the need to allow a young horse to grow and mature.

Indeed every racehorse needs, and must have, a holiday. Grazing and playing in a paddock, particularly in the company of other horses is, for the horse, a mental and physical tonic after the stress of racing. The length of the holiday and the time of the year when it is taken is determined by the above factors, by the length of time a horse has been "up" since its last spell, and the future racing program set for it.

During its spell the horse may be kept at grass or on a combined "at grass" and stable system. On the combined system it spends part of its time at grass and part stabled.

Even during its holiday the valuable racehorse needs proper management and care. Services are best provided by specialist spelling farms.

Section 32.13
Length of Spell

The length of the common spell is a break of about three months from racing. The horse is sent to a spelling farm or paddock for about six weeks and then returns soft-muscled to the training stables. Conditioning the animal for its return to racing usually takes about 6 to 10 weeks.

When the spell is a result of injury or disease, the horse cannot be returned to training or racing until it is considered sound enough. Its break from racing may, therefore be up to a year or more.

Section 32.14
Let-Ups

The term "let-up" refers to a period of about four to eight weeks when a horse is given a break from racing, but kept in training.

Let-ups are generally used to freshen up a horse after a gruelling campaign or when it has shown signs of becoming erratic in its usual racing pattern. They may also be given to horses that have sustained minor injuries and, therefore, must be eased up in their training schedule.

Let-ups may also be given to the sparingly raced horses whose races are spaced over long periods.

Trackwork and barrier trials may indicate the fitness and preparation of a horse resuming from a let-up for a particular race.

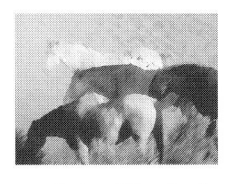

PART 14

FITNESS AND ABILITY OF RACEHORSES

Chapter	33	Fitness
Section	33.1	Fitness and its Components
	33.2	Musculo-Skeletal Fitness
	33.3	Cardiovascular Fitness
	33.4	Respiratory Fitness
	33.5	Psychological Fitness
	33.6	Inherent Courage
Chapter	34	Ability
Section	34.1	Fitness/Ability Relativity
	34.2	Ability
	34.3	Class by Race Eligibility
	34.4	Class by Ability
	34.5	Ability Classifications
	34.6	Horses from Overseas
Chapter	35	Sex in Relation to Racing
Section	35.1	Description of Horses According to Sex
	35.2	Castration
	35.3	The Effect of the Mating Season
	35.4	Fillies and Mares Versus Colts and Horses
	35.5	Sex Allowance in Mixed Sex Races
Chapter	36	Age in Relation to Racing
Section	36.1	Two-Year-Olds
	36.2	Over-Racing of Two-Year-Olds
	36.3	Three-Year-Olds
	36.4	Four- and Five-Year-Olds
	36.5	Six-Year-Olds
	36.6	Aged Horses

CHAPTER 33 FITNESS

Section 33.1
Fitness and its Components

The fitness of a racehorse at any time is one of degree depending on its training program. When, however, a horse is said to be "fit" for a specific race the term means that it is fit in all respects to perform the function of racing in that particular race.

Various factors that contribute to fitness include:
- conformational fitness (explained in Chapters 16 and 17);
- musculo-skeletal or locomotion system fitness;
- cardiovascular or circulatory system fitness;
- respiratory system fitness;
- psychological fitness;
- inherent courage.

Section 33.2
Musculo-Skeletal Fitness

The effectiveness of the locomotion system of the racehorse is all-important.

All the various parts of that system must function in unison — efficiently, effectively, and economically — so that the horse may have the required ability in speed and soundness in action. Its action is geared to the required speed, balance, and lead.

Section 33.3
Cardiovascular Fitness

The cardiovascular or circulatory system of a horse circulates oxygen and nutrients to its organs and tissues and from them removes hormonal and waste products.

When the horse is at rest its pulse rate is about 35 to 40 beats per minute. When it is exercised (and also at other times when it is excited, fearful, feverish, or in pain) the pulse rate and blood pressure increase significantly. When being galloped in early preparation for racing its pulse rate may rise to 200, but immediately after galloping it may fall to about 100 and in a comparatively short time slow down to about normal range. When such pulse recovery time is acceptable — usually no more than 20 minutes — the trainer steps up the horse's program and subjects it to greater stress.

Pulse rate and pulse-recovery time after galloping in trackwork, trials, or races are to the trainer significant measurements of a horse's fitness. Monitoring these therefore is carried out regularly for each of the horses being trained by him or her.

Section 33.4
Respiratory Fitness

The respiratory system consists of the air passages of the head (from nostrils to pharynx), the pharynx (throat), larynx (voice box) and trachea (windpipe), bronchi and lungs. Also included in the respiratory system are the thorax (the chest cavity in which the lungs are situated), the ribs that protect the lungs, the diaphragm and rib muscles that pump the lungs, and the nerves that activate the muscles.

Respiration is the process of taking into the bloodstream atmospheric oxygen (without which living tissue cannot survive) and giving off the cellular-produced waste, carbon dioxide, and other toxic waste.

At rest the horse breathes slowly and shallowly. After movement, excitement, or fright there is a marked increase in the speed and depth of its breathing. After trackwork or racing and use of stored-up energy, the horse breathes fast (as we can see with the heaving flanks) to replace the oxygen lost and dissipate heat generated by the severe muscular effort. The time taken by the horse for its breathing rate to return to the normal resting rate (10 to 15 breaths per minute) and the depth and sounds of such breathing are, to the trainer and the veterinary surgeon, a guide to its normality and a significant measure of its fitness.

Section 33.5
Psychological Fitness

Psychological fitness refers to such phenomena as the horse's liking or disliking for a particular track, distance, state of going, direction of running and so on.

The psychological influence of the stable may well be a problem when the horse is racing on its home track and its stable is close by. This may, in some cases, cause a lack of concentration on racing, the horse being more concerned with returning to its stable and with the prospect of food. Proper training may well eliminate this problem.

Section 33.6
Inherent Courage

A courageous horse may win a race despite not being fit in all respects. Its will to win can drive it beyond the point where less courageous rivals succumb.

PART 14 FITNESS AND ABILITY OF RACEHORSES

CHAPTER 34 ABILITY

Section 34.1
Fitness/Ability Relativity

As indicated earlier, races are most frequently won by horses that are at or approaching full fitness. The fitness factor should always be kept in proper perspective as fitness alone never determines the result of a race. The paramount factor is ability. If a horse does not have the ability to win a particular race, it is purposeless to attempt to ascertain the horse's fitness level because it simply cannot win.

Section 34.2
Ability

The potential of a horse is genetically determined at the time of its conception. Recognition and development of its potential is a matter for the trainer. Without the trainer's essential skills no horse would ever reach its innate ability.

Assessment of true ability and potential cannot be made until the horse has raced and has been tested in competition to the limit of its endurance.

With the exception of the champion whose potential may be obvious from its first start in a race, the relative abilities of most horses are only gradually revealed over a number of races. The number and type of races and the length of time required varies with the individual horse and depends to a great extent upon whether the horse in question is a sprinter, a middle-distance performer, or a stayer. Sprinters, especially those above average quality, may display their ability in their early race starts. On the other hand, stayers take longer to mature and display their latent talents.

Section 34.3
Class By Race Eligibility

Racehorses may be classified according to the type or class of race for which they are eligible.

It is seldom wise for a trainer of a horse (other than a horse showing potential) to start that horse in a race of a class standard higher than that for which it is eligible. In the event of it winning that higher class race it may no longer contest lower class events for which it would otherwise have been eligible. It thus bypasses the opportunity to gain the easier prize money associated with such lower class races.

Trainers may start their horses in races of a higher class than those for which they are eligible, not with the intention of winning, but for the purpose of racing them into condition under light imposts, disguising their progress, and seeking a better advantage when they are started in a future suitable event in their own class standard.

When horses of different race class are nominated for a handicap race, the handicapper, when allotting the handicaps, will take into consideration, among other things, the relative race class weight differences. So, if the topweight in a field is allotted, say, 3kg or more than the second top weight, the top weight is said to be the "class horse of the field". This merely means that the race class standard of the top weight is one or more classes above the class standards of the rest of the field.

Where a horse is entered in a race of a race class standard higher than its own standard, it is said to be "out of class".

Section 34.4
Class by Ability

Within each race class, there are classes of racehorses and the number of such classes is as infinite as the number of horses within the race class. In this sense the term "class" refers to the ability, quality, and potential of a horse compared with other horses. While it is impracticable to express horse classification factors as a simple set of rules, such classification does take into account such factors as the following:

(a) The number and types of races it has won, particularly during the past twelve months. A horse may lose its winning potential and must necessarily be classified on its present potential.

(b) The localities in which it won its races. A horse that wins a number of unimportant or restricted class races in the country may be a "bush champion", but most such horses do not run up to expectations when started in metropolitan events. Locality strengths vary.

(c) The strength of the fields that competed in the races it has won. A horse cannot be classified as champion or high-quality for having won a race of major importance under circumstances where:
- the opposition was weak;
- in a staying event it was the only horse with staying ability;
- it was the only seasoned or fit horse, the others being first-uppers or underdone;
- better horses in the field suffered severe interference;
- and so on.

(d) The age of the horse at the time of winning its races. A horse with any real ability should be out of restricted class at a comparatively early age.

(e) The breeding of the horse. Breeding is very important and often the class of a horse emanates from its breeding — but breeding alone does not make class.

(f) Weights allotted by the official handicapper. The handicapper allots weights to horses in a handicap race according to the merits of their past performances. Thus, more weight is given to the better class horses than to inferior class horses. This is not to suggest that the winner of a race should come from the top weights.

Section 34.5
Ability Classifications

The factors listed above are significant indicators in assessing the differences in ability, quality, and potential of racehorses, but there can be no precise definition for those differences. The over-riding factor is one of personal opinion.

Classes into which horses may be divided are as follows:

(1) Champion Class

(2) High Quality Class

(3) Good Class

(4) Medium Class

(5) Poor Class

(1) Champion Class:

Real top class horses may generally be defined as horses that have won at least three classic or Group 1 events and several other important races.

The performances of these class horses set the yardstick by which the efforts of other gallopers are measured. They possess superior qualities, including courage, the will to win, speed, acceleration, honesty, consistency, versatility, and predictability.

In the assessment of chances for a race these class horses can never be discarded as chanceless. For them class overcomes such things as weight, adverse track conditions, bad barrier positions, running mishaps, interference, lack of racing fitness, and so on. They are the champions.

(2) High Quality Class:

High quality horses are horses just short of champion class because of such things as a slight but chronic conformational defect, a simple but bad character trait, or failure of its trainer to develop its potential to the full.

(3) Good Class:

Horses that may be classified as good class include those that progress steadily and predictably through the race classes and qualify for metropolitan open class events before reaching the peaks of their careers. They contest many of the bettable races run on most Saturdays and may occasionally manage to win a major (listed or group) race.

The number of good class horses far exceeds the aggregate number of high and champion class horses.

(4) Medium Class:

This class includes those horses that, during their careers, advance slowly through the restricted class races, but lack the ability to progress much beyond restricted class. They may eventually contest the weaker open events, particularly those of mid-week meetings. Such a horse may have an ability, under certain circumstances, to rise above its usual moderate standard, for example, when carrying a light weight over heavy going.

(5) Poor Class:

Ninety per cent of all racehorses fit into this catergory.

These are the low, weak, bad, unreliable, or unsound horses. They are called by various vernacular names such as "cockroaches", "cats", "camels", "donkeys" and "snails".

Section 34.6
Horses from Overseas

From time to time horses are brought to Australia from overseas either as short-term visitors or to stay here permanently.

As a general rule a punter should refrain from backing any such import, or from betting in any race in which it competes until it has competed in Australia and assessment made of its ability and potential against our standards and conditions.

The advice does not apply to horses coming from New Zealand. Particulars of the race performances of these horses and their respective weight ratings may be well known to Australians or, if not, they are readily available from Australian Racing Services.

PART 14 FITNESS AND ABILITY OF RACEHORSES

CHAPTER 35 SEX IN RELATION TO RACING

Section 35.1
Description of Horses According to Sex

Youngsters of both sexes are called:
- "foals" (filly foals or colt foals) from date of birth on or after 1 August until the following 1 March which, for *ASB* purposes, is the age of weaning; then
- "weanlings" (filly weanlings or colt weanlings) from 1 March until their first birthday on the following 1 August; then
- "yearlings" (filly yearlings or colt yearlings) until their second birthday.

Male racehorses are called:
- "colts" if they are entires under four years of age;
- "geldings" if both of their testicles have been removed;
- "entires" if they have both testicles in the scrotum;
- "rigs" in cases where one or both testicles may be retained permanently in the abdominal cavity.

Female racehorses are called:
- "fillies" if they are less than four years of age;
- "mares" if they are four years of age or older.

Breeding stock comprise stallions (sires) and broodmares (dams).

The term "horse" used in a racing sense, means any male horse four years old or older; used in a specific stud book sense, means an entire male four years old or older; or used in a general everyday sense, means a male or female of the equine species.

Section 35.2
Castration

If a colt is not required for breeding purposes, it is castrated. Whether or not the horse should be gelded and the timing of the operation are matters to be determined by the owner after consultation with a veterinarian. The operation may be performed when the horse is a weanling, yearling, or two-year-old, depending on circumstances, including its behaviour towards fillies and mares and whether or not it can be kept separated from them.

Section 35.3
The Effect of the Mating Season

The mating or covering season in the equine world occurs during late spring and summer and during that season fillies that have turned three years of age and started to mature and the matured mares turn their minds to certain attractions of nature. Because of this natural phenomenon they are usually, for racing, unpredictable and inconsistent.

Colts and horses also have their mating urge in that season, but seem to put the business of racing before sex, so that generally their racing is not much affected.

During the silly season, fillies and mares continue to compete in races restricted to their sex and also in mixed-sex races. In a mixed-sex event the punter's selection preference should be given to a male galloper unless there is a consistently racing mare or filly well weighted or with a significant advantage.

Section 35.4
Fillies and Mares Versus Colts and Horses

Two-year-olds are not affected by the mating season, but three-year-old fillies and the mature mares display their best and true racing form during the period from about March to the end of July, that is, outside the mating period.

During the autumn and winter period such fillies and mares are able racing competitors with the colts and horses.

A mare, on completion of her racing career, may have some residual value if she has broodmare qualities. On the other hand, an entire is unlikely to have any future as a stallion unless he has outstanding qualities — but most do not.

Section 35.5
Sex Allowance in Mixed-Sex Races

Under the Standard Weight-for-Age Scale, mares are allowed 2.5kg from 1 August to 31 December; 1.5kg from 1 January to 31 March; and 1kg from 1 April to 31 July.

In other set-weight races, conditions usually provide for an allowance for fillies and mares.

In allotting weights for handicap events, the official handicapper has a discretionary power to give weight allowances to the female entrants.

CHAPTER 36 AGE IN RELATION TO RACING

Section 36.1
Two-Year-Olds

On officially turning two years, a thoroughbred becomes eligible to begin its racing career. As many youngsters are, however, less than twenty four months of age at such time, Principal Clubs do not program races for two-year-olds until late September or early October.

Usually a racehorse begins its career as a two-year-old in races restricted to horses of that age. Under conditions of early races, set-weights are carried over distances from 800m to 1000m. After some weeks races are run under handicap conditions over gradually increasing distances up to 1600m. The two-year-old youngsters are referred to as "babies" and the races in which they compete are called "nurseries".

Two-year-old races may be open to both sexes or restricted to fillies or colts and geldings.

Well-trained and mature two-year-olds improve quickly in condition and speed and may be race-fit after barrier trialling. Once they strike top form they are able to carry high weights over the short distances of their races.

Bred and trained to race, they appear to enjoy it and are keen, honest and consistent. Because of this the favourites and likely winners of two-year-old races are usually at very short odds.

Section 36.2
Over-Racing of Two-Year-Olds

Many horses have had their racing potential ruined because of the pressures of premature training and over-racing as two-year-olds.

The problem mainly stems from the desire and impatience of owners to race their sprinting-bred youngsters as soon as practicable in an effort to win back their purchase outlay.

While it is common practice to race horses as two-year-olds it is important that a youngster should not be started until it is sufficiently developed to withstand the rigours of racing and then it should be raced only lightly. Staying-bred youngsters should only be raced for the purpose of giving them experience for middle- and long-distance racing in later years.

Section 36.3
Three-Year-Olds

Horses that race as three-year-olds comprise those that were raced, lightly raced, or over-raced as two-year-olds and those that only begin their racing careers after turning three. The last-mentioned group includes horses that were prevented for one reason or another (set back, castration, and so on) from starting as two-year-olds, late maturing youngsters, and those with staying potential.

The distance of races for three-year-olds are gradually increased up to 2400m so that their staying ability can be measured.

The distance ability of these young horses is established and they become readily identified as sprinters, middle-distance runners, or stayers. Such measured ability determines the horses' future training and racing programs.

Three-year-olds race true to their form and ability, but to a lesser extent than two-year-olds. It is wise, however, for the punter to watch and wait until a three-year-old's distance ability is established before considering it as a reliable betting proposition.

Section 36.4
Four- and Five-Year-Olds

The ability and potential, if any, shown by a horse as a two- or three-year-old will be fully developed as a four- or five-year-old. This is the age during which horses classed as good, high quality, or champion horses win their best races. They provide the best and safest betting opportunities because their class, courage, form, ability, racing style, preference for courses, and so on, are usually well disclosed.

Section 36.5
Six-Year-Olds

At this age a horse takes much more time and racing after a spell to reach its best form than does its younger rival. After reaching peak form, better class horses may still be able to produce some predictable betting propositions — particularly when suitably placed at their favoured track.

Generally, however, performances of horses of this age group are not comparable with their performances of the previous season.

Section 36.6
Aged Horses

Many horses, mostly geldings, are raced by their connections until they are seven, eight, nine, or even ten years of age. These, seven years old or older, horses are officially described as "aged". Because of declining ability associated with old age, strenuous careers, and the cumulative effects of injuries, diseases, or set backs, they win few races.

Aged gallopers lose early speed and consistency, but usually acquire increased weight-carrying ability and stamina. For that reason they usually compete in middle-distance or long-distance events. With progressively declining ability they become unable to compete with any chance of success in metropolitan races. They may, however, be raced with some success during their twilight racing careers in country areas where fields are of lower class and strength. They may also continue their careers in jumping races.

Like everything else, there are exceptions and some aged horses seem to have cast-iron constitutions. Indeed, some horses are reliable betting propositions long after they reach seven years of age. This especially applies to those that have been lightly and patiently raced during their career and that are in the hands of a good trainer.

One factor that must be considered with aged horses is that they normally take much time and racing to attain top racing condition after a spell and then quickly lose that condition.

On completion of their flat-racing careers, racehorses may be sent to stud (if suitable), used for jump racing, put to various uses as hacks, put to green pastures to enjoy a life of leisure, or sadly allowed to degenerate under poor conditions.

… PART 15

STABLES AND STABLECRAFT

Chapter	37	Stables and Stablecraft
Section	37.1	Training Stables
	37.2	Care of the Stabled Racehorse
	37.3	Stable Routines
	37.4	Grooming
	37.5	Bedding
	37.6	Mucking-Out
	37.7	Clipping
Chapter	38	Saddlery
Section	38.1	Meaning of Term
	38.2	Racing Gear
	38.3	Some Items of Saddlery
Chapter	39	Stable and other Vices of the Racehorse
Section	39.1	Causes of Vices
	39.2	Common Vices

PART 15 STABLES AND STABLECRAFT

CHAPTER 37 STABLES AND STABLECRAFT

Section 37.1
Training Stables

During its racing career the racehorse needs somewhat elaborate and sophisticated stabling.

While the design and construction of stables may vary greatly, certain features of good stables are essential and constant and include such things as: good siting; strong construction, preferably of fireproof materials; suitable roofing that is a poor conductor of heat and sound; non-absorbent, hard-wearing, non-slipping flooring; good insulation, drainage, ventilation, and lighting; centrally located and properly equipped rooms for the storage of feed, bedding, saddlery, clothing, veterinary supplies, stable maintenance equipment, and so on; and properly surfaced and well-ordered stable yards.

A separate box (that is, a stall provided in a stable) must be provided for each horse and each box must have such features as: sufficient space for the horse to turn around, lie down, or roll comfortably; divided doors; slightly sloping floor to direct fluids into drains; waist-high inset manger; and individual water bowl.

A sick bay of one or more loose boxes should be set aside for the isolation or quarantining of sick horses.

(There are various requirements of state and local governments and Principal Clubs about the registration, maintenance and inspection of stables and premises so that man and horse can co-exist in these modern times. Unfortunately there is at times laxity in the observance of those requirements.)

Section 37.2
Care of the Stabled Racehorse

In the moulding of a good horse genetic influence is important, but there is another, perhaps more important, influence and that is environment.

Racehorses spend the greater part of their racing careers confined to an artificial stable environment. This is contrary to their natural environment of free-roaming, herd living. Racehorses are, therefore, required to adjust both mentally and physically to the man-imposed, stressful environment of the stable, and in doing so they need much care and attention to compensate for the loneliness, boredom, and confinement. Their experiences within that environment may well make or break them.

In the matter of stablecraft or care of the racehorse, experts may lay down scientific guidelines, but because of the individuality of racehorses those guidelines must be treated with flexibility rather than as hard and fast rules. There must be a balance between science on the one hand and the instinct, experience, knowledge and understanding of, and observation by, the practical horsemen of the stables on the other.

Just as horses are individuals so are stable horsemen. While one person being a qualified horseman may well control horses without difficulty, another person lacking the qualities of a good horseman may be incapable of exercising control.

Section 37.3
Stable Routines

Good management of the training establishment requires the institution and observance of proper stable routines.

Routines are necessary not only for the efficient conduct of the business of training, but also because horses, like humans, are creatures of habit. Any variance from usual routine will agitate and disturb them.

The trainer and employees:

(a) Through care routines, ensure the regular watering, feeding, grooming, inspection, clothing, and exercise of the horses for which they have responsiblity, including exercising the horses on the stable walking machine, allowing them sand rolls, swimming them in a pool, hosing, and so on..

(b) Through sanitation routines, ensure the cleanliness of the stables, yards, feed bins, watering vessels, bedding, and so on, as necessary preventative measures against disease.

(c) Through other routines, ensure the proper cleanliness and maintenance of all the equipment that is a necessary part of the training establishment.

Section 37.4
Grooming

Grooming of the stabled racehorse is one of the several important factors that combine to bring the horse to a state of bodily fitness as near perfect as practicable.

Improved efficiency is demanded of the racehorse's skin because of the horse's unnatural stable environment and higher than natural levels of work and energy food. Grooming is vital to promote that efficiency by the preservation of good health and the prevention of disease by cleaning and massage. Cleaning removes body waste, scuff, dandruff, grease, parasites, mites, dirt, dust, mud, grass, stable stains and so on. Massage is therapeutic and stimulates blood circulation, the roots of the hair, and also tones up the muscles.

Section 37.5
Bedding

In order to protect a horse from a hard floor, to encourage it to lie down and rest properly, and to help keep it warm and clean, and as free as practicable from the effects of excreted urine and dung, a layer of suitable material must cover the floor of its loose box at all times.

The material or bedding should be of good quality and quantity — springy, light, absorbent, free of dust and offensive odours, dry and changeable. Materials used include wheat straw, oat straw, barley straw, grass hay, wood shavings, shredded paper, and the like.

Section 37.6
Mucking-Out

The horse's bedding naturally becomes fouled from the horse's excretion. It is necessary therefore to "muck-out" the stables regularly. This process includes the removal of all soiled bedding and manure to the compost heap, drying and aerating reuseable bedding in the sun, sweeping or washing the stable floor, and when the floor has dried, replacing the reusable bedding or supplying new material.

Section 37.7
Clipping

The coat of a racehorse in training may be clipped because long coat hair causes the horse to sweat excessively; to lose condition; and to dry off so slowly after sweating or hosing that it may become chilled.

Clipping is a time-consuming, delicate process and is usually carried out by professional clippers. There are various standard clips, but usually the racehorse is given a full clip of all coat hair. The time for clipping varies with the individual horse and with the season.

PART 15 STABLES AND STABLECRAFT

CHAPTER 38 SADDLERY

Section 38.1
Meaning of Term

The term "saddlery" means the saddles, bridles, and various other items of equipment, apparatus, or gear which may be fitted to a riding horse or, for the particular purposes of this book, to a racehorse during its handling, grooming, exercising, training, racing, transport, and so on. Horsemen may refer to such equipment as "tack" which is an abbreviation of the word "tackle".

An important part of horsemanship is the fitting of saddlery on the horse efficiently and comfortably. Saddlery that is dirty, worn, or ill-fitting is not only uncomfortable and unpleasant for the horse, but also potentially dangerous for the rider.

Section 38.2
Racing Gear

The basic racing gear attached to a racehorse is the light racing bridle and saddle. Generally speaking, the less gear that a horse carries apart from that basic equipment, the better it is for it and also for the rider. In some cases, however, additional equipment may be used by trainers in an attempt to get their horses to do their best in races.

If a trainer wishes to use additional or special racing gear on a horse for a race, notification of its intended use in a race must be given at the time of acceptance for that race. Once any such additional or special gear has been approved by the stewards for use on a horse, its use on that horse must be continued without variation until permission to remove or to vary it is granted by the stewards.

Any loss or breakage of gear during a race or any unusual happening in connection with the gear must be reported by the trainer or rider to the stewards immediately after the race.

Section 38.3
Some Items of Saddlery

Some items of saddlery are described to give the reader who may not have knowledge of the subject some idea of their purposes and possible benefits.

Bridle: The term refers to the equipment (usually consisting of a headstall, bit, and reins) attached to the head of a horse for control and guidance of the horse.

There are many types of bridle, but for racing purposes, a lightweight, single-rein bridle with rubber grips is used.

Bit: There is an enormous range of bits, but all such bits are variations of two principal types — the snaffle and the curb.

For racing purposes only the jointed or straight-bar snaffle bit, with rings or D fittings to take the reins, may be used. Steel bits may be rubber-covered, but rubber bits must be steel-reinforced. Half-spoon attachments may be used under certain circumstances.

A special lugging bit or a special tongue bit may also be used under certain circumstances.

Cheekers: Rubber or leather attachments to the bridle, called "cheekers", may be used to prevent the bit from slipping through the horse's mouth or to ensure that the horse does not get its mouth over the bit.

Tongue Ties: Sometimes the tongue of a horse may be tied down by a tape, stocking, or strap looped over the tongue and secured around the jaw. The purpose of such tongue tie is to stop the horse getting its tongue over the bit or swallowing it.

Cross-over Noseband: This is a "Y" strap fitted down the nasal bone and attached to both rings of the bit. It is used on hard pullers.

Drop Nosebands: There are several varieties of drop nosebands all of which have in common the object of bringing pressure to bear on the horse's nose to prevent evasion of the bit and to help maintain a correct position of head carriage.

Nose Rolls: Nosebands with thick lambswool or sheepskin covering the front, are used to help prevent the horse from being distracted by, or shying from, shadows in front, or throwing its head up and becoming unbalanced. They may also be called shadowrolls.

Martingales: There are three types of martingale — the standing, the running, and the Irish — each of which has the purpose of lowering and controlling faulty head carriage.

Blinkers: These are used to restrict a horse's field of vision. They may be used on a wayward, erratic runner in an attempt to make it concentrate on racing and to run straight. They may also be used on a field-shy horse to give it confidence.

Muzzle: To prevent a horse biting or eating, a device of straps may be placed over its mouth.

Eye-fringe: When flies are particularly troublesome, an eye-fringe may be attached to a brow band incorporated in the bridle or head collar.

Saddle: The racing saddle is designed to avoid, as far as practicable, adding to the rider's weight. It is particularly lightweight and skimpy with forward flaps. It has aluminium stirrups and can weigh as little as 250g.

Girth: This is the broad strap encircling the horse's belly and attached to the saddle to keep it in place.

Stirrups: Stirrup irons, in which the rider's feet are placed, are attached to the saddle by leather straps. Very light stirrups are specially made for the racing saddle.

Saddle Cloth: For racing purposes a saddle cloth being a square of linen or cotton with a distinguishing number on it is used partly for protection purposes, but mainly to indicate the number of the horse in the race in question as it appears in the race book. The cloth is supplied to the rider at the time of weighing-out.

Breastplate: A breastplate may be fitted to a horse to prevent the saddle slipping backwards.

Crupper: This is used to prevent a saddle slipping forwards — but not in racing.

Boots: Boots are leather or padded leather coverings designed to be strapped around either front or hind legs to protect them from injury during travel, training, or racing.

When used for racing purposes boots are not a good sign. They could indicate bad leg conformation, weakness, fatigue, or just plain awkward swinging leg action. Their use, however, does not prevent a horse from winning.

Padded Cups and Heel Tapes: These are used where a horse gets down on its bumpers (that is, where a horse's fetlocks strike the ground) when galloping and become sore.

Clothing: Horse clothing includes such items as quarter sheets, hoods, blankets, rugs, and bandages.

The purposes of the different types of clothing include such things as protection from inclement weather, the provision of warmth, guarding against injury or disease, and protection from flies and other insects.

Rugs: Types of rugs include: the New Zealand rug made of waterproof canvas or flax and lined with blanket; other canvas rugs with different designs and linings; woollen rugs; bag rugs; light rugs made of cotton, satin, or other light material; and the cooling or anti-sweat mesh rugs.

Bandages: The term "bandages" includes all the various bandages used on the horse when in the stable, travelling, exercising, or racing.

Racing bandages made of woollen crepe or stretch cotton material, or elastoplast or adhesive-type material may be applied to the legs to prevent damage.

PART 15 STABLES AND STABLECRAFT

CHAPTER 39 STABLE AND OTHER VICES OF THE RACEHORSE

Section 39.1
Causes of Vices

As indicated previously, racehorses spend most of their time in the stressful, lonely, boring, confined environment of the training stable which is completely contrary to their natural environment. They are, by nature, free-roaming, gregarious, peaceful animals. It is not surprising, therefore, that some of these stabled animals, generally because of lack of proper care or attention, become neurotic and develop bad habits or behavioural vices. Specific factors that contribute to the development of such vices include: boredom; loneliness; nutritional deficiency; lack of exercise; insufficient interest; excessive energy; discomfort; ill health; mishandling; or fear.

It is vital for the welfare of horse and handler that as soon as practicable after a vice is observed that the cause be diagnosed and appropriate action be taken to eliminate that cause and cure the vice. If a vice is neglected, complications may arise.

Section 39.2
Common Vices

Here are the more common vices.

Air swallowing: A windsucker generally swallows air by setting its teeth into a fixed object, usually wooden, pulling its neck into an arch and bringing its muzzle back to its body. Some "cribbers" or "crib biters" also gulp air in this manner. The windsucker may also swallow air merely by arching its neck.

The swallowing of air may cause indigestion, loss of appetite, or colic. In addition the cribber wears its upper incisors. This vice is really a disease and constitutes an unsoundness.

Bed eating: Horses because of greediness or a nutritional deficiency may eat their straw bedding. As a consequence they may develop colic.

Dirt or dung eating: The habit of eating dirt or dung is not a common one. It may be a symptom of colic or indicate a dietary nutritional deficiency.

Wood eating: Because of boredom, insufficient bulk feed, or nutritional deficiency, horses may develop the habit of chewing and eating wood. In fact most horses will chew and eat wood at some time.

Grain bolting: Swallowing grain without chewing it, sometimes accompanied by swallowing air with the unchewed grain, causes digestive problems and loss of food value.

Cloth tearing: Some horses, using their teeth, tear off materials placed upon them such as bandages and rugs.

Biting and nipping: Stallions are notorious for biting viciously, and by such act may cause severe injury to the hapless person the subject of their attack. Nipping refers to the less serious action resorted to occasionally by some mares or geldings.

Weaving: This is one of the worst vices. It is a sway or an oscillating motion of the horse while standing in the one place or while marking time with its feet in rhythm with the weave. The habit may indicate a nervous disorder because of boredom and may well tire the horse — impairing its performance.

Crowding in the box: Some horses may make a practice of pressing or attempting to press a person against a wall, and may do so quite aggresively. This can be dangerous for handlers.

Tail rubbing: This action may be caused by lice or fungoid growth about the tail, pinworms about the rectum, dirty sheaths in colts, horses and geldings, and dirty udders in mares. If none of those causes is evident, the rubbing is probably just habit.

Turning tail: When a confined horse does not want to be handled it may "turn tail" at close quarters to the handler and thereby place itself in a dangerous position. Such a horse needs proper education.

Pull back: A horse, improperly broken to tie, may pull back habitually on a halter or rope. The consequences of this habit could be very dangerous for the horse and corrective action should be taken.

Pawing: Pawing or stamping with the forefeet before feeding or during feeding is said by some authorities to be an evolutionary trait. Horses that evolved in a cold climate would have pawed while searching for, or eating, snow-covered food.

Kicking: Horses, because of various causes, may practice the habit of kicking the stable wall. Apart from being noisy, the habit is a dangerous one as the kicker may well injure its foot, particularly the coffin bone.

Rearing or striking: A horse may instinctively rear and strike when cornered or frightened, when getting acquainted with another horse, or during teasing at stud. The stallion, too, may use the action to assert his masculinity. Some horses, however, cultivate the action and these are dangerous and unpredictable. The stallion has a strong tendency to rear and strike on occasions other than when exercising masculinity, even without provocation. The habit may be acquired by a mare or a horse that has been gelded after stallion traits have developed.

Getting cast: Some horses are prone to getting cast, that is to say, lying down in their box and getting so close to the wall that they cannot rise.

Other vices or bad habits include: bolting, baulking, shying, pulling, tongue over bit, fighting the bit and tossing the head, and so on.

PART 16
JOCKEYS AND JOCKEYSHIP

Chapter	40	Jockeys
Section	40.1	Authorised Riders
	40.2	Jockeys
	40.3	Apprentice Jockeys
	40.4	Apprentices' Allowances
	40.5	Restrictions on Jockeys and Apprentices
	40.6	Jockeys' Dress and Equipment
	40.7	State Jockey Poll
	40.8	Assessment of Jockeys' Ability
	40.9	Never Bet on Jockeys
	40.10	At the End of a Jockey's Career
Chapter	41	Financial Viability of Jockeyship
Section	41.1	Income of Jockeys
	41.2	Riding Fees
	41.3	Retainer Fees
	41.4	Other Income of Jockeys
	41.5	Matters Affecting Earning Capacity of Jockeys
	41.6	Conclusion
Chapter	42	Jockeyship
Section	42.1	Jockey and Horse Must Act as Combined Unit
	42.2	Horsemen and Mere Riders
	42.3	Qualities of Top Jockeys
	42.4	Stirrup Lengths
	42.5	Race Tactics
	42.6	Use of the Whip
	42.7	Use of Spurs

PART 16   JOCKEYS AND JOCKEYSHIP

CHAPTER 40 JOCKEYS

Section 40.1
Authorised Riders

The only persons permitted to ride in a race at a registered race meeting are: (a) jockeys or apprentice jockeys holding a current licence or permit to ride granted by the Principal Club or the District Racing Association having jurisdiction in the area where the race meeting is held; or (b) a visiting jockey or apprentice jockey holding a licence or permit to ride granted by another Principal Club or District Racing Association, who is granted permission to ride by the stewards officiating at the race meeting concerned.

Even so, certain other persons may be authorised to ride in certain races under special circumstances, that is, amateur riders; owner or lessee of a horse; or any person authorised by the officiating stewards to ride at a country race meeting or picnic race meeting.

Before a person is granted any licence, permit, or permission to ride the applicant must undertake to submit to any tests that are intended to detect in his or her body the presence of any alcohol or drug or its metabolites or artefacts. Such tests may be carried out before, during, or after, the fulfilment of a riding engagement in any race, trial, or trackwork.

Section 40.2
Jockeys

A "jockey" (that is, a fully fledged jockey as opposed to an apprentice jockey) is a person licensed by a Principal Club or a District Racing Association to ride for hire, subject to any conditions of the licence. The licence may authorise the jockey to ride in any flat race run on courses of clubs within the jurisdiction of the licensing authority, or on the other hand, the licence may be provisional, or restricted as to locality, duration, and so on.

Jockeys may offer their services to all trainers or owners, or they may contract to ride exclusively for, or be given first priority to ride horses of, a particular trainer or owner. To be recognised officially, any such contract (called a "retainer") must be in writing, signed by the parties concerned, and lodged with the Principal Club or Association. In a case where a jockey enters into more than one retainer, the respective employers have precedence according to the priority of their retainer.

In many cases jockeys are inclined towards the use of paid agents to arrange their rides.

Section 40.3
Apprentice Jockeys

An "apprentice jockey", usually referred to in the racing industry simply as an "apprentice", is a trainee jockey indentured to a trainer or owner, the "master", in accordance with the Rules and subject to the approval of a Principal Club or an Association having jurisdiction over the area in which the master resides. Under the contract deed, referred to as the Articles of Agreement or Indenture, the apprentice is bound to serve the master in return for training. The parents or legal representative of the apprentice may be a party to the agreement.

The usual requirement is that at the time of entering into the apprenticeship agreement an apprentice must be under the age of 25 years. Further, the agreement must be for a period of five years or if the period terminates on the apprentice reaching 21 years, it must be for a period of not less than three years.

A person who has been an apprentice cannot be granted or hold a fully fledged jockeys' licence while under the age of 21 years unless that person is in, and continues to be in, the employment of an approved trainer or owner.

A permit to ride granted to an apprentice may be restricted as to duration and locality or both. All engagements for an apprentice to ride in races must be made through the master and not by the apprentice.

Subject to any related industrial law, the rate of wages payable to an apprentice is fixed by the Principal Club or the Association.

A bank account is required to be opened by the licensing authority or an approved person under the Apprenticeship Agreement and certain earnings of the apprentice are required to be paid and held in trust for such apprentice.

Section 40.4
Apprentices' Allowances

Apprentices begin learning the art or skill of jockeyship through riding work regularly and riding in barrier trials. Then they start riding in races on country racetracks. When stewards are satisfied as to their ability they become eligible to ride on metropolitan racetracks.

To compensate apprentices for their lack of experience they are entitled, where the Local Rules or the conditions of a race permit, to claim a weight advantage or allowance in the form of specified weight reduction from their mounts' allotted weights.

There are two schemes of entitlement — a country area scheme and a metropolitan area scheme. Each scheme is separate and distinct.

If apprentices are entitled to ride in the country area then they may, when permitted by the conditions of a race, claim an allowance for that race under the scheme for that area. In addition, if they are entitled to ride in the metropolitan area, they also have a weight entitlement allowance under the metropolitan scheme. Their allowance under each of the schemes depends upon their riding results in those areas. (See Section 49.5.)

Notwithstanding the apprentices' allowances schemes, no horse may have its weight reduced below 43.5kg by reason of any such apprentice's allowance. With the prescribed bottom limit weights for races nowadays it is most unlikely that an apprentice's allowance would reduce a horse's weight to 43.5kg let alone take it below.

Section 40.5
Restrictions on Jockeys and Apprentices

Licensed jockeys or apprentices, among other things, may not

- bet, or have an interest in a bet, on any race (and no person may bet with, or for, a jockey or apprentice);
- during the conduct of a race meeting be present in the betting ring of the racecourse on which such race meeting is being conducted or in the immediate vicinity of such ring;
- misconduct themselves in any way;
- own, take a lease of, or have any interest in any racehorse;
- without authority of the licensing authority concerned write any article for publication or, except in respect of past events, grant an interview about racing for inclusion in any radio or television program;
- accept any pecuniary or other gift or consideration contrary to the Rules.

Section 40.6
Jockeys' Dress and Equipment

Jockeys wear silks in the colours of the owners whose horses they ride, white breeches, lightweight black or brown leather boots, skull cap, and goggles.

The forward-cut jockey saddles vary in weight from the super-light "dot" weighing about 250g to the heavier saddles of the lightweight riders weighing up to about 6kg.

When required to make up the weight a horse is to carry, a bag containing the required quantity of lead is placed on the horse's back under the saddle.

Section 40.7
State Jockey Poll

In each State a Jockey Poll is published regularly in the news and sporting papers indicating the number of wins, minor placings, and unplaced rides of jockeys during the racing year within that State or as the case may be, within the metropolitan area of that State. At the end of the year the jockey who tops the poll is the winner of the Jockeys' Premiership. Because of various factors — absences, lack of opportunities, weight restrictions and so on — the winner of a Poll, while a top rider, however, is not necessarily the best rider in that State or metropolis.

Section 40.8
Assessment of Jockeys' Ability

For the application of the weight-rating method of selection (see Part 25) it is important to know who the best riders are and how much better one jockey is than another. The Jockey Poll is not suitable for this purpose

One weight-rating service known to me, the author, maintains and regularly updates a list of jockeys and apprentices, showing the difference in the abilities of those riders in terms of weight, called "Jockey Ratings". To differentiate among, and express the ability of, the various riders, a rating method is used with a scale ranging from 0kg to 5kg — the better the rider the lower the rating. Top riders have ratings from 0kg to 2kg. Less competent jockeys rate from 2.5kg to 5kg.

The ratings are determined from records of riding results and consideration of experience and past performance.

Riders are credited with 1.5kg for a win on a frontrunner and 2.5kg for any other win. (Less skill is needed to pilot a frontrunner to the post.) Riders are debited for losing margins at the rate of 1.5kg per length up to five lengths.

Riders not listed in the ratings either have not ridden often enough in the past six months, or well enough, to merit a rating.

At each period of review the net total number of kilograms for each rider is divided by the number of mounts for that period. The result is the rider's rating expressed in kilograms.

Calculations are made first for Saturday metropolitan mounts only and then for all mounts — metropolitan and provincial. The purpose of this is to effect adjustments for jockeys who are bush champions, but rarely win in town.

Section 40.9
Never Bet on Jockeys

Many punters base their selections on jockeys only. An analysis of jockeys' records indicates that the punter may win over certain but unpredictable short periods, but in the long term such a punter is a certain loser. It is good advice that punters should never bet on jockeys only but on the combination of rider and horse if the horse is fit for the race and has the ability to win it. Even the best jockey cannot win on a horse that is neither sound nor fit.

Section 40.10
At the End of a Jockey's Career

Of the many, many people who aspire to be jockeys and get on the first rung of the ladder by becoming indentured to a trainer, very few make it in this hazardous, unpredictable profession. Many retire along the way because of weight problems, riding inability, injuries, and so on. Those who stay on are imbued by their occupation and may continue to ride until they are about 50 years of age.

Many jockeys may, during their careers, follow part-time employment in other occupations and after retirement may have full-time employment in such occupations. Many obtain employment in training establishments or take up second careers as trainers. Some may be successful but it would be safe to say that not many have succeeded as trainers.

CHAPTER 41 FINANCIAL VIABILITY OF JOCKEYSHIP

Section 41.1
Income of Jockeys

Most jockeys in the metropolitan areas would be regarded as full-time, that is, available to ride at all race meetings. The hours which jockeys work in provincial and country areas, however, provide scope for them to undertake some other forms of employment. Within the racing industry the income of jockeys and apprentice jockeys is derived from several sources, including: riding fees (in races and official barrier trials); percentage of prize money won by their mounts; retainers; gifts; fees for riding trackwork, and so on.

Section 41.2
Riding Fees

In the absence of a special registered agreement the fees payable to jockeys and apprentices are prescribed from time to time by the Principal Club. Such prescription is based on

(a) a set riding fee for the rider of every horse competing in a race;

(b) plus, in the case of a winning mount, an additional fee of 5 per cent of the value of the prize to the winner; or in the case of a mount placed second, third, fourth or fifth, an additional fee of 5 per cent of the value of any prize of a prescribed amount or over to such placed horse.

A sum equivalent to the set riding fee is required to be lodged in cash with the race club secretary or other appointed official before the rider weighs out. The fee to which any rider becomes entitled for riding the winner or other placed mount is deducted by the club from the prize money otherwise payable to the owner. Total riding fees are paid in due course to the riders entitled thereto.

The same level of fee applies for both jockeys and apprentice jockeys. One quarter of the fees earned by an apprentice, however, must be paid to the apprentice's master.

An apprentice is not entitled, without the consent of the master, to charge any fee for riding a horse trained by such master.

Section 41.3
Retainer Fees

An agreement for retention of a jockey's services may provide for a retaining fee in addition to any riding fee or percentage of prize money earned.

Section 41.4
Other Income of Jockeys

Many owners give the jockey of their horse an amount additional to the riding fee and percentage of prize money when the jockey is successful in riding a winning race. The

Darren Beadman served his apprenticeship at Randwick under "Master" Theo Green in the 1980's. He has developed into a skilled, leading jockey and has achieved personal distinction, admiration and respect.

(Refer to Section 42.1)   Photo courtesy Steve Hart Photographics.

Finish of the 1996 STC Rosehill Guineas for three-year-olds over 2 000 metres at set weights. The race was won by Octagonal (by Zabeel from Eight Carat) (centre) from Saintly (outside) and Nothin' Leica Dane (inside). Class does not have a precise definition but there is no doubting the top class of these three placegetters.

(Refer to Section 34.5)   Photo courtesy Steve Hart Photographics.

Saintly (by Sky Chase from All Grace) ridden by Darren Beadman, is shown winning the 1996 VRC Foster's Melbourne Cup over 3 200 metres. Saintly's win gave trainer "Cups King" Bart Cummings his tenth Melbourne Cup success — a most extraordinary training achievement — and also gave him honour as breeder and senior part-owner of the horse.

(Refer to Section 43.13)   Photo courtesy Steve Hart Photographics.

amount of these gifts is at the discretion of the particular owner. A jockey is prohibited from accepting any pecuniary gift from any person other than the nominator of the horse ridden or to be ridden without the consent of such nominator.

All gratuities for apprentices are required to be paid to the club to be held in trust in accordance with the Apprenticeship Agreement.

Fees are also payable to riders of horses participating in organised trials. No fee is payable under the Rules for riding trackwork, but riders may be paid by trainers for such service. The level of any such trial or trackwork fees or charges is comparatively small.

Section 41.5
Matters Affecting Earning Capacity of Jockeys

Matters of concern to jockeys or apprentices, or matters affecting their earning capacity as jockeys or apprentices include:

- the low level of "bottom limit weights" used in handicap races;
- their own weights;
- the need to reduce their weight by diet, sauna sweating, or other measures and the possible health problems associated with excessive weight reduction;
- the handicapping of horses which they regularly ride or may ride at weights below their riding weights;
- their riding ability;
- the number of race meetings in the area in which they ride, the number of races at each such meeting, the number of horses in each race, and the value of prize money;
- suspensions, illnesses, injuries, and other absences.

Section 41.6
Conclusion

Considering relevant facts or factors, it can only be concluded that:

(a) there is a severe limitation on the earning capacity of jockeys and apprentices (particularly in the geographically larger and less populous states and in the provincial or country areas of States);

(b) because of such limitation, many jockeys and apprentices are involved in the racing industry on a part-time basis and must necessarily seek income from outside the industry.

Unless they themselves have financial management skills, jockeys will have a need to obtain professional services in the matter of endorsements, investments, and personal appearances.

CHAPTER 42 JOCKEYSHIP

Section 42.1
Jockey and Horse Must Act as Combined Unit

Success or failure in any race depends upon the fitness and ability of the horse, the skill of its jockey, the jockey's confidence in his or her ability to handle the horse and the horse's confidence in the jockey. That is to say, the basis of success depends upon the combination of horse and jockey and their mutual understanding.

The underlying principle is clear. The greater the skill of a rider, the greater the winning chance of a horse that he or she rides. Conversely, no matter how fit and able a horse may be, its chances of winning are greatly reduced or negligible if ridden by a jockey lacking in skill. There are good and bad riders. Indeed there are two broad categories of jockeys — horsemen and riders.

Section 42.2
Horsemen and Mere Riders

A horseman has a natural affinity with a mount and has knowledge and understanding of the horse's physical and psychological needs and so acts in such a manner that horse and horseman operate as one. By communication through proper use of riding aids, the horseman signals requirements to the horse, and the horse having confidence in the rider responds with willing obedience.

Riding principles are based on controlling the natural impulsion of the horse, and riding aids are the means of such control. These are the natural aids of hands, legs, seat (position of rider's weight), and voice, and the artificial aids such as the bit, whip, spurs, nosebands, rings (martingales) and similar appliances. All of those aids are regarded by the horseman purely as means of communicating to the horse what is required of it — and not means of force or punishment. The horseman controls the horse by management and equestrian skill and not by brute strength.

The mere rider sadly lacks the qualities of the horseman.

Section 42.3
Qualities of Top Jockeys

The qualities of top jockeys are seen in their race techniques and tactics. Good jockeys are alert at the barrier and have their mounts well positioned and balanced soon after the start; are good judges of pace and are aware of what is going on in a race, instinctively doing the right thing at the right time; have knowledge of the habits and abilities of other horses and riders competing in the race; use their hands lightly on the reins; properly balance their weight to assist their mounts' movement; adjust their riding tactics according to the style of running of their horses; properly time their mounts' finishing run; use the whip only to let the horse know what is required of it, rather than as a means of force or punishment; and use vigour and strength in a hard finish.

Above all, top jockeys are experienced horsemen who have confidence, a love of horses and the racing game, and the will to win!

Section 42.4
Stirrup Lengths

In the distant past horses carried huge imposts over long distances and races tended to be leisurely run, with accelerated pace over the last two furlongs. Jockeys in those days rode with long stirrups. Through time horses have been bred for speed at the sacrifice of "stoutness" and weights allotted have been reduced. Nowadays most races are run over sprint distances. Jockeys now use short stirrups and short reins, and crouch low on their mounts.

Australian jockeys usually ride two holes of the stirrup leather longer than their English and American counterparts. The slightly longer stirrups give them better balance and enable them to kick their mounts with their heels, so they say.

Section 42.5
Race Tactics

In order to ascertain knowledge of the characteristics of their mounts in coming races and also those of the other competing horses and jockeys, top jockeys may spend lengthy periods of research into historical data about performances in past races. It is vital for them to know the good and bad habits of such horses and riders.

Jockeys have usually ridden the horses for which they hold race engagements previously, in races, track gallops, or trials and have knowledge of their fitness, ability, and characteristics.

Tactics for a particular race may be discussed between trainer and jockey well before a race, but trainers issue final instructions to jockeys in the mounting yard before a race. Many trainers do not tie down good jockeys with fixed instructions as it is not possible to forecast accurately how a race will be run. While a riding plan may be made by trainer or jockey before a race it often has to be disregarded when the race is run differently from what had been anticipated.

The most important part of a race is from the home turn to the winning post, a distance of some 400m to 600m. This is the real test of the horse's ability, the rider's skill, and the understanding between horse and jockey.

Section 42.6
Use of the Whip

Every rider carries a whip which must conform in design and size to a regulation description.

Successful jockeys position themselves over the horse's centre of gravity, keep their mounts well balanced, and ride them with hands and heels with as little use of the whip as is practicable. Occasionally they will shake up a lazy horse with some whip punishment or, when desperate, use the whip to extract maximum effort from their mounts in a tight finish. But they realise that, on the whole, the less use that is made of the whip the better the overall results; its use may hinder a horse that has been doing its utmost without whip persuasion.

Under recently issued Rules jockeys are required to refrain from using the whip where a horse is past the post; is clearly winning; is out of contention for a place; is showing no response; or is likely to be injured. Use of the whip forward of the shoulder or in the vicinity of the head is prohibited as is use of the whip in a two-year-old race before the 200m mark.

Stewards may punish a rider for excessive use of the whip or spurs.

Section 42.7
Use of Spurs

Blunt spurs, as approved by the stewards, may be worn by a jockey at his or her discretion or that of the trainer concerned. Many horses, particularly the thin-skinned ones, resent being spurred, and react by racing erratically. Some horses only win when the rider is not wearing spurs.

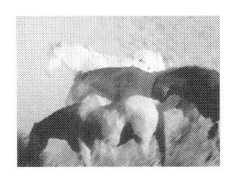

PART 17

CLASSES OF RACES ON THE FLAT

Chapter	43	Classes and Types of Races
Section	43.1	Definitions of Terms
	43.2	Division of Races into Classes
	43.3	Races for Two-Year-Olds
	43.4	Races for Three-Year-Olds
	43.5	Standard Restricted Class Races — Old Format
	43.6	Standard Restricted Class Races — New Format
	43.7	Statistics Underpinning Scheme for Restricted Class 1–6 Races
	43.8	Special Restricted Races and Special Condition Races
	43.9	Open Fillies and Mares Races
	43.10	Open Class Races
	43.11	Group and Listed Races
	43.12	Classic Races
	43.13	The Melbourne Cup
	43.14	Picnic Races
Chapter	44	**Weight-for-Age Scale**
Section	44.1	Weight-for-Age Scale
	44.2	Use of Weight-For-Age Scale for Handicapping

PART 17   CLASSES OF RACES ON THE FLAT

CHAPTER 43   CLASSES AND TYPES OF RACES

Section 43.1
Definitions of Terms

A "race on the flat" means a race held at a registered race meeting in which two or more registered galloping horses compete one against the other or others in a test of speed over a designated distance, not less than 800m, for prize money or for the purpose of providing a contingency on which bets may be made. The term does not include a trial, a race for hurdlers or steeplechasers, or any contest, event or contingency in which any obstacle has to be overcome or in which skills other than speed alone are tested.

A handicap race is one for which the official handicapper allots weights to competing horses according to their race class, merit of past performances, and other relevant factors, with the theoretical objective, so far as circumstances will allow, of equalising their chances and resulting in all runners crossing the finishing line in a mass dead-heat. One of the circumstances referred to is that the handicapper must frame the weights for a handicap race within prescribed top limit and bottom limit weights.

A set-weight race is one in which the weights the competing horses are required to carry are fixed by the conditions of the race usually without regard to performance. In some cases, however, weight penalties or allowances are imposed or allowed for performance (number and class of races won), sex or age. The official handicapper has no influence on the allocation of the weights.

A "stakes" or "sweepstakes" race is one in which the prize or part of it is contributed by the owners of the competing horses.

Section 43.2
Division of Races into Classes

Provision is made by the Australian Rules of Racing for the division of races into classes. Subject to those Rules, clubs may divide races into classes and attach conditions to those races about various matters such as: restrictions on entries for age, sex, breeding, number and types of races won, prize money won, and so on; the allocation of weights on a handicap or set-weight basis; and weight penalties and allowances to be imposed or allowed. The term "type of race" refers to the categories of races within each "class".

The object of the division of races into classes and types is to match horses with others of similar ability or standard of performance. It is one of the basic elements of thoroughbred racing.

During the racing year, starting on 1 August, races are appropriately programmed by clubs for all classes of horses in all racing areas — metropolitan, provincial, and country. These races are explained in some detail in this chapter.

Section 43.3
Races for Two-Year-Olds

Horses, as yearlings, are not permitted to race. After attaining the age of two years on their common birthdate, 1 August, they are permitted to start:

(a) in races for two-year-olds when such races are permitted to be programmed, that is, on or after 1 October or such earlier date as may be approved by the Principal Club;

(b) in races in which horses over the age of two years are also eligible to run (that is, open races) on or after 1 January or such earlier date as may be approved.

The important races for two-year-olds are usually programmed during the Autumn months — March, April and May.

The above provisions consider that youngsters need some time to develop before subjecting them to full racing pressures. Remember that, as horses are usually foaled in Australia between August and December, a horse officially turning two years on the artificially imposed common birthdate, 1 August, may actually be one or more months less than twenty-four months of age.

Races for two-year-olds:

- may be run on metropolitan, provincial, or country racecourses;
- may be run over distances ranging from 800m to 1600m;
- may be "open" races or restricted as to sex, breeding, races won, or prizemoney won, restricted as to class (Class A–D or Class 1–6) or restricted by special conditions;
- may be handicap races or set-weight events with or without weight penalties or allowances relative to sex, races won, or prize money won;
- may have other conditions imposed as indicated in the approved programs.

Where conditions allow and subject to their eligibility, two-year-olds may start in open races.

The important group or listed races for two-year-olds include such events as the Blue Diamond Stakes (VATC); Champagne Stakes (AJC); Golden Slipper Stakes (STC); Marlboro Stakes (QTC); and Sires Produce Stakes (of the various clubs).

Section 43.4
Races for Three-Year-Olds

Races for three-year-olds:

- may be run on metropolitan, provinical, or country racecourses;
- may be run over distances from 1200m to 2800m;
- may be "open" or restricted as to sex, breeding, races won, or prize money won, or restricted as to class (Class A-D or Class 1-6) or restricted by special conditions;

- may be handicap races or set-weights events with or without weight penalties or allowances relative to sex, races won, or prizemoney won;
- may have other conditions imposed as indicated in the approved programs.

Subject to their eligibilty, three-year-olds may also start in open races.

The major races for three-year-olds are the Derbies, Oaks, Guineas, and St.Legers. These events are the "classics".

Section 43.5
Standard Restricted Class Races — Old Format

Before the 1989 – 1990 racing year when horses reached three years of age they were able, subject to eligibility according to Local Rules of each State, to compete in races termed "Restricted Class". These races were designed to match horses three years old and older with others of their own class or standard of performance.

These races were run as handicaps restricted to horses of the same or lower class, or run as set-weight events restricted to two or more classes. Any such race may also have been restricted as to age or sex.

The various classes through which the restricted class horses advanced were termed as follows:
- Maiden
- Improvers
- Progressive
- Intermediate
- Advanced
- Approved
- Novice
- Transition
- Encourage
- Trial.

Under the conditions of those races it was possible for a horse to win up to 15 or more restricted class races if its racing was restricted to provincial or country circuits where restricted class conditions were mainly used.

Section 43.6
Standard Restricted Class Races — New Format

There were many difficulties associated with the practical application of the Local Rules because the old format of standard restricted class races varied as between States.

In an attempt to resolve those difficulties and to provide a restricted class scheme that was easy to understand and uniform throughout Australia, rules for the old scheme were repealed and replaced in 1989 – 1990 by a new uniform set of rules in all States of Australia.

A summary of those uniform rules is as follows.

"Maiden Race": a maiden race is one restricted to horses that, at the time of starting, have never won on the flat a race at a registered meeting, or any advertised race in any country.

"Class A–D Races": a class A,B,C, or D race is one restricted to horses that, at the time of starting, have not received in the aggregate more than a "prescribed amount" for wins in races on the flat and have never won a race on the flat outside Australia.

The "prescribed amounts" as from 1 January 1997, are as follows:

Class A Race – $1500

Class B Race – $3000

Class C Race – $4500

Class D Race – $6000

The value of the prize to the winner in a Class A, B, C, or D race cannot exceed such prescribed amount.

Programming of Class A-D races is limited.

A "Class 1–6 Race", subject to provisos, is one restricted to horses that, at the time of starting, have won not more than one race or, as the case may be, two, three, four, five, or six races on the flat.

In determining the eligibility of any horse for a Class 1–6 race

(a) no account is taken of any wins in Class A–D races other than where such win constitutes the first win of the horse and as such is classified as the winning of a "maiden race";

(b) no horse is eligible for a Class 1, 2, 3, 4, 5, or 6 race if it has won any race in Australia, New Zealand, or any other country of the description specified in the Rules for the respective class.

Section 43.7
Statistics Underpinning Scheme for Restricted Class 1–6 Races

In adopting the scheme for Class 1–6 restricted races, Principal Clubs had regard to several facts and factors including statistical results disclosed by an analysis of the completed careers of retired racehorses. Those results, summarised, indicate that 90 per cent of horses fail to win more than six races.

	%
Horses that fail to win a race	41
Horses that win only one race	21
Horses that win only two races	10
Horses that win only three races	7
Horses that win only four races	5
Horses that win only five races	4
Horses that win only six races	2
	90
Horses that win more than six races	10
	100%

Section 43.8
Special Restricted Races and Special Condition Races

Metropolitan clubs may program:

(a) "Special Restricted Races" that restrict the eligibility to horses that have not won a race or a prescribed number of races on the flat in a metropolitan area of Australia or in any other country;

(b) "Special Condition Races" that restrict the eligibility to horses that, during a preceding specified period (say, one year or two years), have not won a prescribed number of races on the flat in a metropolitan area of Australia or in any other country.

Eligibility for these special restricted races or special condition races may be further restricted as to age, sex, or value of prize money of races won.

These races may be run under handicap or set-weight conditions.

Section 43.9
Open Fillies and Mares Races

Races restricted to fillies and mares are regularly programmed by clubs. They may also be nominated for open class handicaps and weight-for-age events.

Section 43.10
Open Class Races

Following the restricted class events there are races which are open to any horse of any age (usually excluding two-year-olds) or of any class. These are called the "Open Class Races" and comprise races of the following description:

- Highweight Handicaps
- Welter and Flying Welter Handicaps
- Open Sprint Handicaps
- Open Distance Handicaps
- Standard Weight-for-Age Events.

Highweights and Welters are the lowest types of open class races and are programmed for horses which do not possess the speed or acceleration necessary to win an Open Sprint Handicap or an Open Distance Handicap. In these races horses having such limitation of speed or ability to accelerate at the end of a race carry comparatively big weights and compete against other horses having the same limitation.

Many horses, having graduated to open class, never win beyond welter or highweight class.

Open Sprint Handicaps are events for horses possessing or geared for high speed, and acceleration where necessary, over distances ranging from 1000m up to and including 1600m. Sprints up to and including 1200m are called "Flying Handicaps" while sprints of 1600m are referred to as "mile" events.

Open Distance Handicaps may be run over distances from in excess of 1600m up to 3200m. Such races up to 2200m are called "middle-distance" races and those in excess of 2200m, "staying" races.

Weight-for-Age Races are programmed for the better class horses that, because of their proven class, are highly weighted in handicaps. Such races range in distance from 1000m to 2500m. Weights are allocated to horses according to their age or sex as indicated in the Standard Weight-for-Age Scale. In cases the conditions of a Weight-for-Age race may provide for penalties or allowances or the race may be confined to horses of the same age.

Some authorities maintain that Weight-for-Age racing is the pinnacle of thoroughbred racing.

Section 43.11
Group and Listed Races

A worldwide uniform classification has been developed for the purpose of measuring the true performance standard of thoroughbreds, particularly those with a stud future. The system was started in Europe where a program of races was developed (called the "Pattern System") and those races were divided into three groups. Group races are now used in most countries including Australia where the system was adopted in the early 1970s.

Group 1 comprises the most prestigious races in the racing calendar. Group 2 consists of races which are just below championship level. Group 3 races are down another level and their significance is generally more local than national. Prize money is the main basis of assessing gradings.

Listed races are more important than ordinary events, but are not of sufficient significance to justify group rating.

In pedigrees and sales catalogues horses that have won group or listed races are shown in black type (bold) capital letters while horses that have been placed in such events are shown in black type (bold) lower case letters. "Black type" is highly regarded in a pedigree.

Because the system of group and listed races is international, "black type" is a simple and fairly reliable guide to the merit of a horse whose bloodlines might be unfamiliar.

Group and listed races run in Australia are those published as such by the Australian Conference of Principal Racing Clubs. Group and listed races run outside Australia are published as such by the International Cataloguing Standards Committee.

Section 43.12
Classic Races

In England five famous races are run each racing season to test the quality of the three-year-old crop. These races, known as the "classics", were first run in the latter half of the eighteenth century. They comprise:

- the Derby for colts and the Oaks for fillies each run at Epsom over one-and-a-half miles (2.4km);
- the Thousand Guineas for fillies and the Two Thousand Guineas for colts each run at Newmarket over one mile (1.61km);
- the St Leger open to both fillies and colts run at Doncaster over one-and-three-quarter miles (2.8km).

The Derby was named after the 12th Earl of Derby who was an early influential member of the English Jockey Club and the Oaks after the Derby family home at Epsom.

Similar classic tests were introduced into France, the USA, and other countries. Each State of Australia has its own classic program for the three-year-old colts and fillies.

Nowadays while those tests are the only true classics, other important group races with very high prize money are commonly referred to as "classic events".

Winning a true classic is enormously prestigious and the winners are assured of their future as breeding stock.

Section 43.13
The Melbourne Cup

Cup Day, the first Tuesday of November, is the day Australia comes to a standstill for the running of the Melbourne Cup, the climax of the Australian racing season.

The first Melbourne Cup, as we know it in this age, was run in 1861. Since then it has become part of our national identity.

Section 43.14
Picnic Races

Picnic race meetings are authorised for country areas each racing year. Races programmed for those meetings comprise maiden, class A–D, class 6, and open races.

Except that the first win of a horse always counts as a maiden win, class A, B, C and D wins at picnic meetings do not count in determining the race class of a horse for professional meetings.

Class 6 races provide for horses classed 1–6 but there is no concession for professional meetings for the winning of any such race at a picnic meeting.

In some cases picnic meetings are primarily traditional social assemblages of people from far and wide for a few days of revelry, feasting, drinking, and so on, with some rough-and-ready horse racing. In other cases the meetings are orderly and well conducted with good racing.

PART 17 CLASSES OF RACES ON THE FLAT

CHAPTER 44 WEIGHT-FOR-AGE SCALE

Section 44.1
Weight-for-Age Scale

The Standard Weight-for-Age (WFA) scale for flat races is a table in the Rules of Racing.

The sporting gentry of England long ago learnt that the running ability of a horse was considerably influenced by its age and sex. Accordingly, they developed a weight compensation condition for the purpose of bringing horses of both sexes and of all ages together on an equitable basis. The scheme was drawn together in a scale designed by Admiral Henry Rous soon after his appointment in 1855 as handicapper to the Jockey Club of England. Since then the scale has been used internationally with only slight changes, some of which were necessarily made in Australia at the time of changeover from imperial to metric weights and distances.

Standard Weight-for-Age races are programmed by race clubs for the better class horses that, because of their proven class, are highly weighted in handicaps. Weights carried by horses competing in WFA races are those set by the scale according to age and sex of the horse, the distance of the race, and the season of the year.

The original scale, as amended and used in Australia, allows for improvement in maturing horses, deterioration in ageing horses, seasonal disadvantages of fillies and mares, and age disadvantages of horses sired "north of the line" and foaled between 1 January and 31 July. (Northern Hemisphere official foaling time is 1 January: Southern Hemisphere official foaling time is 1 August.)

Features of the WFA scale are indicated in the following table which is an abridgement of part of the scale.

PART 17 CLASSES OF RACES ON THE FLAT

AGE	DISTANCE m	AUGUST kg	JANUARY kg	JULY kg	IMPROVEMENT DETERIORATION kg
2	1200	...	43	48.5	}
	1600	...	41.5	47	} + 5.5 for half year
	2200	...	40.5	45.5	}
3	1200	50	53	56.5	}
	1600	49	52	55.5	}
	2200	47	51	54.5	} + 7
	2600	46	50.5	54	}
4	1200	57	57	57	}
	1600	57	57	57	}
	2200	57	57	57	}NIL
	2600	57	57	57	}
5+	1200	58	57.5	57	}
	1600	58.5	58	57	}
	2200	59	58.5	57.5	} – 1.5
	2600	59.5	59	58	}

Allowances for Mares — 2.5kg from 1.8 to 31.12
1.5kg from 1.1 to 31.3
1.0kg from 1.4 to 31.7

Section 44.2
Use of Weight-For-Age Scale for Handicapping

Admiral Rous intended that the standard WFA scale be used as a guide to a handicapper when assessing weights for races to be run under handicap conditions. The scale provides, however, only for a broad pattern of improvement or deterioration in horses generally, and does not, and cannot, provide for the individual ability or race fitness of each horse at any time — factors which are vital for handicapping. Accordingly official handicappers usually do not use the scale, except for the single purpose of allotting weights to horses nominated for WFA events. Some may use the scale as a guide when assigning weights to three-year-olds racing in open company.

"When the jockeys are out with the whips... and the backers grow white to the lips". Whips were out at the finish of the 1994 AJC Epsom Handicap. (Refer to Section 42.6) Photo courtesy Steve Hart Photographics.

The finish of the 1997 STC Golden Slipper Stakes. This race for two-year-olds over 1 200 metres at set weights was won by the colt Guineas (by Crown Jester ex Foreign Bank) from the colt Encounter with filly Regal Chamber third. The Golden Slipper is the richest race for two-year-olds run in Australia.
(Refer to Section 43.3) Photo courtesy Steve Hart Photographics.

"I'm St Jude, a well-bred stallion (by Godswalk USA from Out of Danger) standing at stud in Queensland. I'm well-equipped genetically and otherwise to carry out my duties and I'm looking forward to an increase in demand for the production of racehorses."

(Refer to Section 14.3)
Photo courtesy Alan Peach Photography.

Nearing the finish of the 1997 AJC Australian Derby. This classic race for three-year-olds run at Royal Randwick over 2 400 metres at set weights was won by the colt Ebony Grosve (Grosvenor-Dusky Rosa) from Danendri and Intergaze. Shane Dye rode the winner and Darren Beadman the second horse.

(Refer to Section 43.12)   Photo courtesy Alan Peach Photography.

PART 18
RACETRACKS

Chapter	45	Racetracks Generally
Section	45.1	Meaning of Terms "Racecourse" and "Racetrack"
	45.2	Racetrack Design
	45.3	Horses for Courses
	45.4	Barrier Stalls
	45.5	Barrier Positions
	45.6	Importance of Barrier Positions
	45.7	Limitation on Size of Fields
	45.8	Meaning of Term "Distance"
	45.9	State of the Going
	45.10	Cutaway Rail
Chapter	46	Metropolitan Racetracks and Barrier Guides
Section	46.1	Diagrams of Tracks and Barrier Tables

PART 18 RACETRACKS

CHAPTER 45 RACETRACKS GENERALLY

Section 45.1
Meaning of Terms "Racecourse" and "Racetrack"

While the terms "racecourse" and "racetrack" may be used synonymously, technically they have different meanings.

Reference to a "racecourse" as a racing venue is reference to a defined area of land licensed by a licensing authority (being a State Government or an instrumentality of that Government) for the particular purpose of holding lawful race meetings. In that sense the term "racecourse" includes all such licensed land and the buildings and facilities on it.

On the other hand, a "racetrack" or "racecourse proper" is the prepared track, course or route, usually as indicated by running rails, laid out on a racecourse and on which races are run. The main track is called the "track proper" or "course proper" while chutes, auxiliary to the track proper, may join it either from the inside or the outside.

Application for a racing venue licence is made by a race club to its Principal Club which forwards the application, together with its recommendation to the licensing authority. The authority, in the exercise of its powers and functions, may grant or refuse the licence and, if granted, may at any time suspend, cancel, or transfer that licence.

While the racing venues used by most metropolitan and provincial race clubs are used exclusively for racing purposes many racing venues, particularly those in country areas, serve other interests as well as racing. Such interests include those of show societies, sporting bodies, local industry, and so on.

Section 45.2
Racetrack Design

A racetrack is designed to test the speed and stamina of racehorses over various distances, usually on a circuitous course. Circuitous racing began in the reign of Charles II in the seventeenth century. The predominant factor considered in any design is the safety of competing horses and riders. The track must be reasonably level with negotiable turns banked at about 7 degrees. It must have a surface that will cushion or lessen the jarring or jolting effects of galloping on the gallopers' legs, and a good drainage system.

With one notable exception (the Darwin sand track), Australian metropolitan racetracks have surfaces of grass growing on a mix of soil and sand. Training tracks, and racetracks outside the metropolitan areas, may have surfaces of grass, sand, dirt, wood fibre, or cinders.

Each racetrack has its own peculiarities that make it different from every other track.

Section 45.3
Horses for Courses

Horses, too, are different. Some horses may race well at one track and poorly at others. Some horses, called "course specialists", have a special liking for one particular track at which they record most of their wins. Conversely, there are horses that have an absolute dislike for a certain track or tracks on which they never run well. High quality or class horses usually run well at any track.

There is an old adage "horses for courses" and this remains valid today. The reasons for such liking or disliking of courses include:

- Long, free-striding horses gallop well on big, roomy tracks, but have difficulty handling tracks with sharp turns and short stretches.
- Short-striding horses have the ability to handle sharp turns at speed and are at an advantage on tracks designed with such turns and short stretches.
- Some horses run best right-handed or clockwise, others left-handed or anti-clockwise. Races are run clockwise in New South Wales and Queensland. In other States, the running is anti-clockwise.
- Some horses like to lead, others like to sit in on the pace while others like to drop out in the early stages and make their final runs from behind. Different tracks suit their different styles.
- Frontrunners usually falter where a track has an upward inclination, particularly in the straight; and so on.

The fact that a horse is trained at a particular track does not indicate that it will perform best at that track. It may. Many horses show a preference for a track other than their home track.

Section 45.4
Barrier Stalls

Barrier stalls are in use at all race meetings on which the TAB operates. They are also used at most other race meetings, although it well may be that the old line-up method is still used at some country or picnic meetings.

The barrier stalls are fitted with a row of starting stalls or compartments with gates at the front and back. The design provides for all front gates to be opened simultaneously by the starter and so give all runners an even chance at the start.

If the stewards are of the opinion that a horse is prevented from starting by any failure of the mechanical barrier at the time the horses are dispatched, they may declare such horse not to be a starter.

Barrier stalls are usually set at a 90 degree angle to the inside running rail.

Section 45.5
Barrier Positions

After declaration of acceptances for a race, the barrier draw is made by lot. In the case of subsequent scratchings the barrier draw number of each starter is reduced by the number of scratchings, if any, of horses drawn inside it. There could be a considerable difference between a barrier draw number and the barrier stall number or position that it occupies at the start of the race.

Sometimes there are a large number of scratchings particularly at race meetings during holiday periods, or when a racetrack becomes rain-affected.

Section 45.6
Importance of Barrier Positions

Barrier positions are usually an important factor in the outcome of a race. This is clear from a study of racetracks and their peculiarities; the location of starting posts; and statistical data about barrier position numbers from which winners started.

Factors that may accentuate or negate the importance of barrier positions include:

(a) The distance of the run from the starting point to the first turn and the tightness of that turn:
- Where the distance is long, horses will have time to take up their appropriate running positions before entering the turn.
- Where, on the other hand, the distance is short and the turn is tight, horses need the ability not only to begin well, but also to negotiate the turn, otherwise they will be pushed wide. Those drawn at wide barriers are at a disadvantage. Indeed the closer the starting point to the first turn the more hazardous the path of runners from wide starting positions. But slow beginners drawn near the rails may also be disadvantaged by being cut off and pushed back to the rear of the field.

(b) The erection of a temporary false running rail on the track and the distance of that false rail from the permanent rail. The effect of this is a narrowing of the track and a tightening of the turns.

(c) The surface conformation of the track particularly at, or soon after, the starting point (that is to say, whether the track is level or inclined upward or downward).

(d) The ability of a horse to handle the track or the going. Some horses are course specialists while some have an absolute dislike for a certain track or tracks. Some horses can only handle fast or good surfaces while some can handle dead tracks, some slow, some the heavy going. If a horse does not have the necessary ability, its barrier position is not likely to affect its winning chance.

(e) In wet weather, particularly on tracks that are well banked and drain towards the inside, the inside going becomes more affected than the outside. In such a case widely drawn horses have the advantage of the better going.

(f) The manner in which the race is run. In a distance race the pace may be dawdling, but in a short sprint there is likely to be a helter-skelter dash.

(g) The size of the field. There is a limit on the number of horses that may start from each starting point.

(h) Where a horse has a weight advantage and also has the ability to begin smartly and take up and hold a good running position early without great effort, its barrier position is not of great importance. On the other hand, slow beginners and average horses starting from outside barrier positions are disadvantaged. Indeed slow beginners can also suffer from inside barrier positions.

(i) The wider the barrier position the longer the distance from the starting point to the winning post, and so on.

Factors mentioned above may also be affected by a race club, having regard to the circumstances of the day, moving the starting stalls backward or forward one or more panels of the running rail from the advertised starting point.

Figures are published from time to time indicating the number of times horses starting from each barrier position at each starting point on a racetrack were successful. Any comparison is not meaningful unless such statistical results are expressed on a percentage basis. The sizes of fields vary hence only percentages allow proper comparison.

Section 45.7
Limitation on Size of Fields

The number of horses permitted to start from each starting point at each racetrack is prescribed by Local Rules. That number varies according to the position of the moveable rail, that is, whether such rail is in the true or normal position or, if moved out from normal, the number of metres by which it is out.

In some cases, when the rail is moved out from normal position, the distances of certain races are marginally altered by relocation of the starting point.

The Rules for this are based on safety factors.

Section 45.8
Meaning of Term "Distance"

The term "distance", unless the context in which it is used indicates otherwise, is the distance of a race.

The minimum distance of a race is 800m. Races over that and other short distances are programmed for two-year-olds early in the season.

When a person closely associated with racing, particularly a race caller, uses the term "at the distance", however, the reference is to the 200m mark or pole in the home straight; in imperial distance, the old furlong pole. In that context the term derives from the past when races were conducted in heats with heat winners going into a final. If, in any heat when the winner reached the winning post any other runner had not reached the distance pole, then it was judged to have been "distanced" and was disqualified from that heat and subsequent heats.

Section 45.9
State of the Going

The condition of the track, that is, the state of the going, is determined and announced by stewards in charge of a race meeting on the morning of that meeting. The weather is not controllable by man (thank God!) and a lot can happen to the weather and the track rating between time of first inspection of the track and time of the first race... and also after. Accordingly stewards may change the original rating if, in their opinion, there is any change in the track condition.

In making their rating assessment, stewards make a visual inspection of the track and may have penetrometer measurements made by track management. They may also consult with jockeys during the course of a meeting about the track.

The penetrometer is a device used for measuring the firmness of the track surface by measuring the extent to which it is penetrated by a given force. These measurements are a guide only. They are affected by variables such as type of grass, type of soil, rate of drainage, and so on. Readings may vary from track to track and season to season, hence it is necessary for an operator to develop penetrometer statistics over a period before using them to calculate track ratings with any accuracy. As a general rule penetrometer ratings are as indicated in the following table:

Less than 3.00	Fast
3.01 to 3.50	Good
3.51 to 4.00	Dead
4.01 to 4.50	Dead/Slow
4.51 to 5.00	Slow
5.01 to 5.50	Slow/Heavy
5.51 and over	Heavy

After a race meeting has started a good indication of the state of the going may be obtained by a comparison of running times for early races at the meeting with comparable standard times for various conditions at that track. Standard times for the track concerned, calculated from historical records, may be somewhat as indicated in the following table:

TABLE OF TIMES FOR VARIOUS TRACK CONDITIONS AT TRACK "X"

DISTANCE	GOOD	DEAD	SLOW	HEAVY
1000m	59.5	61	62.5	64.5
1200m	71.5	73	74.5	76.5
1400m	83.5	85	87	89
1600m	97	98.5	100.5	102.5
2000m	124	126	128	130
2400m	150	152	154	157

Tracks with grass surfaces deteriorate when they are rain-affected and jockeys may be observed searching all over the track for the better or firmer going. This may be in the centre or along the outside rail. In such cases the difference between the inside and the outside going may be expressed in lengths. Punters cannot bet with any confidence under such conditions.

Section 45.10
Cutaway Rail

When a false running rail is used it may be put out from the true rail the same distance around the entire track, or put out for a certain part of the track with gentle curving back to the true rail.

The Australian Jockey Club has been experimenting at Randwick Racecourse with what is called the "cutaway rail". In such a case the false rail cuts back at a sharp angle to the normal or true running rail at the 400m mark just after the entrance to the home straight. The rail has been used when considered "necessary", particularly when the weather conditions were poor.

It has been reported that wear and tear of the track when the cutaway rail is not in use is mainly just before the home turn. However when the cutaway rail is in use, wear and tear of the track is mainly at the end of the turn into the straight. This would indicate that when such rail is in use jockeys are delaying their runs.

Those in favour of the cutaway rail point out that it provides open spaces for horses that otherwise would be locked away on the rail; it offers horses a clear run in the home straight; it assists in the elimination of interference and so assists in the welfare of competing horses and jockeys; it provides better racing by evening up the chances of all runners being particularly helpful for horses drawn wide at the barrier; and so on.

On the other hand, those not in favour of the use of the cutaway rail point out that it takes away a lot of the initiative and skill of jockeyship; it causes races to be run slowly to the corner into the straight, that is, just before the cutaway rail; it causes horses to become confused when they move from galloping alongside the rail to galloping in the open space; frontrunners and horses drawn wide are disadvantaged; use of the rail for some meetings and not others causes inconsistency — the rail should be used for all meetings or not at all; on a wet day the inside running where the rail cuts back is slower than the outside; and so on.

CHAPTER 46 METROPOLITAN RACETRACKS AND BARRIER GUIDES

Section 46.1
Diagrams of Tracks and Barrier Tables

When carrying out a selection process for a race it is vital that an astute punter has a good knowledge and understanding of the characteristics of the track on which such race is to be run, the ability of horses starting in the race to handle that track, and the advantage or disadvantage that accrues to each starter from its barrier position.

Diagrams of racetracks and comment on their features are usually published in sporting papers at times when race meetings are programmed to be held at the respective tracks. As a convenient source of reference for punters, however, diagrams (not necessarily drawn to scale) of Australian metropolitan racetracks follow, together with some comment on the peculiarities of each of those tracks and a guide to the relevance of barrier positions from the various starting points (or approximate starting points) of races. Unless otherwise indicated, barrier positions from starting points in staying races are not significant.

PART 18 RACETRACKS

RANDWICK, SYDNEY

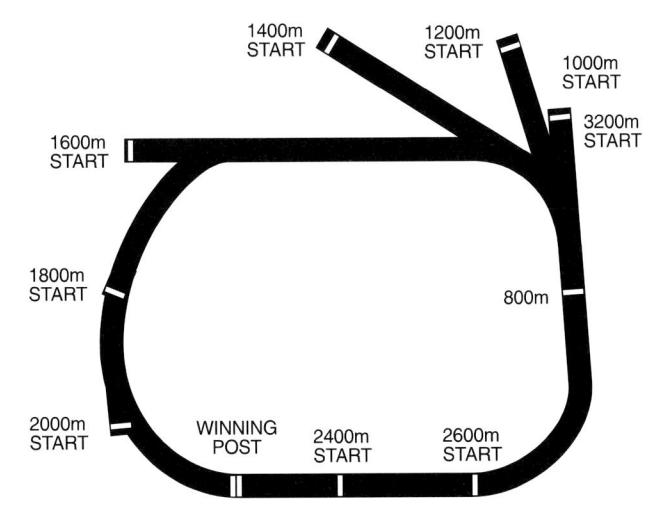

Licensee: Australian Jockey Club
Direction of Running: Clockwise
Circumference: 2213m
Straight: 410m
Width: 30m

BARRIER GUIDE		
STARTING POINT m	STARTING POSITIONS Good to Fair	Poor to Bad
1000	1–11	12–13+
1200	1–13	14–15+
1400	1–13	14–15+
1600	1–14	15–16+
1800*	1–11	12–13+
2000	1–11	12–13+

* Horses drawn close inside at the 1800m starting point run the risk of being cut off by outside horses.

There is a slight inclination between the 2000m mark and the 1600m mark. There is a declination at the entrance to the home straight followed by a significant 3m rise between the 400m and 200m marks.

The track is roomy and the turns sweeping. Its long and difficult straight is stamina-testing. It suits good, long-striding horses that make their final runs from behind the field.

Inside Track: Measurements of the inner grass track are: circumference 2100m; straight 401m; width 20m.

ROSEHILL, SYDNEY

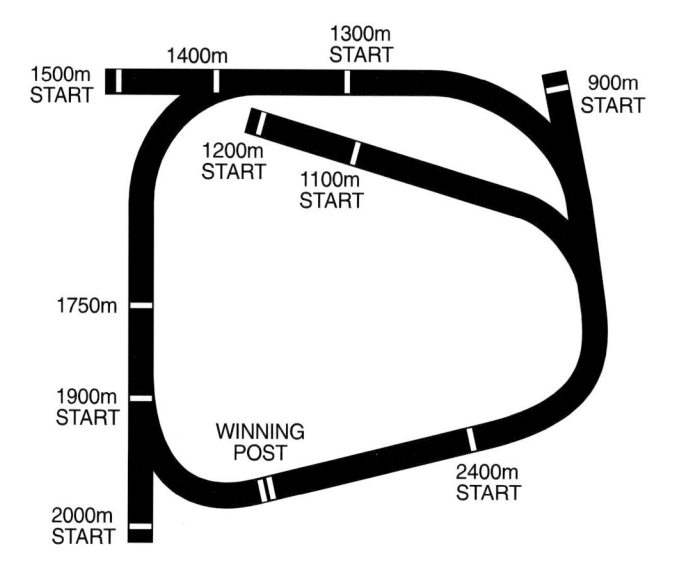

Licensee: Sydney Turf Club
Direction of Running: Clockwise

Circumference: 2048m
Straight: 408m
Width: 26m

BARRIER GUIDE		
STARTING POINT m	STARTING POSITIONS Good to Fair	Poor to Bad
1100	1–8	9–12+
1200	1–9	10–12+
1300	1–10	11–14+
1500	1–11	12–15+
1900	1–9	10–11+
2000	1–10	11–12+

The turn from the in-course 1200m chute to the course proper is sharp. Other turns are moderately tight.

The surface conformation is mostly level, but there is a slight rise in the long straight.

Inside barriers are an advantage from every starting point, but particularly from starting points in the 1200m chute.

All types of runners are suited by the "easy" track.

PART 18 RACETRACKS

WARWICK FARM, SYDNEY

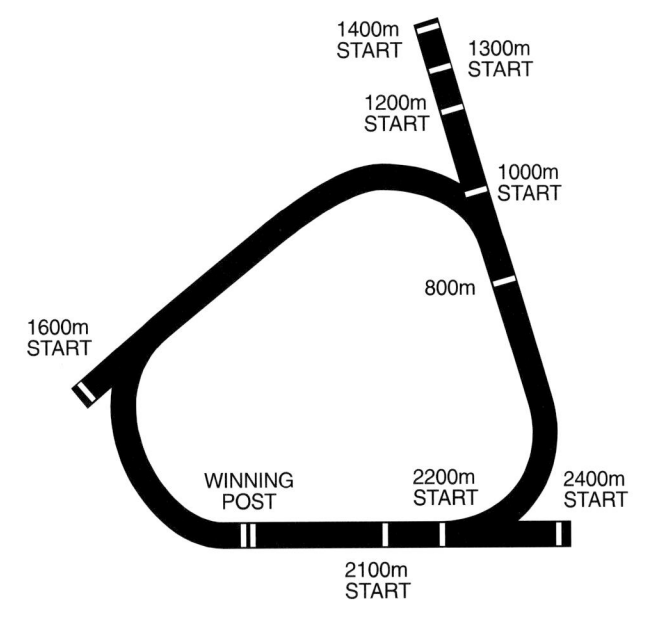

Licensee: Australian Jockey Club
Direction of Running: Clockwise
Circumference: 1937m
Straight: 326m
Width: 23m

BARRIER GUIDE		
STARTING POINT m	STARTING POSITIONS Good to Fair	Poor to Bad
1000	1–9	10–13+
1200	1–11	12–15+
1400	1–13	14–16+
1600	1–11	12–15+
2100	1–9	10–12+
2200	1–9	11–12+

The turns are moderately tight, but all are cambered.

The surface is mostly level with a very slight rise in the straight.

Inside barriers are an advantage from every starting point, particularly from the 1000m point and the middle-distance starting points in the straight.

Horses that can be up with the leaders at the turn into the home straight are suited. It is a track for specialists.

CANTERBURY, SYDNEY

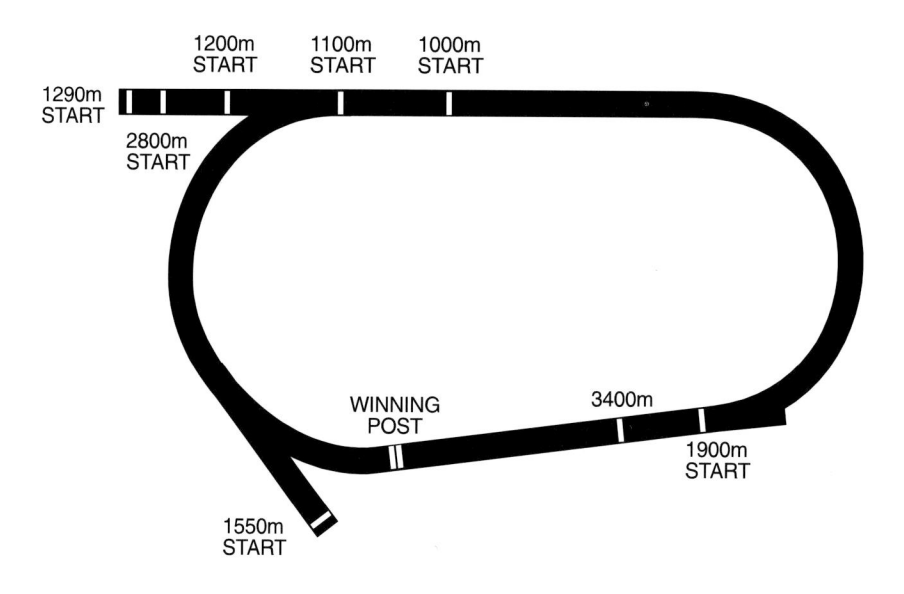

Licensee: Sydney Turf Club
Direction of Running: Clockwise

Circumference: 1578m
Straight: 317m
Width: 23m

BARRIER GUIDE		
STARTING POINT m	STARTING POSITIONS Good to Fair	Poor to Bad
1100	1–10	11–13+
1200	1–11	12–14+
1290	1–12	13–14+
1550	1–8	9–10+
1900	1–10	11–12+

The track is small and the turns tight.

There is a slight declination in the back straight followed by an inclination from about the 800m mark to the entrance into the home straight.

Inside barriers are an advantage, particularly from starting points in the 1550m chute.

Track specialists being short-striding, front-running horses are suited. Horses that are long-striding, or that get back in a field, or that are unfamiliar with the track, invariably run wide at the home turn.

PART 18 RACETRACKS

FLEMINGTON, MELBOURNE

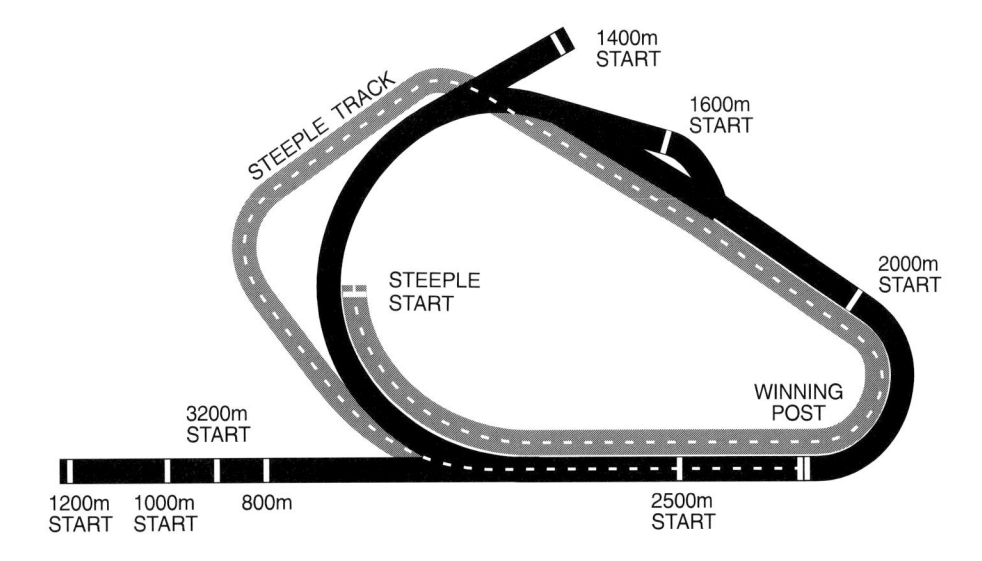

Licensee: Victoria Racing Club
Direction of Running: Anti-clockwise
Circumference: 2312m
Straight: 448m
Width: 30m

BARRIER GUIDE		
STARTING POINT m	STARTING POSITIONS Good to Fair	Poor to Bad
Sprints up to 1200	*	*
1400	1–10	11–14+
1600	1–10	11–14+
2000	1–12	13–15+
2500	1–10	11–12+

* Barriers for sprint races down the straight track are of little significance.

Track Proper

There is a sharp turn out of the straight into the back stretch. For this reason, in staying races, it is vital for success from starting points located in the straight, or in an extension of the straight, that a runner take up a position close to the running rail and handle the sharpness of that turn.

To lessen the disadvantage of outside barrier positions, races are run over 2500m, rather than the traditional classic distance of 2400m.

The track proper is relatively level with a sweeping home turn into the long straight. Good horses that are long striders and make their runs from behind the field are suited by the testing courses of races on the track proper.

"Straight 1200" Track

A long chute, being an extension of the home straight, provides for races up to 1200m to be run over a straight course called the "Straight 1200". It also provides a starting point for races run over 3200m — including the Melbourne Cup.

Generally, barriers are of little significance for races down the Straight 1200 track. Horses drawn in the centre usually cross for easy guidance to the inside or outside running rail. Some horses may be disadvantaged because of the practice of such "crossing".

When the track is wet, the going is better near the outside running rail than the inside.

If a horse drawn near the outside rail in a race down the Straight 1200, runs a diagonal course and finishes near the inside rail, the extra distance of such course is 10 metres.

CAULFIELD, MELBOURNE

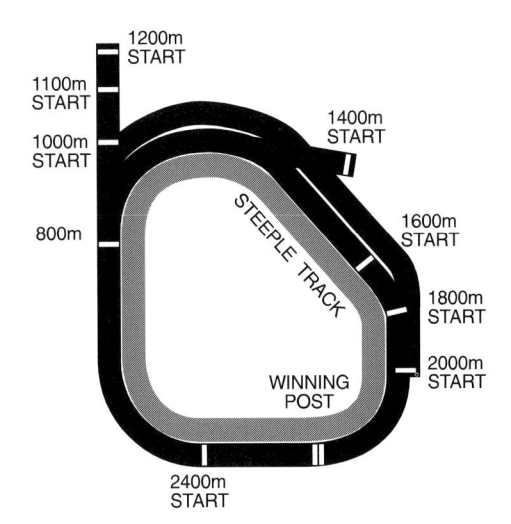

Licensee: Victoria Amateur Turf Club
Direction of Running: Anti-clockwise

Circumference: 2080m
Straight: 367m
Width: 30m

BARRIER GUIDE		
STARTING POINT m	STARTING POSITIONS Good to Fair	Poor to Bad
1000	1–10	11–13+
1100	1–11	12–14+
1200	1–12	13–15+
1400	1–10	11–13+
1600	1–11	12–13+
1800	1–9	10–11+
2000	1–9	10–11+

The new Caulfield track was opened in April 1996. It features an outer circuit for 1700m, 1800m and 2000m races.

The track is somewhat like a right-angle triangle with turns rounded and cambered. There is an inclination in the back stretch, the rise from the 1400m mark to the 1200m mark being quite significant. This is followed by a declination for a few hundred metres. The home turn is banked at about 6°.

Inside barriers are an advantage from every starting point.

Horses that can race with the leaders are suited. It is a track for specialists.

During wet weather the going is very difficult and unpredictable.

MOONEE VALLEY, MELBOURNE

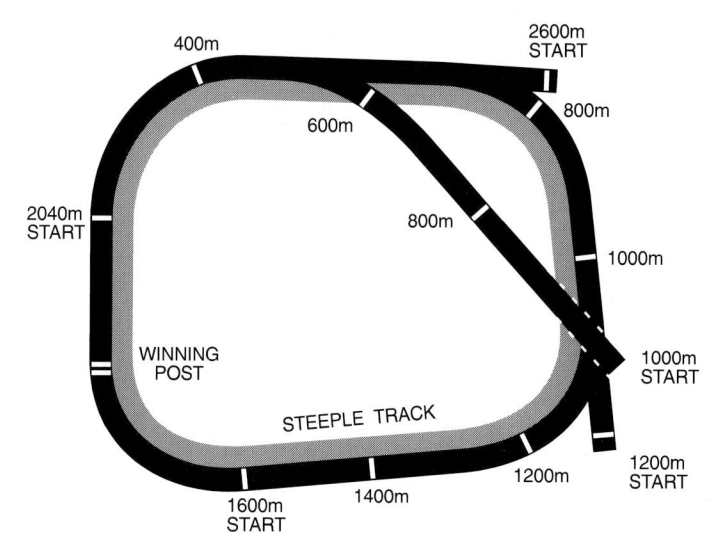

Licensee: Moonee Valley Racing Club
Direction of Running: Anti-clockwise
Circumference: 1805m
Straight: 173m
Width: 23m

BARRIER GUIDE

STARTING POINT m	STARTING POSITIONS Good to Fair	Poor to Bad
1000	1–11	12–13+
1200	1–10	11–12+
1600	1–9	10–11+
2040	1–9	10–11+
2600	1–9	10–12+

The track was reconstructed during the period from October 1994 to October 1995. It incorporates sand mesh elements and is said to now provide a consistently good all-weather racing surface. Nevertheless, the track is small, narrow, and tricky with short and tight turns.

Turns are banked at 7.5° and the track rises 8.5m from the 800m to the winning post.

The number of starters from every starting point is limited to 14 or 15. Inside barriers are an advantage from every starting point.

To have any winning chance horses must be in front or with the leaders when entering the short straight. Horses that are heavily weighted and unfamiliar with the track have very little chance of winning. It is a case of "horses for courses" — many horses just do not handle the track.

SANDOWN, MELBOURNE

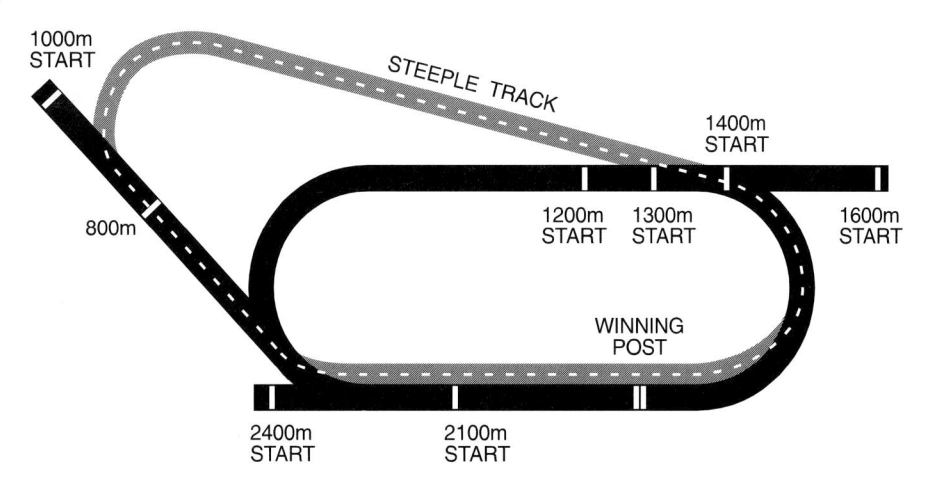

Licensee: Victoria Amateur Turf Club
Direction of Running: Anti-clockwise

Circumference: 1891m
Straight: 407m
Width: 30m

BARRIER GUIDE		
STARTING POINT m	STARTING POSITIONS Good to Fair	Poor to Bad
1000	1–10	11–12+
1200	1–10	11–12+
1400	1–11	12–13+
1600	1–12	13–14+
2100	1–9	10–11+

The track proper is undulating: It
- rises about 4m from the 1200m mark to the 800m mark;
- drops about 3.5m from the 800m mark to the 400m mark;
- rises more than 0.6m from the 400m mark to the winning post.

The 1000m chute drops about 6m to the 400m mark on the track proper. Times for races run from that chute are understandably fast. Inside barriers are an advantage from every starting point when the going is good.

In wet weather, because of well-banked turns, water flows or seeps to the inside making the going there very heavy. In such a case, riders keep their mounts well out on the track and barrier positions are then of little consequence. It is, nevertheless, considered to be a good wet-weather track. Good horses that make their runs from behind the field are suited by the track.

MORPHETTVILLE, ADELAIDE

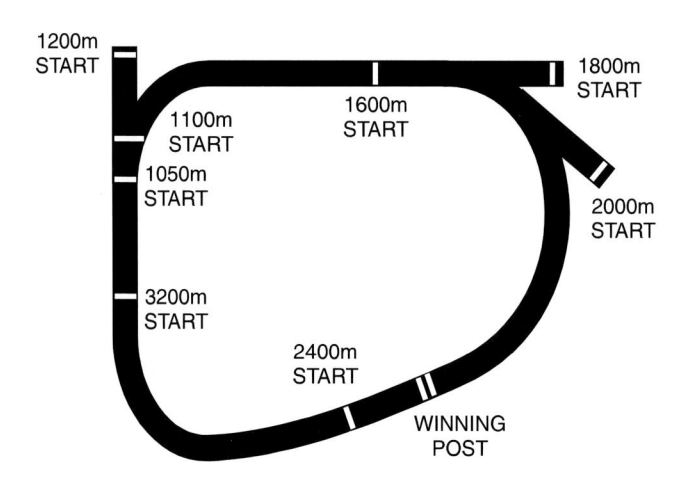

Licensee: South Australian Jockey Club
Direction of Running: Anti-clockwise
Circumference: 2327m
Straight: 330m

BARRIER GUIDE		
STARTING POINT m	STARTING POSITIONS Good to Fair	Poor to Bad
1000	1–8	9–11+
1200	1–10	11–13+
1600	1–9	10–11+
1850	1–10	11–12+
2000	1–9	10–12+

The track is level. The turn into the straight is fairly tight, otherwise turns are fairly gradual and banked.

Inside barriers are an advantage from every starting point.

The course is considered roomy and all types of gallopers are suited.

CHELTENHAM, ADELAIDE

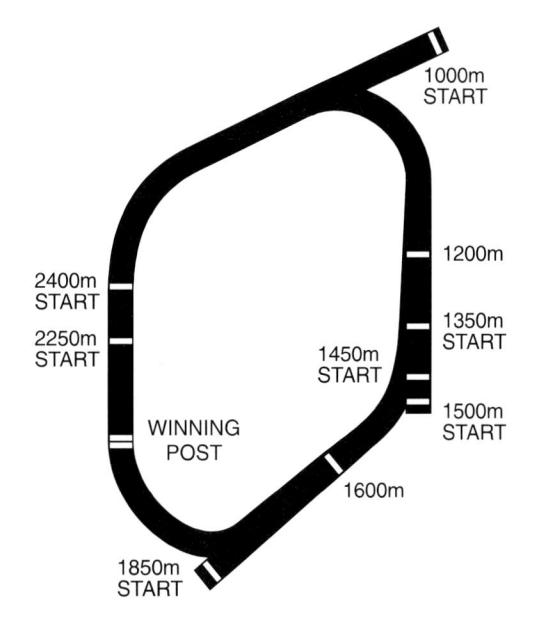

Licensee: South Australian Jockey Club
Direction of Running: Anti-clockwise
Circumference: 2000m
Straight: 325m

BARRIER GUIDE		
STARTING POINT m	STARTING POSITIONS Good to Fair	Poor to Bad
1000	1–9	10–11+
1350	1–9	10–13+
1450	1–10	11–13+
1850	1–10	11–12+
2250	1–8	9–11+

The track is oval-shaped with two tight turns and two much better turns.
Horses near the lead on the gentle turn into the straight are favoured.
Inside barriers are an advantage from every starting point.
Cheltenham is a track for specialists.

VICTORIA PARK, ADELAIDE

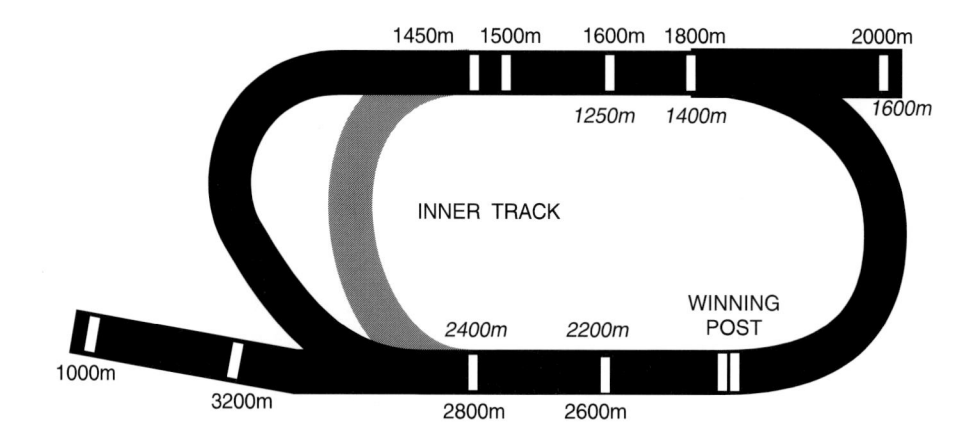

Licensee: South Australian Jockey Club

Direction of Running: Anti-clockwise

Circumference: Inner 1960m
Outer 2360m

Straight: Inner 428m; Outer 601m

BARRIER GUIDE		
STARTING POINT m	STARTING POSITIONS Good to Fair	Poor to Bad
1000	1–12	13–15+
1200–1250*	1–8	9–11+
1400*	1–9	10–12+
1500	1–10	11–12+
1600	1–10	11–12+
1800	1–11	12–13+
2000	1–12	13–14+

* Inner Track

The racecourse features a main or outer track with a shorter inner track.

A long chute, being an extension of the home straight, provides for races up to 1000m to be run over a straight course.

There is a gradual declination down the 1000m straight track, including the straight of the track proper. Otherwise the track is relatively level. Turns are gradual.

The downhill going in the straight assists the front runners.

Inside barriers are an advantage from every starting point although less so from the 1000m starting point.

EAGLE FARM, BRISBANE

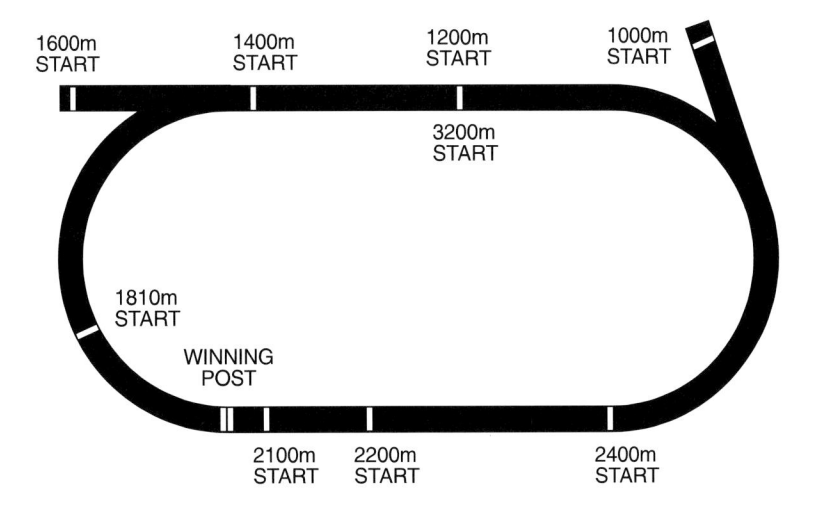

Licensee: Queensland Turf Club
Direction of Running: Clockwise
Circumference: 2027m
Straight: 435m

BARRIER GUIDE		
STARTING POINT m	STARTING POSITIONS Good to Fair	Poor to Bad
1000	1–10	11–13+
1200	1–8	9–10+
1400	1–10	11–12+
1600	1–10	11–12+
1800	1–7	8–11+
2100	1–8	9–13+
2200	1–10	11–13+

There is a gradual rise of about 5m from the 600m mark down the long straight to the winning post. Otherwise the track is relatively level. Turns are gradual.

Inside barriers are an advantage from every starting point.

Long-striding horses that finish strongly from behind are suited by the long straight.

DOOMBEN, BRISBANE

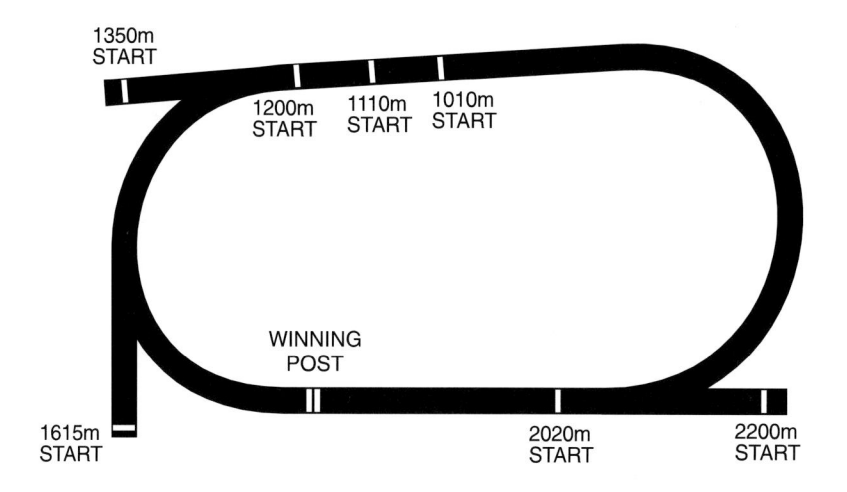

Licensee: Brisbane Turf Club
Direction of Running: Clockwise
Circumference: 1717m
Straight: 354m

BARRIER GUIDE		
STARTING POINT m	STARTING POSITIONS Good to Fair	Poor to Bad
1010	1–8	9–10+
1110	1–9	10–11+
1200	1–10	11–12+
1350	1–12	13–14+
1615*	1–8	9–10+
2020	1–9	10–13+
2200	1–10	11–12+

* Slow beginners from inside may be cut off.

The old problematic track was dug up in 1996 and replaced with a completely new track which has been well acclaimed by the racing fraternity.

The new track is level with a banked home turn and a good drainage system.

Inside barrier positions are an advantage from every point.

While good horses can come from behind and win, the front runners are advantaged.

PART 18 RACETRACKS

ASCOT, PERTH

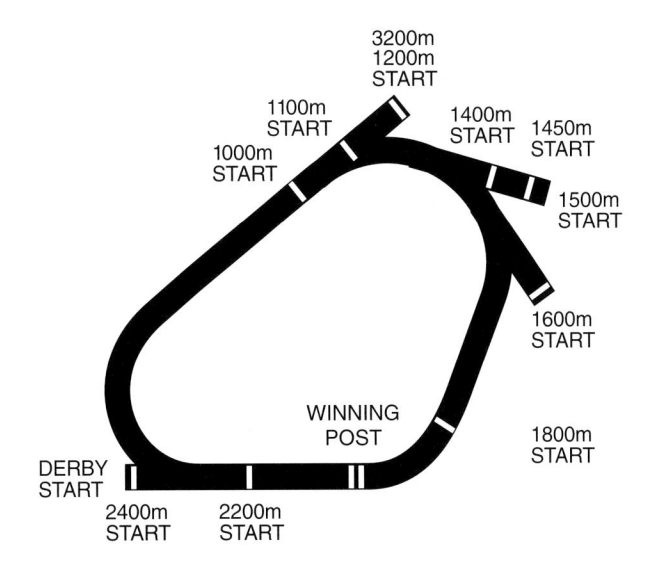

Licensee: Western Australian Turf Club
Direction of Running: Anti-clockwise
Circumference: 2022m
Straight: 302m

BARRIER GUIDE		
STARTING POINT m	STARTING POSITIONS Good to Fair	Poor to Bad
1000	1–9	10–13+
1200	1–11	12–14+
1400	1–10	11–13+
1500	1–11	12–14+
1600	1–11	12–14+
1800	1–11	12–14+
2200	1–8	9–11+

Ascot is Perth's major racecourse and racing is conducted there during the dry summer months. The Group races run there attract good gallopers from the east of Australia.

The course is a testing one. After the winning post, through the turn out of the home straight to about the 1800m mark, there is a gradual inclination. This is followed by a slight declination to about the 1600m mark. The home turn is tight, but well cambered and is followed by an uphill straight.

Inside barriers are an advantage from every starting point.

BELMONT PARK, PERTH

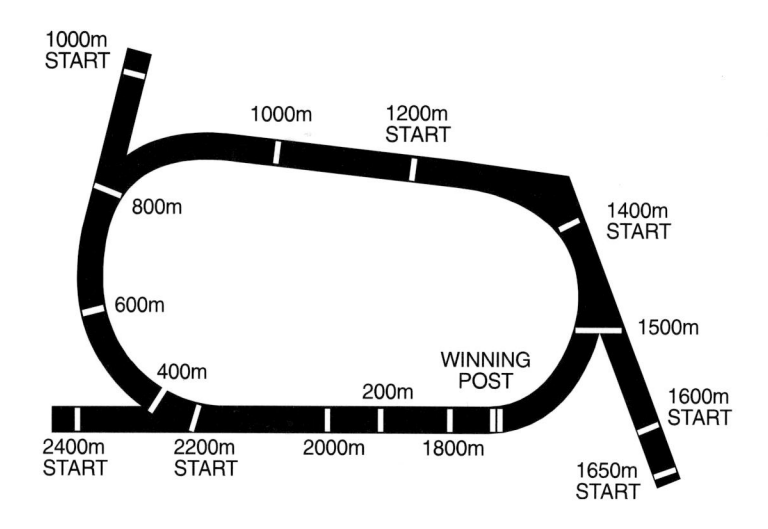

Licensee: Western Australian Turf Club
Direction of Running: Anti-clockwise
Circumference: 1699m
Straight: 333m

BARRIER GUIDE		
STARTING POINT m	STARTING POSITIONS Good to Fair	Poor to Bad
1000	1–11	12–15+
1200	1–12	13–15+
1400	1–11	12–13+
1600	1–11	12–13+
2200	1–11	12–13+

Belmont Park, because of its good drainage, is extensively used during the wet winter months. Races there normally attract only local horses as major events (with one or two exceptions) are not programmed for the course.

Inside barriers are an advantage from every starting point.

All types of gallopers are suited.

ELWICK, HOBART

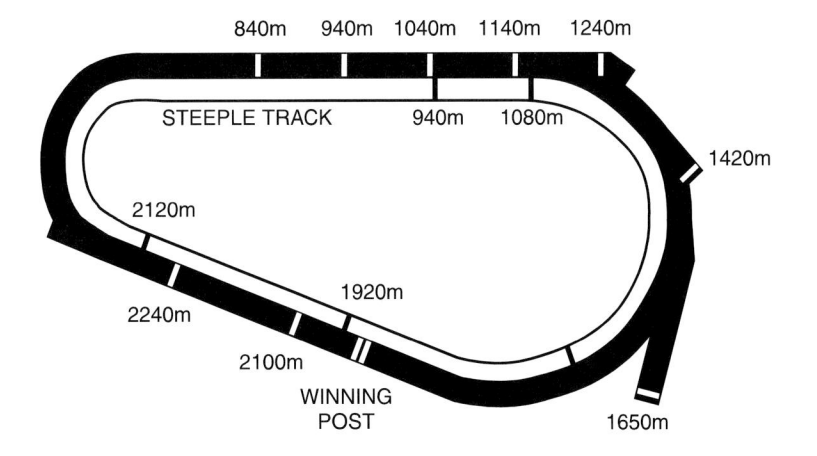

Licensee: Tasmanian Racing Club
Direction of Running: Anti-clockwise
Circumference: 1984m
Straight: 300m

BARRIER GUIDE

STARTING POINT m	STARTING POSITIONS Good to Fair	Poor to Bad
1040	1–9	10–11+
1240	1–10	11–13+
1420	1–8	9–11+
1650	1–8	9–11+
2100	1–7	8–9+
2240	1–7	8–9+

An inclination in the straight to the winning post is followed by a gradual declination to about the 1000m mark.

There is one wide, sweeping double turn from the straight into the back stretch and one tight double turn from that stretch into the straight.

Inside barriers are an advantage from every starting point.

Front runners are more suited to this track. A course for specialists.

MOWBRAY, LAUNCESTON

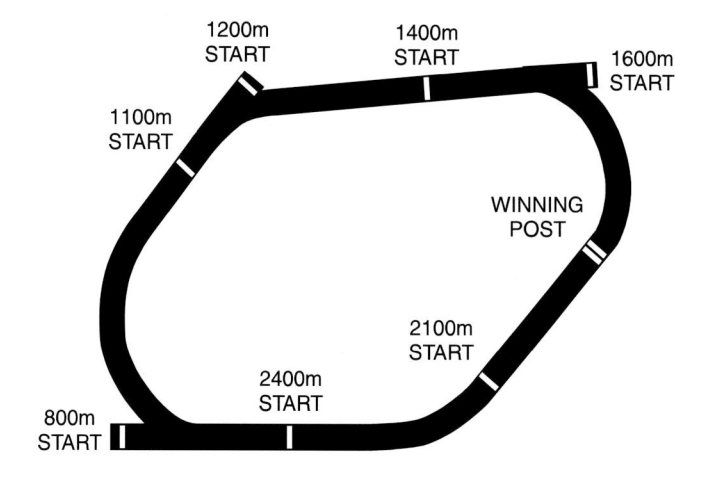

Licensee: Tasmanian Turf Club
Direction of Running: Anti-clockwise
Circumference: 1826m
Straight: 250m

BARRIER GUIDE

STARTING POINT m	STARTING POSITIONS Good to Fair	Poor to Bad
1100	1–10	11–13+
1200	1–11	12–14+
1400	1–9	10–14+
1600	1–10	11–12+
2100	1–9	10–11+

There is an inclination in the straight, otherwise the track is relatively level.
The home turn is gradual, but other turns are fairly tight.
Inside barriers are an advantage from every starting point.
Horses with stamina that finish from behind the field are suited.

FANNIE BAY, DARWIN

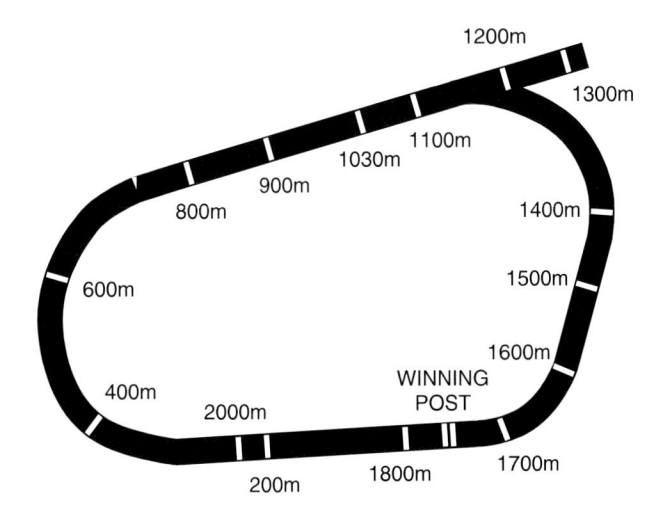

Licensee: Darwin Turf Club
Direction of Running: Anti-clockwise
Circumference: 1776m
Straight: 382m

> **BARRIER GUIDE**
>
> Barriers numbers 1 to 5, inclusive, are a great advantage from every starting point. On the other hand, horses drawn outside barrier number 5 are disadvantaged.

Racing of any note in the Northern Territory is conducted during the dry seasonal period at the Fannie Bay course.

The track surface is sand, well dressed with oil. Its wet weather rating is accordingly excellent.

The back stretch declines to the 400m mark and thereafter sharply inclines to the winning post.

It is a course for specialists.

PART 19

RACE MEETINGS

Chapter	47	Race Meetings Generally
Section	47.1	Registered Race Meetings held by Registered Race Clubs
	47.2	Other Registered Race Meetings
	47.3	Unregistered or Unlawful Race Meetings
	47.4	Postponement or Abandonment of Race Meeting
	47.5	Phantom Race Meetings
	47.6	Novelty Events at a Race Meeting
Chapter	48	Pre-Race Day Procedures
Section	48.1	Race Programs
	48.2	Nominations
	48.3	Allocation of Weights
	48.4	Bottom Limit Weight
	48.5	Minimum Top Weight
	48.6	Race Class Relativity Weight Scale
	48.7	Weights to be Raised
	48.8	Declaration of Weights
	48.9	Declarations of Acceptance
	48.10	Division of Races and Rejection of Entries
	48.11	Emergency Acceptors
	48.12	Barrier Draw
	48.13	Declaration of Riders
	48.14	Withdrawals (Scratchings)
	48.15	Cancellation of Race
	48.16	Race Books

PART 19 RACEMEETINGS

CHAPTER 47 RACE MEETINGS GENERALLY

Section 47.1
Registered Race Meetings Held by Registered Race Clubs

Because of its equable climate, race meetings are conducted in Australia on an all-year-round basis.

In the USA race meetings are also held all the year round but in Europe the flat-racing season runs from March to early November with jump racing during the winter months.)

Before the start of each racing year in Australia, a Principal Club allocates to each race club under its control, dates upon which race meetings may be held during that year.

A race club may only conduct a race meeting on a licensed racecourse on a day allocated to it by the Principal Club.

Section 47.2
Other Registered Race Meetings

The Principal Club may also approve and register certain race meetings, called "picnic race meetings", other than those held by registered clubs.

Application to hold any such meeting must be made in writing by the organisers of the proposed meeting and be accompanied by particulars of the proposed program.

Section 47.3
Unregistered or Unlawful Race Meetings

It is unlawful for a race meeting that has not been approved and registered by a Principal Club, to be held on a licensed racecourse. It is also unlawful for any race meeting to be held at any place which is not a licensed racecourse.

Section 47.4
Postponement or Abandonment of Race Meeting

If, owing to adverse weather conditions or other emergent circumstances, a race club considers it impossible or impracticable to hold a race meeting (or part of it) on a day allotted to that club, the race club concerned, with approval of the Principal Club, may postpone that meeting (or part of it) until such other day as may be approved; or may abandon that meeting (or part of it).

Section 47.5
Phantom Race Meetings

A phantom race meeting is a meeting authorised in accordance with law at which no race is actually conducted or required to be conducted.

A race club may, with the approval of its Principal Club, hold a phantom meeting:
- on a day approved for a race meeting, where such race club postpones or abandons that meeting before the start of it;
- on such day or days as may be approved where such race club, because of track re-construction or other major works, is not allotted what its Principal Club considers is a normal allocation of days upon which it may hold race meetings;
- on any other day with approval, for any reason, of the Principal Club.

Section 47.6
Novelty Events at a Race Meeting

With the approval of its Principal Club, a race club may conduct a novelty event during the progress of, or in conjunction with, a lawfully held race meeting. Betting on the outcome of a novelty event is prohibited by law.

CHAPTER 48 PRE-RACE DAY PROCEDURES

Section 48.1
Race Programs

A race club is required to draw up a proposed program (including the conditions and name of every race) for each race meeting to be conducted by that club, and to submit that proposal to its Principal Club for approval within the prescribed time (usually two or three months before the meeting is held).

In drawing up race programs, clubs have a responsibility to cater adequately for the horse populations of their respective localities. For example, outside the metropolitan areas where some 70 per cent of horses are in maiden or lower restricted classes, it is vital that programs provide races in proportion to such horse classes. The objectives of adequate programming include pushing more horses through the restricted class system; providing more balanced fields; increasing the pool of individual winners from which higher restricted class and open class race fields will be drawn; and giving some incentive to owners to persevere in the racing industry.

The number of races that may be programmed for any one day is a minimum of five and, unless otherwise approved, a maximum of nine.

After the Principal Club has approved a program, particulars thereof are advertised in the Racing Calendar of that Principal Club.

Section 48.2
Nominations

To enter a horse for a race for which it is eligible, a nomination or entry form is required to be submitted to the secretary of the club concerned.

The nomination or entry form is required:

- to give the name and description of the horse which must agree with the Document of Description;
- to give particulars of the owner or lessee of the horse and the trainer;
- to be prepared and signed by a person eighteen years of age or older being the owner, lessee, manager, or trainer, or an authorised agent of any such person;
- to be accompanied by the prescribed fee, if any;
- to be submitted within the advertised time.

Such nomination or entry is subject to approval by the committee of the club concerned or the stewards. The stewards may refuse the nomination of any horse until such horse has trialled, barrier trialled, or passed any required veterinary examination to their satisfaction.

The stewards may also refuse the nomination of a horse, if in their opinion, that horse has been entered in a race with the sole purpose of affecting the weight to be allocated to another horse entered in such race.

After approval by the committee of the race club concerned, and the stewards of that club, the nomination or entry forms are delivered to the club's official handicapper for the allocation of weights to the nominated horses.

Section 48.3
Allocation of Weights

The handicapper's duty is to allocate weights to horses nominated for a race under the conditions attaching to that race, that is:
- if a set-weight race, the prescribed scale;
- if a handicap, the prescribed top weight and bottom weight.

The task is an enormous one because of the number of races that are run, the number of horses that compete in such races, and the important fact that most of the races are run under handicap conditions.

The handicapper's objective for handicap events is to allot weights so far as circumstances will allow, so that, theoretically, all the runners will cross the finishing line together, that is, in a mass dead-heat. In practice that could never be achieved because of many factors: the state of fitness of each competing horse at the time of the race; the ability of each horse to handle its weight over the distance of the race; the state of the going; mishaps and running interference; and so on.

The handicapper has ready access to comprehensive records for every such nominated horse and its performance in every race in which it has started. This information includes significant mishaps or running interference and the manner in which the horse was running at the finish of each such race.

From that stored information, from his own observations when watching races or video tape replays, and drawing on his long years of experience in the racing industry and his in-depth knowledge of racehorses, the handicapper forms his opinions.

The judgment that the handicapper exercises is about the differences between the horses entered for a race so far as their merits, class or ability are concerned and the reflection of those differences in terms of weight. The official firstly selects the horse that in his opinion is the best horse in the race under consideration and then the next best, and so on: and having done so the handicapper expresses in weight his opinion of the degree of difference in the ability of each such horse.

In other words, the handicapper assesses for each entrant the merits or otherwise of its past performances, its ability, and its potential to win the race under consideration, and accordingly places, by his weighting method, a disadvantage or an advantage on each competitor to theoretically equalise their winning chances.

Section 48.4
Bottom Limit Weight

The bottom limit weight for a handicap race is the lowest weight that, in accordance with the Local Rules of Racing or conditions of the race, may be allotted to a horse nominated for that race.

Under the Australian Rules of Racing the prescribed minimum weight to be carried by any horse in a handicap event is not less than 43.5kg.

The prescribed bottom limit weights for handicap events vary among States; metropolitan, provincial and country areas; and among classes and types of races; and prize money for those races.

In various Group or Listed handicap events (usually referred to as "feature events") the bottom limit weight may be set under the conditions of the race at a comparatively low figure — but not less than 43.5kg. This allows the handicapper for any such event to accommodate the large numbers (in some cases, several hundreds) of the horses that may be entered for that event. As pointed out earlier, the handicapper's objective is to express in weight his opinion of the relative degree of difference in the ability of each nominated horse, and unless he has a sufficient margin between top and bottom limits, he would necessarily have to depress all weights to fit in all horses. If, for example, the bottom limit weight was 50kg, most of the nominated horses would be allotted that limit.

Horses allotted the bottom limit weight by the handicapper are those considered by the handicapper to be below the class standard of the race and to have no reasonable chance of winning.

Section 48.5
Minimum Top Weight

Local Rules usually provide that the top weight allotted by the handicapper in any handicap event shall not be less than a prescribed weight. Prescriptions in the several States vary between 54kg and 57kg.

Section 48.6
Race Class Relativity Weight Scale

Each handicapper or handicapping panel, as the case may be, establishes and uses a "Relativity Weight Scale" to express opinion as to the relative difference for the various classes of handicap races in terms of weight, and to do so on a consistent basis. As each handicapper or handicapping panel acts independently in the development of such a scale, there are variations among the scales in use.

The theoretical class values of certain handicap races run at provincial and metropolitan races in New South Wales and Victoria are indicated in the following tables.

TABLE 1

NSW AND VICTORIAN PROVINCIAL MEETINGS	NON-TAB MEETINGS	TAB MEETINGS Fri, Sat, Sun, Mon	TAB MEETINGS Tues, Wed, Thurs.
Restricted Class Handicaps:	kg	kg	kg
Class 1	0.0	0.0	0.0
Class 2	0.5	1.0	1.5
Class 3	3.0	3.5	4.0
Class 4	4.5	5.0	5.5
Class 5	6.0	6.5	7.0
Class 6	7.5	8.0	8.5
Open Handicaps	8.5	9.5	10.5

TABLE 2

SYDNEY AND MELBOURNE MEETINGS	MID-WEEK	SATURDAY
Open Class Handicaps:	kg	kg
Mares	8.0	10.5
Welters	10.0	11.5
Open Sprint and Distance	13.0	15.0

TABLE 3

SYDNEY AND MELBOURNE MEETINGS. GROUP RACES	MARES HANDICAP	OPEN HANDICAP	WFA*
	kg	kg	kg
Listed	12.0	16.5	…
Group 3	13.5	18.0	21.0
Group 2	15.0	19.5	22.5
Group 1	16.5	21.0	24.0

* These WFA events are shown for purposes of comparison.

Note (1)   The above class values relate to races that are unrestricted as to age or sex. In a case where any such restriction applies, the class value should be reduced.

Note (2)   There is no weight relationship between the young, developing horses competing in two-year-old and three-year-old events and events for older horses.

Note (3)   Race class relativity values for special restricted and special condition races (see Section 43.8) vary as shown by handicappers' ratings. The prize money for any such race is a helpful guide when making an assessment of relative class value.

Section 48.7
Weights to be Raised

The Local Rules usually provide that if, after the declaration of acceptances for a handicap event, the highest weight of final acceptors is less than the prescribed top weight allotted by the handicapper then the top weight of the field is to be increased to that prescribed weight (or some other specified weight) and the weights of all other runners are to be increased by the same amount.

Section 48.8
Declaration of Weights

Weights allocated to horses nominated for races to be conducted at a race meeting are duly declared and advertised by the committee of the club conducting that meeting.

Section 48.9
Declarations of Acceptance

After the publication of weights, and before the advertised time for acceptances for a race, notices (called "Declarations of Acceptance") need to be given to the club in question, signifying those horses which are intended starters in such race and for which their nomination was approved and for which they were duly allocated a weight. Such Declarations of Acceptance are required to be in writing, signed by the nominator or trainer or by the authorised agent of either of them.

Declarations are usually required to be made two working days before the day of the race meeting concerned, although in the case of certain important races there are several stages of acceptance.

The nominations of any horses not declared acceptors at the advertised closing time for acceptances, lapse.

Final acceptors in a race are referred to as "runners".

Section 48.10
Division of Races and Rejection of Entries

If more than the prescribed number of horses accept for a race, the committee of the club may reject or ballot out any entry or entries according to any special conditions that may apply to a particular race or, subject to those conditions, to general rejection or ballot conditions.

In some cases where the number of horses that accept for a race exceeds the limit fixed for such race the race may be divided and run in two or more divisions.

Section 48.11
Emergency Acceptors

In any race from which horses have been rejected or balloted, a club may provide for emergency acceptors to replace horses withdrawn or scratched after final acceptances and before the time appointed for scratchings on the day of that meeting.

Such "emergency acceptors" are the last four horses to be balloted out (or such lesser number as may be required).

Emergency acceptors are included in the starters in the sequence of the draw.

Section 48.12
Barrier Draw

After the declaration of acceptances for a race the order in which the horses are to be placed in the stalls at the starting post is determined by lot. Such lots are drawn under the supervision of two persons appointed by the Principal Club conducting the meeting by means of some approved device or system.

The barrier draw number of each acceptor is indicated in the race program immediately after each such acceptor's name.

Section 48.13
Declaration of Riders

An owner, lessee, or trainer, (or an authorised agent of one of them) of any horse that is intended to be run in any race at a race meeting is required to declare by the specified time to the secretary of the club conducting that meeting, the rider of that horse.

The times by which declarations of riders are required to be made is usually a time on the day preceding that race meeting. This enables the names of riders for race meetings in the metropolitan and certain other areas, to be printed in race books, or otherwise advertised.

This requirement is of great advantage to punters because, when making their selections on the day preceding the race meeting, it is important that they have knowledge of the riders.

If changes of riders are made on race days punters may have to revise their workouts and selections.

Once a rider has been so declared, no other rider may be substituted without the permission of the stewards.

All riders must be present in the jockeys' room at least three-quarters of an hour before the time appointed for starting any race in which they are to ride.

Section 48.14
Withdrawals (Scratchings)

A horse that has been nominated for, and declared to be, an acceptor for a race, may later be withdrawn (or scratched):

- before the prescribed scratching time by the nominator or trainer or the authorised agent of either of them by giving notice in writing of withdrawal to the race club.
- after that prescribed scratching time, with the permission of, or on the order of, the stewards, acting on veterinary advice or for other sufficient reason.

Horses withdrawn from a race after being declared acceptors for that race are called "withdrawals" (or "scratchings") or, as the case may be, "late withdrawals" (or "late scratchings").

The term, "late withdrawal" (or "late scratching") includes an acceptor withdrawn from a race after betting on that race has started, or an acceptor declared by the stewards to be a non-starter for that race. The effect of a late withdrawal on betting is dealt with elsewhere in this book.

If a race meeting (or part thereof) is postponed to another day, scratchings made on the day such meeting was to have been held are deemed void and of no effect, and the time of scratching is extended to the prescribed scratching time on the day on which the meeting (or part thereof) is subsequently held.

Section 48.15
Cancellation of Race

The committee of a race club may cancel any race where the number of acceptors or the number of starters does not, in their opinion, justify the running of the race.

Section 48.16
Race Books

Before the start of a race meeting, the club conducting that meeting orders the printing of race books (or race cards) in which it sets out particulars of the program for that meeting. Those particulars are also widely advertised in newspapers and other publications, but in the event of any discrepancy between any such publication and the race book (for example, competing horses), the race book prevails as the official source of information.

Every horse running in a race carries a saddlecloth bearing a number corresponding with its number in the race book. The cloth is supplied to the rider at the time of weighing out.

PART 20

RACE DAY PROCEDURES

Chapter	49	Race Day Procedures Before the Race
Section	49.1	Horses held in Saddling Paddock
	49.2	Weighing-Out
	49.3	Weight to be carried
	49.4	Weight Penalties
	49.5	Apprentices' Allowances
	49.6	Substitution of Riders
	49.7	Saddling and Mounting
	49.8	The Preliminary
	49.9	Barrier Positions
Chapter	50	The Race
Section	50.1	The Start
	50.2	Running
	50.3	Finishing Positions
	50.4	Dead-Heats
	50.5	Losing Margins
	50.6	Weighing-In
	50.7	Correct Weight
	50.8	Protests
	50.9	Other Objections and Complaints
Chapter	51	Post Race Meeting Procedures
Section	51.1	Reports on Race Meetings
	51.2	Payment of Prize Moneys
	51.3	Offences and Punishments
	51.4	List of Disqualifications
	51.5	Forfeit List

CHAPTER 49 RACE DAY PROCEDURES BEFORE THE RACE

Section 49.1
Horses Held in Saddling Paddock

On race day all horses intended to be run in a programmed race are required to be brought into an area of the racecourse, called the "saddling paddock" where stalls and other facilities are provided for their care. They must arrive in that paddock at a prescribed time — usually one to two hours before the time appointed for the start of the race in which they are to compete — and remain there until the time arrives for them to proceed to the starting post. After taking part in the running of the race, they are returned to the saddling paddock where they must remain for half-an-hour before removal, unless otherwise approved by the stewards.

Section 49.2
Weighing-out

Riders are weighed-out by the Clerk of the Scales at least half-an-hour before the start of the race in which they are to ride.

Each rider is weighed in riding gear (excluding skull cap and whip) and carrying the saddle, saddlecloth, and any other gear (martingale, breastplate or clothing) to be put on the horse he or she is to ride, except blinkers, mesh eye protectors, plates and anything to be worn on the horse's legs.

Where the weight of the rider and allowable gear is less than the weight the horse is required to carry, the deficiency is made good by the use of lead bags.

Where, however, the weight of the rider and allowable gear is greater than the weight the horse is to carry, the rider must seek the approval of the stewards to ride overweight. If approval is granted the Clerk of the Scales signifies this fact outside the weighing room. Where, on the other hand, approval is not granted, the stewards substitute another rider at, or nearer, the weight the horse is required to carry.

Section 49.3
Weight to be Carried

The weight required to be carried by a horse competing in a set-weight race is the weight allotted to that horse in accordance with the conditions of that race or the Rules plus any overweight that may be approved by the stewards or, as the case may be, less any allowance that may be claimable by an apprentice rider.

The weight to be carried by a horse competing in a handicap event is the weight allotted to that horse by the handicapper at time of declaration of weights plus, in a case where the weight of every horse in the race is to be increased by an equal amount in accordance with the Rules, the amount of such increase plus any penalty weight that may be applicable under the Rules plus any overweight that may be approved by the stewards or, as the case may be, less any allowance that may be claimable by an apprentice rider.

Section 49.4
Weight Penalties

The conditions of a handicap race usually prescribe that if, after weights are declared for horses entered for that race, any one of those horses wins a race or races, it will be required to carry in that particular handicap race, in addition to the original allotted weight, a weight penalty. The penalty is such additional weight as may be determined by the handicapper (usually not exceeding in the aggregate 3kg) or as may be prescribed.

Section 49.5
Apprentices' Allowances

Until such time as he or she has ridden 60 winners, an apprentice may claim a weight allowance in any handicap flat race for which the total prize money does not exceed a prescribed amount, or unless the conditions of a race state that an apprentice may not claim.

The weight allowance is determined according to the following scale:

3.0kg until 15 winners ridden

2.5kg until 30 winners ridden

1.5kg until 60 winners ridden

nil after 60 winners ridden

In assessing the number of winners ridden:

(a) for a race in the metropolitan area, winners in that area only are taken into account;

(b) for a race in a provincial area, winners in both the metropolitan and provincial areas are taken into account;

(c) for a race in a country area, winners in the metropolitan, provincial and country areas are taken into account.

Notwithstanding that, an apprentice may claim the same allowance during a day of racing to which he or she was entitled at the beginning of that day.

The weight a horse is to carry in a race may not be reduced below the prescribed minimum weight of 43.5kg by reason of an apprentice allowance.

Section 49.6
Substitution of Riders

If, after having been declared the rider of a particular horse in a race, a rider-

(a) is overweight and such overweight is not approved by the stewards;

(b) is prevented by accident or illness, or other cause from riding, the stewards may substitute or approve the substitution of another rider at, or nearer, the weight the horse is to carry, and having somewhat similar experience and ability. In this latter regard, their guidelines are to substitute a jockey for a jockey; a non-claiming apprentice for a jockey or vice versa; or a claiming apprentice for a claiming apprentice.

Apart from these circumstances, another rider may not be substituted for a rider whose name has been declared at time of declaration of riders.

Section 49.7
Saddling and Mounting

After weighing-out, each rider hands to the trainer of the horse the saddle and other gear with which the rider has been weighed, including a saddlecloth. This cloth bears a number corresponding with the number of the mount in the race book.

Trainers (or their employees) then saddle their horses in their allotted stalls in the saddling paddock and, when directed, lead them into the mounting enclosure. Before entering that enclosure the racing plates or tips of each horse are examined by the farrier's supervisor.

Riders, after weighing-out, remain in the jockeys' room until ordered by the stewards to mount their respective horses in the mounting enclosure.

From the time the riders leave the jockeys' room to mount until such time as they dismount or, if required, weigh-in, after the race:

(a) no person other than the nominator or trainer (or the authorised agent of either of them) or an official acting in the course of official duties, or during the race another rider, is permitted to speak to, or otherwise communicate in any way, with such rider;

(b) no person other than an official in the course of official duties or, before the race, the trainer of the horse, may touch any such rider, the horse, or any of its equipment.

(c) such rider is prohibited from speaking to, or otherwise communicating with, any person other than those persons referred to above.

Section 49.8
The Preliminary

On order from the stewards, riders take their horses from the mounting enclosure onto the racetrack. They are then required to walk or canter their horses past the Judge's box (at least once) and then proceed to the starting post where they come under the direct control of the club's official starter.

Section 49.9
Barrier Positions

When so ordered by the starter, the runners are drawn up at the start in starting stalls. Before the introduction of starting stalls some years ago, the open barrier or flag method of starting was used. Such a method may still be used where starting stalls are not available or are not operating.

The number of the starting stall that each runner occupies at the starting point (called its "starting", "post", or "barrier" position) is its number as previously determined at time of barrier draw, reduced by the number of horses, if any, which drew lesser numbers but were scratched from the event. That is, runners drawn outside scratched acceptors move closer to the inside rail at the start. For example, if two acceptors which drew numbers 5 and 10 were scratched, draw numbers 1 to 4 stand; numbers 6 to 9 are reduced by 1; numbers 11 outwards are reduced by 2.

PART 20 RACE DAY PROCEDURES

CHAPTER 50 THE RACE

Section 50.1
The Start

The starter gives all such orders and takes all such measures as he considers necessary for securing a fair start.

Horses are placed in the starting gates in order of the pre-determined draw for positions. The starter starts a race by pressing an electric button which opens the gates simultaneously.

Where a horse is unruly and refuses to enter its starting stall, or having entered its stall, becomes or continues to be unruly, the starter may order the horse to be placed behind the stalls and out of the race. In such a case it is declared a non-starter.

In the event of a false start or a void start (for example, if the gates of one or more stalls open involuntarily) and the stewards are of the opinion that the chances of any horse have been materially prejudiced, they may order its withdrawal and declare it a non-starter.

Again where a horse is riderless at the time a race is started, or where it is otherwise denied a fair start, the stewards may order its withdrawal and declare it a non-starter.

Where, however, a horse is placed in the stalls with the rest of the field but refuses to race away with the field when the stalls are opened, it is officially a starter.

The starter is responsible for starting each race from the proper starting point. If the stewards determine that a race was started in front of, or behind, that proper starting point, they may at their option order the race to be re-run; declare the race void; or deem the race to have been run over the proper course or distance.

The starter is also responsible for reporting to stewards after each race any matters of significance associated with the start, for example, unruly horses, horses left at, or slow away from, the barrier, and the like.

Section 50.2
Running

The Rules of Racing are designed to ensure that every horse that runs in a race, runs on its merits.

A duty is placed by the Rules upon each rider to take all reasonable and permissible measures throughout a race to ensure that the horse is given full opportunity to win or to obtain the best possible place at the finish. If, in the opinion of the stewards, any person breaches, or is a party to the breaching, of that duty, that person may be punished and the horse concerned may be disqualified.

Stewards are positioned at certain advantageous positions to observe the running of each race. In addition, on major racecourses, patrol cameras are located at various positions around the course to film the running action. These action films provide replay records which are vital for purposes of the stewards.

Section 50.3
Finishing Positions

The official finishing order of horses that run first, second, third, fourth and fifth in a race, are decided by the Judge occupying the Judge's box at the time the runners pass the winning post.

A camera installed above the Judge's tower in line with the winning post is used to make photographs of the runners at the finish to assist the Judge in determining their positions as indicated by their noses. The camera records the smallest of margins as indicated on the photographs which are produced promptly after a race is decided. The Judge's decision as to the order of finishing positions is final, subject only to alteration by the stewards in accordance with the Rules.

Section 50.4
Dead-Heats

When two horses cross the finish line exactly level, the result is referred to as a dead-heat. When three horses finish level, the result is called a triple dead-heat.

When horses run a dead-heat for first or any other place, the prize money available for those horses had they finished in successive places and not dead-heated is aggregated and divided equally between the nominators of those horses.

Arrangements are made amicably or by lot as to which nominator is to have any cup, trophy, or other prize that cannot be divided. Such arrangement usually provides for the payment of a sum of money by the recipient nominator to the other nominator.

Section 50.5
Losing Margins

The margins by which a horse loses a race are expressed in terms of lengths (a length being the distance between a horse's head and tail).

Margins up to a length are expressed as follows:
- short half head or nose
- half head
- short head
- head
- long head
- half neck
- short neck
- neck
- long neck

- half length
- three-quarters of a length
- length

After the first length, fractions of lengths are expressed in quarter lengths.

Section 50.6
Weighing-in

After a race is run every rider is required, as soon as practicable, to ride the horse to the mounting and dismounting enclosure and then when ordered by the stewards, dismount.

Riders of the placed horses (and any other riders as may be directed) then proceed to the weighing scales and their weights (including saddle, martingale, breastplate or clothing) are duly checked by the Clerk of the Scales to ensure that they have carried the correct weight. A rider may use the option of weighing the bridle or be allowed a half a kilogram for it.

Section 50.7
Correct Weight

Provided that no protests are lodged and all riders weigh in correctly:
- a signal declaring "correct weight" is promptly and publicly displayed; and
- the horses are led away from the enclosure.

If, however, the weight of a rider is found to be insufficient the horse is automatically disqualified from the race and the rider punished.

Section 50.8
Protests

An objection or protest may be lodged verbally or in writing to a steward or the Clerk of the Scales against the declaration of correct weight pending the hearing of allegations by an authorised person about interference to a placed (including fourth, and fifth placings) runner by another placed runner, or for some other matter associated with the running of that race.

The time when a protest may be made and the people who may make such protest are as follows:
- before the rider of the placed horse weighs in, by the owner, nominator, trainer or rider of that horse;
- at any time before weight is declared by a steward or the starter.

"Interference" occurs where:
- a horse crosses a horse so as to interfere with that horse or any other horse;

- a horse or its rider jostles or in any way interferes with another horse or its rider — unless such jostle or interference was caused by some other horse or rider, or the horse or rider jostled or interfered with was partly at fault.

A signal indicating that an objection or protest has been lodged to the placing of any horse is displayed promptly by the stewards for general information.

If, after hearing evidence about the protest (that is, after questioning riders, viewing the official film of the race, and so on) the stewards are of the opinion that a placed horse or its rider caused interference to another placed horse or its rider during the running of the race and that interference materially affected the chances of that horse they are said to uphold the protest. In such a case they may:

(a) disqualify from the race the horse that caused the interference and any other horse in the same nomination;

(b) if the horses in question finished in first, second, third, fourth, fifth or sixth positions, alter the order of placings so that the horse that caused the interference is placed after the horse interfered with.

For example, if a horse placed fourth successfully protests against the winner the placings would then change so that the horse first past the finishing post becomes fourth, second becomes first, third becomes second, and fourth becomes third.

Where the stewards dismiss the protest they may, if they consider that the allegation or grounds frivolous, fine the person who lodged that protest.

The stewards may also punish a rider in such manner as they see fit (by fine, suspension, or disqualification) if, in their opinion, the rider is guilty of careless, improper, incompetent or foul riding, or used the whip in an improper manner.

Notification by the stewards to the public that a protest has been upheld or dismissed is made promptly after the decision is reached in an appropriate manner.

Section 50.9
Other Objections and Complaints

Objections other than those about the actual running of a race (for example, those dealing with the identity, qualificatioon, nomination, registration or drugging of a runner) may be lodged in accordance with the Rules before the conclusion of the race meeting or, as the case may be, within one month of the conclusion of that race meeting.

Decisions about such objections may affect the payment of prize money and sweepstakes, but do not, in any way, affect the betting on the particular race.

PART 20 RACE DAY PROCEDURES

CHAPTER 51 POST RACE MEETING PROCEDURES

Section 51.1
Reports on Race Meetings

After each race meeting the club holding the meeting and the stewards of the meeting are required to prepare and forward through the relevant District Racing Association to the relevant State Principal Club, reports setting out prescribed information about the meeting and the races conducted there.

The Principal Clubs then furnish this information to the Racing Services Bureau in Melbourne which is a division of the Victoria Race Club and is responsible for the maintenance of the official record of *Australian Race Results*.

The Racing Services Bureau enters the information into its comprehensive computerised database with Bureau subscribers having access to various components of that database.

Until August 1995 the Bureau also compiled and regularly published an official publication called *Australian Race Results* which contained particulars of all races run in Australia and an index of runners and the races in which they competed. Owing to falling numbers of subscribers and rising costs of production, however, it is currently intended that *Australian Race Results* will only be published as an annual volume in future.

Section 51.2
Payment of Prize Moneys

After a race meeting, prize moneys and sweepstakes (if any) due and payable to owners, lessees, trainers, or jockeys of winning or placed horses are promptly paid, in accordance with the Rules and race conditions, by the race club that conducted the race meeting.

In cases where an action at law about such moneys is pending, or where an objection lodged against a placed horse has not been decided, and in other like cases, the race club holds those moneys in trust, pending the outcome of the hearings.

Section 51.3
Offences and Punishments

The committee of any race club or the stewards of any race meeting:

- may punish by suspension, disqualification, and/or fine, any person who in their opinion is guilty of an offence under the Rules of Racing;
- may disqualify any horse in connection with which an improper practice or dishonourable action is found to have been committed.

Upon imposing any punishment by suspension or disqualification, the committee of the race club or the stewards are required to issue a certificate, setting out the facts upon which such punishment is founded, and to forward such certificate to a District Racing Association or, as the case may be, the committee of the Principal Club.

A person aggrieved by any punishment imposed by a race club or the stewards may, subject to the Rules, appeal to a District Racing Association or, as the case may be, the committee of the Principal Club.

Usually, however, there is no right of appeal against such matters as:
- any decision concerning the eligibility of any horse to race or the conditions upon which it can race;
- any disqualification or suspension of a horse from racing (except where that disqualification or suspension is imposed in conjunction with a penalty imposed upon a person);
- the imposition of a fine not exceeding a prescribed amount.

An appeal must be instituted within a prescribed time of the imposition of the punishment. It must specify the grounds of appeal and must be submitted in writing to the District Racing Association or, as the case may be, the committee of the Principal Club, and a copy of it served on the race club and stewards concerned.

An appeal operates as a stay of any fine, disqualification, suspension, or warning-off from participating in racing in any capacity until the appeals body determines the appeal or the appeal is allowed to be withdrawn.

The appeal body may:
- set aside or vary the penalty, decision, or order, of the stewards or the race club;
- disallow the appeal.

In some cases a person may appeal to a higher Racing Appeals Authority (consisting of judges or legal practitioners) against the decision of an Appeals Committee of a District Racing Association or a Principal Club.

The racing industry is mainly self-regulating although, in cases, appeals from decisions of Principal Clubs may be brought under certain circumstances in Supreme or other appropriate courts of the several States.

Section 51.4
List of Disqualifications

A list of people suspended, warned-off, or disqualified, and of horses disqualified, is kept by each Principal Club and, from time to time, published in the Racing Calendar.

A disqualified person is not permitted during the period of disqualification:
- to enter upon any racecourse at which a race meeting is being held;
- to subscribe to any sweepstakes;
- to enter any horse for a race or a barrier trial;
- to be employed in any racing stable or to ride a horse in any exercise or trial without appropriate permission.

Further, during the period of disqualification, no horse that is owned or leased by the disqualified person or person's spouse is permitted to race or be placed or remain in the care of any licensed trainer.

A person warned-off by a Principal Club is subject to the same disabilities as a person disqualified.

Section 51.5
Forfeit List

Persons who fail to pay subscriptions, fines, fees, stakes, recoverable prize moneys, and certain other moneys due to a racing club or body, forfeit their right to participate in racing. A list setting out particulars of such persons, moneys payable, and the horses for which moneys are so payable, called the "Forfeit List" is kept by each Principal Club and from time to time published in the *Racing Calendar*.

So long as any person's name remains on the Forfeit List that person is subject to the same disabilities as a disqualified person, and that person's listed horse is subject to the same disabilities as a disqualified horse.

PART 21
BOOKMAKERS AND BOOKMAKING

Chapter	52	**Bookmakers**
Section	52.1	Introduction
	52.2	Licensing of Bookmakers
	52.3	Bookmakers' Clerks
	52.4	Bookmakers' Associations
	52.5	Indemnification of Bettors
Chapter	53	**Bookmaking**
Section	53.1	Services Provided by a Bookmaker
	53.2	Betting Tickets
	53.3	Betting Sheets
	53.4	Betting Ring Strategies
	53.5	Bookmakers' Percentages
	53.6	Financial Viability of Bookmaking
Chapter	54	**Betting with Bookmakers**
Section	54.1	Betting Law
	54.2	Play or Pay Principle
	54.3	Dead-Heats
	54.4	"Win Only" Betting
	54.5	"Place Only" Betting
	54.6	"Win and Place" Betting
	54.7	Doubles Betting
	54.8	On-course Starting Price Betting
	54.9	Compulsory Maximum Amount of Bet
	54.10	Disputes or Claims relating to Bets

CHAPTER 52 BOOKMAKERS

Section 52.1
Introduction

A bookmaker is a licensed professional betting person who, at odds offered by him or her, accepts the bets of others on the result of a race; pays winning bets, taxation and other expenses; and, as a result of such transactions gains or endeavours to gain a livelihood either wholly or partly.

Bookmakers have always been an integral part of Australian racing. Indeed, Australia is one of the few countries in which bookmakers legally operate, others being the United Kingdom and South Africa. The USA and European countries operate all tote betting.

Bookmaking is highly controlled by State Government legislation to protect the interests of Crown revenue, club income, and the public.

Section 52.2
Licensing of Bookmakers

After a person has gained experience in carrying out the various duties of a bookmaker's clerk; has acquired a thorough knowledge of the Racing Rules and the Betting Rules; has joined the Bookmakers' Association; and has the necessary finance or bank guarantee, that person may apply to the appropriate licensing authority for a bookmaker's licence.

Where an applicant does not have the necessary liquid assets, he or she needs to obtain financial backing to meet the shortfall. Finance for the hazardous purpose comes dearly from behind-the-scenes characters called "Mikes".

If the licensing authority is satisfied that the applicant has the necessary qualifications and is of good repute, then the authority members consider the application, along with others that may be before them, for suitable vacancies as they arise. The first licence is usually restricted to fielding at comparatively small betting rings at provincial or country courses. Later when the licensee proves an ability he or she may apply for, or be moved into, a larger ring. The yardstick for promotion is the quantum of turnover.

The licensing authority limits the number of bookmakers' licences that may be current at any time, based on the demand for bookmakers' services in the racing area under its jurisdiction, and the financial viability of bookmaking. Licensees are expected to field regularly and if they fail to do so without reasonable cause, their licences may be cancelled. By its policy, the licensing authority seeks to encourage keen betting and to stimulate competition.

Successful bookmakers possess exuberant, energetic, personal qualities that are partly innate, but these are mostly acquired by effort and experience . They gain such experience in the first instance while carrying out the various duties of a bookmaker's clerk.

Section 52.3
Bookmakers' Clerks

Bookmakers' clerks, duly licensed, assist the bookmaker to make a book and give an efficient service by setting up the bookmaker's stand; receiving stakes; issuing tickets; recording bets; advising the bookmaker of the holding and payout liability for each horse and the total holding on all such horses; and paying out winning tickets.

The clerks are usually called by the nature of the duties they perform, that is to say, bagman, penciller, equipment operator or pay-out person.

If authorised by proper authority, a clerk may act as a bookmaker's remote clerk for the purpose of conducting part of the bookmaker's business at a place remote from the bookmaker's authorised stand; or when the bookmaker is temporarily absent, act as the bookmaker's agent.

Section 52.4
Bookmakers' Associations

A licensed bookmaker is required to be a member of a Bookmakers' Association. These associations exist at both State and local levels. The main functions of the State associations are to liaise with racing control bodies and the government on matters affecting members (for example, taxation, levies and fees) and to operate a scheme that allows members to comply with requirements about indemnification of bettors.

Section 52.5
Indemnification of Bettors

A bookmaker is always required to maintain in full force and effect one or more than one policy of insurance or bond indemnifying bettors for winning bets and refunds payable to them against loss suffered by them by reason of the bookmaker carrying on bookmaking. The amount of the indemnity and the terms and conditions of such policy of insurance or bond must comply with the requirements of law.

As well as protecting unpaid bettors, the bond is also a protection for unpaid Crown revenue and club income.

PART 21 BOOKMAKERS AND BOOKMAKING

CHAPTER 53 BOOKMAKING

Section 53.1
Services Provided by a Bookmaker

The type of betting service provided by a bookmaker at a race meeting conducted by a race club is that stipulated by the licensing authority, that is, win only, win and place, place only, doubles, and so on.

The bookmaker and clerks set up their bookmaking stand in the enclosure in which the bookmaker is permitted to field and exhibit a notice indicating the type of the betting service being provided.

Section 53.2
Betting Tickets

When a person makes a bet with a bookmaker, the bookmaker is required to issue a betting ticket to that person indicating particulars of the bet and the name of the bookmaker issuing the ticket. A separate ticket must be issued for each bet except that particulars of a win and place bet on the one horse may be recorded on the same ticket.

A tax (stamp duty) is payable by the bookmaker on each ticket.

Section 53.3
Betting Sheets

Particulars of all bets, including both cash and credit bets, made by a bookmaker at a race meeting must be recorded completely and accurately on approved betting sheets.

Particulars required to be recorded on betting sheets for each race are (a) for each bet, the amount bet by the bookmaker, the amount bet by the bettor, the number of the betting ticket issued and, in the case of a credit bet, the name of the bettor; (b) for each horse, the progressive total liability and the progressive sum held.

Where a bookmaker backs a horse against which he or she is offering odds, that is, where the bookmaker reduces liability for that runner by betting with another bookmaker, or the on-course tote, the bookmaker is required to enter particulars of such bet on the betting sheets under the name of the horse he or she backed.

When a bettor claims a winning bet and presents the betting ticket to the bookmaker or clerk, the clerk finds the entry for the number of that ticket and pays the bettor the sum of the bet as recorded. Paid bets are indicated on the betting sheets by a single line drawn through the ticket serial number recorded.

After the meeting, the bookmaker must forward the originals of the betting sheets for that meeting, together with a remittance of turnover tax and club levy payable on it, to the State Government taxing authority. The bookmaker is also required to advise the club conducting that meeting of certain particulars of the day's betting, particularly the total amount of turnover. The club then must inform the taxing authority of the names of bookmakers who fielded at the meeting and the aggregates of their individual turnovers as advised by the bookmakers.

The copies of the betting sheets must be retained by the bookmaker for two years and must be made available at any time for inspection by the taxing authority or its betting inspector, a police officer, or the race club.

Section 53.4
Betting Ring Strategies

The object of a bookmaker is to lay horses in each race of a race meeting so that irrespective of which horse wins, the payout on the winner will be less than the total "hold" on the race and the net total of such profit margins in all races of the meeting will be sufficient to meet all bookmaking expenses and leave an acceptable net profit return for the practice of a very hazardous profession financially.

The bookmaker's ring strategy, therefore, is to get the better of adversaries (you and me, the punters) and develop a book that will give the bookmaker the best chance of attaining this objective.

When betting on a race begins, the bookmaker sets the odds displayed on the price board very cautiously (well "overround" at about 135 per cent), taking into account the price market prepared by the bookmaker or a professional market-framer; and the bookmakers' professional or secret service as to the fitness or otherwise of competing horses, pre-post betting trends, and anticipated betting moves. Prices fluctuate constantly as betting on the race progresses.

Some bookmakers do in-depth pre-race research and prepare their own betting market, based on facts, factors, and opinion about the ability and fitness of each competing horse, and they are not unduly influenced by betting trends. Some rely on markets prepared by professional market-framers. Some are primarily concerned with finding out what horses are likely to be backed and keeping those prices short, rather than researching the degree of chances of such horses. Some try to attract bets on the chanceless horses and avoid bets on the good chances. Some "take on" a horse in a case where they consider the horse is not as good as its prevailing odds indicate.

No matter what strategies bookmakers employ, for them to be successful it is vital that as far as practicable they observe the bookmakers' percentage scheme. It is also vital that the astute punter has knowledge and understanding of such a scheme because it is from such awareness that he or she knows when to bet and when to wait for prices to ease.

Section 53.5
Bookmakers' Percentages

Under the percentage system a bookmaker determines the amount he is prepared to risk on a race and makes a book accordingly, that is one in which no horse will take out more than the amount of that risk. Prices are set so that theoretically there will be a percentage of the total hold left after meeting the payout liability. On a percentage basis the bookmaker's chances of winning are 'over' the punters' chances.

When a bookmaker bets "round", prices are set so that theoretically the pay-out liability for each horse is the same and is equivalent to the total hold on the race. That is, the bookmaker neither wins nor loses from his or her betting transactions.

It would be most unusual for a bookmaker's board to indicate that betting is "under round" or geared to losing figures. Bookmakers don't bet this way.

Examples of "round", "over round", and "under round" prices are indicated in the following table:

No.	NAME	ROUND Odds	%	OVER ROUND Odds	%	UNDER ROUND Odds	%
1	Joshua	13–2	13.3	5–1	16.7	7–1	12.5
2	Samuel	5–1	16.7	4–1	20.0	5–1	16.7
3	Jonah	16–1	5.9	9–1	10.0	16–1	5.9
4	Micah	16–1	5.9	10–1	9.1	16–1	5.9
5	Amos	11–2	15.4	4–1	20.0	11–2	15.4
6	Daniel	12–1	7.7	10–1	9.1	14–1	6.7
7	Isaiah	5–1	16.7	3–1	25.0	5–1	16.7
8	Joel	12–1	7.7	11–1	8.3	14–1	6.7
9	Hosea	8–1	11.1	9–2	18.2	8–1	11.1
Total			100		136		97
Potential profit					36		
Potential loss							3

The percentage for each horse's odds may be calculated as follows: (a) add the odds on offer about a horse together; (b) divide the total into 100; and (c) multiply the answer by the right-hand figure of the odds.

For convenience prices are expressed as percentages in some detail in the following table:

PRICE	%	PRICE	%	PRICE	%	PRICE	%
1–10	90.9	7–10	58.8	9–4	30.8	9–1	10.0
1–9	90.0	8–11	58.8	24–10	29.4	10–1	9.1
1–8	88.9	4–5	55.6	5–2	28.6	11–1	8.3
1–7	87.5	9–10	52.6	26–10	27.8	12–1	7.7
1–6	85.7	1–1	50.0	11–4	26.7	13–1	7.1
1–5	83.3	11–10	47.6	28–10	26.32	14–1	6.7
2–9	81.8	10–9	47.4	3–1	25.0	15–1	6.3
1–4	80.0	12–10	45.5	32–10	23.8	16–1	5.9
4–15	79.0	5–4	44.4	13–4	23.5	17–1	5.6
2–7	77.8	13–10	43.3	34–10	22.7	18–1	5.3
3–10	76.9	11–8	42.1	7–2	22.2	19–1	5.0
4–13	76.5	14–10	41.7	15–4	21.1	20–1	4.8
1–3	75.0	6–4	40.0	38–10	20.8	25–1	3.9
4–11	73.3	16–10	38.5	4–1	20.0	30–1	3.2
2–5	71.4	13–8	38.1	9–2	18.2	33–1	2.9
4–9	69.2	17–10	37.0	5–1	16.7	40–1	2.4
1–2	66.7	7–4	36.4	11–2	15.4	50–1	2.0
8–15	65.2	18–10	35.7	6–1	14.3	60–1	1.6
4–7	63.6	15–8	34.8	13–2	13.3	66–1	1.5
6–10	62.5	19–10	34.4	7–1	12.5	75–1	1.3
8–13	61.9	2–1	33.3	15–2	11.7	80–1	1.2
4–6	60.0	22–10	31.3	8–1	11.1	100–1	1.0

Section 53.6
Financial Viability of Bookmaking

Of the bookmakers' total turnover, 65 per cent is estimated to be recorded by a comparatively small percentage, say 30 per cent of bookmakers.

Bookmakers incur many expenses in carrying out their profession including: tax on turnover, stamp duty on betting tickets, club levies, fielding fees, interstate betting fluctuation service fee, clerks' wages, and various miscellaneous expenses for betting boards, betting books, tickets, electronic equipment, premiums on insurance policies or bonds for protection of punters, and so on. Government tax and club levies and fees would approximate 3 per cent of a bookmakers turnover, and wages and other expenses 2 per cent.

As indicated by bookmakers, it is evident that the financial viability of bookmaking has become increasingly difficult owing to several factors, particularly the introduction of legal off-course betting in the late 1960s and early 1970s in all States of Australia; the computerisation and proliferation of such totalisator operations; the amalgamation of all off-course and on-course totalisator pools of the respective State TABs; the telecasting of races to TAB offices, clubs and hotels; the falling attendances at race meetings; the significant increase in the number of race meetings; competition from other forms of gambling, for example, casinos, poker machines, scratch caskets, Bingo, Lotto and football pools; the state of the Australian economy; and so on.

The main saving factor for bookmakers in the 1990s has been the relaxation of regulations by the various State governments about the use of telephones on-course. Off-course clients of bookmakers are now permitted to make legal bets with on-course bookmakers in most jurisdictions, provided that the value of those bets meets the minimum amount (usually some hundreds of dollars) set by regulation.

Even taking this factor into account it is clear that the hey-day of bookmakers in the Australian racing industry was from its inception up until about 1970. Times and conditions have since changed markedly.

CHAPTER 54 BETTING WITH BOOKMAKERS

Section 54.1
Betting Law

The law on betting in each State is to be found in Acts or subordinate law of the State or in Racing Rules of the Principal Club concerned. The following general requirements apply on an Australia-wide basis.

Betting is lawful when made by a person 18 years of age or over with (a) a totalisator that is lawfully operated either on-course or off-course, or (b) a bookmaker lawfully carrying on the business of bookmaking on a racecourse for programmed races. Betting on the outcome of a trial or novelty event is unlawful.

A person who carries on bookmaking contrary to law commits a criminal offence. Nevertheless, illegal starting price bookmaking has always been part of the Australian racing scene. Indeed competent authority in the mid 1990s assessed and reported that this market was worth some $4 billion per year.)

Section 54.2
Play or Pay Principle

All bets are "play or pay" unless otherwise agreed between the parties when the bets are made or otherwise provided by the Rules. That is:

(a) A bet made on a horse before the day of the race is forfeited to the bookmaker if that horse is later scratched.

(b) A bet made on the day of the race on a horse that is later scratched or declared by the stewards not to be a starter is refundable to the bettor.

(c) If a race is abandoned, postponed to another day, declared a no-race, ordered to be re-run, or becomes a walkover, all bets made on the day of the race for that race are refundable to bettors.

In a case where:

- a horse is withdrawn from a race after the time fixed for scratching;
- the starter fails to put a horse in its starting stall;
- a horse is prevented from starting in the race by failure of the starting gate to open; or
- a start of the race is effected while a horse is riderless,

the stewards may declare off all bets made on any such horse on the day of the race.

Stewards, if they are of the opinion that the withdrawal or non-starting of any such horse would have any material effect on the odds of the remaining horses, may also declare that all bets made before such withdrawal or race start (whichever is applicable) on the horses remaining in the race stand subject to a deduction calculated in accordance with the Rules.

Section 54.3
Dead-heats

In the event of a dead-heat for first place, the sums bet as recorded on a betting ticket on a dead-heater must be put together and divided into as many equal parts as there are winners of that dead-heat and one such part is payable to the bettor. Somewhat similar rules apply for place and other types of betting.

Section 54.4
"Win Only" Betting

A bookmaker betting "win only" will accept bets on any of the competing horses at the odds indicated on the betting board to win.

Section 54.5
"Place Only" Betting

A bookmaker betting "place only" will accept bets on any of the competing horses at the odds indicated on the betting board to run a place, that is, to run first, second, or third if there are eight or more runners at the time the bet is made, or first or second if there are five, six, or seven runners at the time the bet is made.

Section 54.6
"Win and Place" Betting

A bookmaker betting "win and place" will accept bets on competing horses to win. Such bookmakers will also accept bets on competing horses to win or run a place provided that the bet is on an "each way" basis (that is the place bet is for an amount equal to the win bet) or that the amount bet for a place is less than the amount bet for a win.

Where a bookmaker so bets for a win and a place and -

(a) there are eight or more runners at the time a bet is made, the odds for the place must be at least one-quarter the odds for the win bet and payable on the first, second, and third places;

(b) there are 5, 6, or 7 runners at the time a bet is made, the odds of the place must be at least one-third the odds for the win bet and payable on the first and second places.

There is no requirement for a bookmaker to bet win and place on a two-year-old race, a weight-for-age race, a set-weight race, or a race where the odds offered about any runner are odds-on.

Section 54.7
Doubles Betting

Double events bets are subject to the play or pay principle, except where otherwise agreed when the bets are made, or where otherwise provided by the Rules.

Included in such Rules are the following provisions:

(a) Bets are determined when the first event is lost.

(b) Where both events are run on the one day, bets made on the course on that day are void and the stake refundable to the bettor:
- if the horse backed for the first event does not become a starter;
- if the horse backed for the second event is scratched before the first race is run;
- if the horse backed for the first event wins and the horse backed for the second event is scratched or withdrawn before the advertised starting time of the first event;
- if the first event is abandoned or declared a no-race (even though re-run).

(c) Where both events are run on the one day then, for bets made on that day where the horse backed for the first event wins and the horse backed for the second event is scratched or withdrawn after the advertised starting time for the first event, or the second event is abandoned or declared a no-race, the bettor is paid starting price odds (as determined by the stewards) on the first horse.

In the case of doubles on feature events not run on the same day, betting (referred to as pre-post or ante-post betting) is on an "all in" basis. There are no refunds for non-starters.

Section 54.8
On-course Starting Price Betting

Winning bets made at race meetings at starting price odds, on races run inter-State or elsewhere, must be paid the odds determined by trained assessors and declared to be the starting price odds by the club conducting the meeting where the race is run, except that certain limits may be applied to such prices, for example, 33/1 for minor events and 100/1 for major events.

Section 54.9
Compulsory Maximum Amount of Bet

In the event of a bettor wanting to bet for an amount greater than that which the bookmaker is willing to accept and which is greater than the maximum bet the bookmaker is required to accept in accordance with the Rules, the bookmaker must inform the bettor of that maximum amount and offer to accommodate the bettor to at least that amount. This amount varies according to the locality and the ring where the bookmaker bets.

Section 54.10
Disputes or Claims Relating to Bets

Every race meeting is attended by one or more bookmakers' supervisors and any dispute or claim (for example, about a lost ticket) that arises should be referred to a supervisor as soon as practicable.

Under the Rules of Betting of the Principal Club, a dispute or claim about a bet made at a registered race meeting may be heard and decided by -

(a) the committee of the club holding the meeting;

(b) the stewards acting at the meeting either on referral of the matter to them by the committee of the club holding the meeting or of their own volition;

(c) the committee of the Principal Club having jurisdiction in the area concerned on referral to them by the committee of the club holding the meeting.

Any decision made by the committee of the club, the stewards, or the committee of the Principal Club, referred to above, is final and not subject to appeal.

PART 22
TOTALISATORS AND THE TABS

Chapter	55	Totalisators
Section	55.1	Meaning of "Totalisator"
	55.2	Off-course Totalisator Operators
	55.3	On-course Totalisator Operators
	55.4	Classes of Totalisators
	55.5	Modes of Investing on Totalisators
	55.6	Totalisator Investments
	55.7	Totalisator Pools
	55.8	Deductions from Totalisator Pools
	55.9	Calculation of Dividends
	55.10	Fractions
	55.11	Amalgamation of Pools
	55.12	Payment of Dividends and Refunds
	55.13	Unpaid Dividends and Refunds
	55.14	Government Control
Chapter	56	Totalisator Administration Boards (TABs)
Section	56.1	Constitution of State TABs
	56.2	Service provided by TABs
	56.3	Achievements of TAB's
	56.4	TAB Operations Predominantly Relate to Thoroughbred Racing
	56.5	Operating Results of TABs
	56.6	Distribution of TAB Profits to Clubs
	56.7	Accountability of TABs

CHAPTER 55 TOTALISATORS

Section 55.1
Meaning of "Totalisator"

The term "totalisator" means a scheme under which investments are accepted and aggregated, and dividends are calculated, declared, and paid on a proportional basis depending on the result of a race or a series of races in accordance with prescribed formulae. In a sense, totalisator punters bet against each other rather than against a predetermined book, and approximate odds will fluctuate with betting patterns up to the time of race close.

In each State totalisators may be operated for racing events staged within the State concerned, in other States, or, in the case of international events, in other countries. Totalisators can also be operated on other sporting events or contingencies.

Any device, instrument, or computer used to effect such a scheme and any place where a scheme is operated is also called a "totalisator".

Section 55.2
Off-course Totalisator Operators

Off-course totalisators are operated in each of the several States by the Totalisator Administration or Agency Board (TAB) constituted under the law of the State concerned. That is, the TAB in each State is separate and distinct from TABs in other States, except that TAB pools may be amalgamated (see Section 55.11).

Section 55.3
On-course Totalisator Operators

On-course totalisators are operated at metropolitan, provincial, and certain country race meetings by the race club conducting the meeting or by an authorised agent acting on behalf of the club. The authorised agent may be the TAB, or a private company contracted by the club to provide this service.

Section 55.4
Classes of Totalisators

Detailed information for each class of off-course totalisator is available from the TAB and for each class of on-course totalisator, from the on-course totalisator operator.

General information is given in this section about common classes of totalisator that may be operated for thoroughbred racing and the purpose of each such class, and in the following section, the modes of investment on those classes are explained.

CLASS OF TOTALISATOR	PURPOSE: To provide a pool for the payment of dividends to investors who select the following:
(a) Win	The runner (or runners in the case of a dead-heat) placed first in a race.
(b) Place	Runners filling first, second and third places in a three-dividend race or first and second in a two-dividend race (depending on the number of starters).
(c) Quinella	A combination of runners placed first and second in a race irrespective of the order of finishing.
(d) Forecast	A combination of runners placed first and second in a race in the correct finishing order.
(e) Trifecta	A combination of three runners placed first, second, and third in a race in the correct finishing order.
(f) Double	A combination of the runners placed first in each of the two races of the double.
(g) Treble	A combination of the runners placed first in each of the three races of the treble.
(h) Quadrella or Fourtrella	A combination of runners placed first in each of the four races of the quadrella or fourtrella.

Section 55.5
Modes of Investing on Totalisators

On the win or place totalisators any number of units may be invested on any runner to win or, as the case may be, for a place.

On the quinella totalisator, modes of investment include: single, boxed, and banker quinellas.

Cost of a boxed quinella is as follows:

    3 selections at 1 unit = 3 units
    4 selections at 1 unit = 6 units
    5 selections at 1 unit = 10 units
    6 selections at 1 unit = 15 units
    7 selections at 1 unit = 21 units
    8 selections at 1 unit = 28 units
    9 selections at 1 unit = 36 units
    10 selections at 1 unit = 45 units

Cost of a banker quinella is equivalent to the number of selections other than the banker for example, banker and four selections = 4 units.

On the forecast totalisator modes of investment are similar to quinella investments (except that the first and second placegetters must be placed in correct order). Consequently, the cost of including multiple selections in a boxed forecast is double that for a boxed quinella.

On the trifecta totalisator modes of investment include: single, boxed, multiple, and banker trifectas.

Cost of a boxed trifecta is as follows:

   3 selections at 1 unit = 6 units
   4 selections at 1 unit = 24 units
   5 selections at 1 unit = 60 units
   6 selections at 1 unit = 120 units
   7 selections at 1 unit = 210 units
   8 selections at 1 unit = 336 units
   9 selections at 1 unit = 504 units
   10 selections at 1 unit = 720 units

Cost of a multiple trifecta varies according to the number of runners chosen for each placing and whether or not there are common selections.

Cost of a banker trifecta (one only banker for first followed by any number of selections to run second or third in any order) is as follows:

   3 selections at 1 unit = 6 units
   4 selections at 1 unit = 12 units
   5 selections at 1 unit = 20 units
   6 selections at 1 unit = 30 units
   7 selections at 1 unit = 42 units
   8 selections at 1 unit = 56 units
   9 selections at 1 unit = 72 units
   10 selections at 1 unit = 90 units

Cost of a double banker trifecta (one selection for each of two specified places with two or more selections for the other placing) is equivalent to the number of selections other than the bankers.

On the double totalisator the modes of investment are single or multiple. The cost of a multiple double is equivalent to the number of selections in the first leg multiplied by the number of selections in the second leg.

On the treble totalisator the modes of investment are single or multiple. The cost of a multiple treble is equivalent to the number of selections in the first leg multiplied by the number of selections in the second leg and again multiplied by the number of selections in the third leg.

On the quadrella totalisator the modes of investment are single or multiple. The cost of a multiple quadrella is equivalent to the number of selections in the first leg multiplied by the number of selections in the second leg and again multiplied by the number of selections in the third leg and again multiplied by the number of selections in the fourth leg.

Section 55.6
Totalisator Investments

Moneys that are placed (invested) on totalisators by persons (investors) are officially called "investments". The basic monetary unit that may be invested and on which a dividend is declared and paid is called a "unit of investment".

Particulars of all investments made at the various offices and agencies of each State TAB are relayed to a central computer of that TAB for processing.

Any person may invest on a totalisator except totalisator operators; employees of the totalisator operators; jockeys; and persons under the age of 18 years, all of whom are prohibited from making investments either on their own behalf or on behalf of any other persons.

Section 55.7
Totalisator Pools

All investments on a particular class of totalisator are aggregated and such aggregate is called the "totalisator pool". Excluded from such pool are investments made on that totalisator on horses that become scratchings, late scratchings, or non-starters and which investments consequently become refundable in full. (In the case of certain classes of totalisators, investments on non-runners in the race concerned are not refundable, but are transferred to the declared totalisator favourite for that race).

Usually, if a race is abandoned, postponed, or declared a no-race, or is ordered to be re-run all investments on that race are refundable in full to the investors concerned and do not form part of any totalisator pool.

Section 55.8
Deductions from Totalisator Pools

From each totalisator pool there are deducted the amounts respectively payable by, or retainable by, the totalisator operator, being:

- Totalisator Turnover Tax, payable to the State Government for the credit of the Consolidated Revenue Fund (on average 6.5 per cent)
- Racecourse Development Fund Levy, payable to the State Government for the credit of that Fund and to be used for the development of racecourse facilities (on average 0.5 per cent)

- Totalisator Operator's Commission (on average 8.5 per cent), retainable by the operator to meet operating expenses and to provide for distributions to the racing industry.

The rates of deduction from the totalisator pools are prescribed by the respective State governments and vary among classes of totalisators, on-course and off-course totalisators, and also among States. The overall or aggregate rate of the deductions specified above varies from about 14 per cent to about 20 per cent.

Section 55.9
Calculation of Dividends

After the prescribed deductions are made from the totalisator pool, the balance of the pool, that is, the net pool, is available for the calculation of dividends.

Dividends per unit of investment payable to winning investors are calculated by the totalisator operator by dividing the number of units representing all winning tickets sold in relation to the pool in question, into the net pool and, in cases, adjusting such calculated amount fractionally downwards.

Section 55.10
Fractions

Fractional adjustments are made in accordance with prescribed conditions to pay a guaranteed minimum dividend, or to pay in multiples of 5 cents or 10 cents, and so on.

Sums being dividend fractional adjustments downwards are paid into a separate account of the totalisator operator and are used in the first instance to meet sums required for dividend fractional adjustments upwards. Any accumulation in the Fractions Account is paid to the State Government or is retained by the TAB in some cases.

Section 55.11
Amalgamation of Pools

In a case where the TAB and one or more race clubs in the same State operate the same classes of totalisator for the same race or series of races, the net pools are usually amalgamated to form common net pools and to declare common dividends. In other words the establishment of computer lines linking TAB off-course totalisators, metropolitan on-course totalisators, and totalisators at racecourses at various cities and towns throughout each State where race meetings are held enable the amalgamation of the net pools of all such totalisators within the one State and the declaration of common dividends.

Monetary adjustments are necessarily made among totalisator operators participating in an amalgamation.

Where the on-course totalisators and the off-course totalisators operate independently, that is, where there is no common pooling, dividends differ.

Again, under certain circumstances the TAB in one State may enter into arrangement with a corresponding body in another State in order to amalgamate the pools of any class of totalisator operated by both Totalisator Boards. For example, the Victorian TAB now accepts into its pools, investments from the Tasmanian, South Australian, Western Australian and ACT TABs, the pooling system being named "SuperTAB".

Section 55.12
Payment of Dividends and Refunds

Declared dividends and refundable investments are available for collection by investors shortly after the declaration of correct weight for each race concerned.

Section 55.13
Unpaid Dividends and Refunds

Dividends or refunds that remain unpaid by a totalisator operator after a race meeting may be claimed by the persons entitled to them by presentation of the relative tickets:

- if issued by an on-course totalisator operator, to such operator within 28 days of its issue, or after that date, to the State government department concerned;
- if issued by the TAB, to a TAB office at any time.

All unpaid dividends and refunds that remain unclaimed, are in due course paid by totalisator operators to the State Government concerned or in some cases they are retained by the TAB. That procedure does not alter the above claiming arrangement for investors.

TABs will also accept lost ticket claims from customers.

Section 55.14
Government Control

After each race meeting on which totalisators are operated, or at regular intervals of time, totalisator operators (the TAB, and the race clubs or race club agencies) are required to furnish to the State Government, a declaration of transactions for all classes of totalisators operated at that meeting or during that time. The declaration is required to be accompanied by a remittance for the particular tax or levies payable.

Authorised officers of the government have wide powers and functions to supervise the operation of all totalisators and to inspect the accounts and records of totalisator operators.

Totalisator operations are a primary source of revenue for State governments. The amounts involved are huge.

CHAPTER 56 TOTALISATOR ADMINISTRATION BOARDS (TABS)

Section 56.1
Constitution of State TABs

Until a few decades ago, illegal off-course starting price bookmaking flourished fairly openly throughout the Australian States. Recognising those illegal operations and the interests of the public and the racing industry, each of the several State governments passed legislation during the 1960s and early 1970s providing for the establishment of legal off-course totalisator betting.

In each State an authority called the Totalisator Administration Board or the Totalisator Agency Board (in brief, the TAB) was constituted under the legislation for the purpose of controlling, supervising, regulating, and promoting such betting on events conducted by the three racing codes — gallopers, harness horses, and greyhounds. In Victoria, the State Government and the racing industry agreed to privatise the TAB and, for this purpose, a public company called Tabcorp Holdings Limited was formed and duly listed on the Australian Stock Exchange on 15 August 1994. This company operates subject to government legislation and to a joint venture arrangement with the State racing industry. Some other States are considering privatisation.

Section 56.2
Service Provided by TABs

A TAB aims to provide a high quality off-course totalisator service to the public throughout the State for which it is responsible. For this reason it has established numerous offices and agencies (including facilities in clubs and hotels) and, in addition, a telephone betting branch. TAB branches are operated by TAB employees while agencies operate on a commission basis.

All investments from all sources are relayed through an extensive communications network to computers situated at the Board's Head Office. Dividends are centrally calculated and declared after correct weight declaration for each race on which it operates and this is automatically notified to all branches and agencies to enable payments to be made promptly to winning investors.

Section 56.3
Achievements of TABs

Since inception of the TABs, they have grown to a position of prominence in the Australian racing industry. During that time their operations have expanded throughout their State areas; systems for investments and payments of dividends have been greatly improved; turnover has markedly increased; profit results have been buoyant; and distributions made from profits for the assistance and development of the three racing codes have been significant. During those decades when the progress and achievement of TAB operations has been so spectacular, racecourse attendances have fallen significantly.

Section 56.4
TAB Operations Predominantly Relate to Thoroughbred Racing

Operations of the TABs predominantly relate to the Thoroughbred Racing industry. Of the total turnover of all State TABs for all racing codes, about 85 per cent is for Thoroughbred Racing and the balance for Harness Racing and Greyhound Racing.

Section 56.5
Operating Results of TABs

Income is predominantly earned from commission deducted from totalisator pools. Commission expressed as a percentage of total investment turnover for a year would roughly approximate 10 per cent. Expenditure is made up of salaries, wages and auxiliary costs, agents' commission, telephones and communications, rentals of premises, depreciation, promotion and sundry other items. From the operating profit, amounts are set aside for necessary provisions and reserves and the balance is available for distribution to clubs of the three racing codes.

Section 56.6
Distributions of TAB Profits to Clubs

Totalisator Agency/Administration Boards have an incumbent duty to distribute annual profits to clubs of the three racing codes at as high a rate as prudent business accounting principles allow. In other words, after the TAB has set aside part of the annual profits for necessary provisions and reserves, the balance (indeed the bulk) of the profits are available for such distribution.

The distributions are made according to a formula or scheme of distribution approved by the particular State Government often linked to prize money paid by the clubs concerned. The basis of such scheme varies as between States. All clubs that conduct race meetings benefit from the distributions irrespective of whether any such club conducts any races on which the TAB does not operate.

In some cases TAB distributions to clubs are supplemented to some extent by State Government distributions or capital advances from Racing Development Funds.

The aggregate of sums so distributed to clubs would roughly equate to 3 per cent of the total investment turnover of the TAB.

Section 56.7
Accountability of TABs

Each State TAB is required to keep proper accounts and records, to prepare annual financial statements, and to have such statements audited by a qualified person.

It is also required to prepare a report on its operations for each year and to submit that report to the government concerned and to the Parliament through the responsible Minister.

PART 23
PUNTERS AND PUNTING

Chapter	57	Punters and Punting
Section	57.1	Punters
	57.2	Marks of an Astute Punter
	57.3	Historical Data Basis of Selection Procedure
	57.4	Selection Systems
	57.5	Selection Services
	57.6	The Consumers' Annual Guide to Punting Publications and Services
	57.7	Relevance of Probability to Punting

CHAPTER 57 PUNTERS AND PUNTING

Section 57.1
Punters

A punter is a person who punts, gambles, wagers, bets or "invests" with a bookmaker or on the totalisator on the outcome of a chance event, a horse race.

Most punters have a gambling approach to punting. These punters follow the money, that is, shorteners; follow the leading stables; follow the selections made by others; follow their own haphazard methods; and so on.

Over a period, being gamblers, most punters are losers, ranging from heavy losers to marginal losers. Through their losses, punters provide large sums of money annually to State governments, race clubs, bookmakers, the totalisator agency boards and, indirectly, to many other participants in the racing industry.

Losing punters (not you or me, of course) are subject to negative psychological influences. They have haphazard methods of selection and staking; do not know price values; blame jockeys, trainers and someone other than themselves for what are really their own errors. Punters become angry, upset or regretful after losing; after a series of losses they increase the size of their bets and back the longer priced runners in the hope of striking a larger return. Sometimes they bet outside their means; do not have any specific long-term goal for their punting activities; are subject to misinformation and deceptive conjecture; and so on.

On the other hand a small percentage of punters eliminate the gambling approach to punting and apply a sound, disciplined, logical, businesslike approach to achieve regular profit from punting.

Set forth in this book are various matters to assist punters to gain knowledge and understanding of the racing business, to develop a businesslike approach to betting, and with time and experience, to achieve proficiency in punting.

Section 57.2
Marks of an Astute Punter

The marks of an astute punter include confidence, discipline and patience, allied with the use of sound methods of selection and betting.

Most successful punters depend totally on their own logical techniques of selection and staking. They are in no way dependent upon the ceaseless stream of racing propaganda or misinformation that emanates from the self-styled experts.

Their realistic aim is to make and maintain a profit (excess of wins over losses) of about 10 per cent on turnover.

Section 57.3
Historical Data Basis of Selection Procedure

Any assessment of chances of horses competing in a race must be based upon historical data about past performances of the competing horses. The quality of historical data used for such assessment is, therefore, of vital importance.

It can be readily appreciated that the gathering, analysing, measuring and recording of information about the performances of all horses that compete at metropolitan, provincial and the more important country race meetings are very demanding, time-consuming and laborious and mundane tasks. Such detailed research is just not practicable for the vast majority of punters. Accordingly, a punter may consider, among other things, the following options:

(a) buying a "Selection System" (see Section 57.4)

(b) subscribing to a "Selection Service" (see Section 57.5)

(c) subscribing to a "Weight-Rating Service" (see Section 58.2)

Section 57.4
Selection Systems

A "Selection System" is a one-package set of rules compiled by a person and offered for sale to punters for a fixed sum on a "sight unseen" basis. The rules set out the methods the punter needs to apply to ascertain the events at a race meeting suitable for selection analysis and the methods for carrying out that analysis to ascertain the main chance or, in some cases, the main chances in each such event. The buyer usually has no communication with the author.

Section 57.5
Selection Services

A "Selection Service" is one under which the service undertakes for a prescribed payment by the punter, to provide to that punter over a certain period, selections (usually singletons) for specified events at specified race meetings. In some cases the service will provide relevant information such as the fair price for any selection, its ability to handle the going, and so on. The method used by the service to ascertain selections may or may not be disclosed to the user. Such method may be based on a selection system, on weight ratings or speed rating or otherwise.

Services include telephone 0055 and 1900 selections.

Section 57.6
The Consumers' Annual Guide to Punting Publications and Services

While some selection systems, selection services and rating services are logical and soundly based (some more so than others) and marketed by fair and honest persons, there are some so-called systems and services (including clubs and syndicates to which punters are invited to subscribe for investment on their behalf) that are marketed by scoundrels, cheats, tricksters, swindlers, liars, rogues, robbers, and the like. These unprincipled, dishonourable "gentlemen" advertise quite extensively through the print and electronic media, and in such advertisements make wild, reckless, fanciful, unethical, misleading or false claims about their so-called system or service and their racing knowledge, skill, ability, experience, technological backing, access to inside information, and so on.

How does a punter seeking to gain knowledge of available systems and services ascertain which are sound and logical and which are not? The answer is simply by studying the findings of *"Punters' Choice"*.

Punters' Choice of P.O. Box 70, Roseville, 2069, examines all advertised selection systems and selection services and tests each "reasonable" system for some months. It then reports frankly to consumers the results of those tests and the feasibility of the advertised products. This it does through *Punters' Choice Annual*.

Section 57.7
Relevance of Probability to Punting

Statistically, the term "probability" means the relative frequency of the occurrence of an event as measured by the ratio of the number of cases or alternatives favourable to the event to the total number of cases or alternatives.

The theory of probability was formulated some centuries ago as a means of expressing chances in card games. For example, tables indicating statistical data about chances of combinations in poker hands and the chances of improving them were compiled as a guide to play and not as an infallible key to skill.

The theory can be applied to situations where turnover factors can be expressed in statistical terms and can be subject to analysis.

It can be argued that as each race has its own problems (few facts and many unknown factors) that cannot be easily expressed in mathematical terms, the theory is not suitable to make fixed-rule systematic selections. Those problems can only be resolved by a sound, logical and flexible approach.

On the other hand, some punters who have mathematical knowledge and who understand the theory may use a systematic selection system based on the theory — and enjoy some degree of success.

PART 24

WEIGHT RATINGS

Chapter	58	Introduction to Weight Rating
Section	58.1	Weight-Rating — Definition
	58.2	Weight-Rating Service — Definition
Chapter	59	Calculation and Recording of Weight Ratings
Section	59.1	Method of Calculating Weight Ratings
	59.2	Losing Margin Adjustment
	59.3	Barrier Position Adjustment
	59.4	Missed the Start Adjustment
	59.5	Blocked-for-Room Adjustment
	59.6	Running-Wide Adjustment
	59.7	Hanging or Veering Adjustment
	59.8	Eased Down at Finish Adjustment
	59.9	Easy Win Adjustment
	59.10	Race Class Relativity Value
	59.11	Horse Class Locality Quality Difference
	59.12	Field Strength
	59.13	Contingencies Affecting Race Times
	59.14	Time Factor in Weight Rating
	59.15	Speed Rating — Time Adjustment
	59.16	Recording of Weight Ratings for Future Use
Chapter	60	Data Not Included in Weight Ratings but Noted for Future Selection Procedure
Section	60.1	Introduction
	60.2	Manner of Horses' Finishing Run
	60.3	Improvement
	60.4	Conditioning Runs
	60.5	Horses on the Decline
	60.6	Casting a Plate
	60.7	Cut-Throat Tactics

CHAPTER 58 INTRODUCTION TO WEIGHT RATING

Section 58.1
Weight Rating — Definition

"Weight Rating" is a system that provides for the:

- analysing of past performances of racehorses;
- assigning of numerical measurements in terms of weight to those performances;
- recording of those performances and measurements;
- use of those records in future race selection procedures to compare horses entered in a race even though their previous performances may have been in different races, in different classes or types of races, or in different localities.

Included in the various factors taken into account in the assessment of weight ratings as described in this book are the matters of "horse class" and "race class" relativity values. These matters have been dealt with earlier in this book.

Weight ratings as described herein are thus a basic indicator of "class" and are accordingly sometimes referred to as "class ratings" or "class and weight ratings".

Where the time adjustment figures as calculated for speed ratings are also used in the assessment of weight ratings in accordance with Section 59.15, such weight ratings are in fact a combination of class, weight, and speed ratings - all expressed in terms of weight.

Section 58.2
Weight-Rating Service — Definition

A "Weight-Rating Service" is one that:

(a) gathers all available information about the performances of horses that competed in races at all, or selected meetings (say, all metropolitan meetings and the more important provincial and country meetings in one or more States);

(b) analyses and assesses such performances in the light of pertinent facts and factors assigning weight equivalents and thereby calculating "weight ratings";

(c) records particulars of such performances and weight ratings of those performances in a database in a manner that makes it easy to refer to when selection procedures are being carried out for future race meetings;

(d) supplies to subscribers details of the rating database, leaving it to those subscribers to carry out their own selection procedures; or in some cases, carries out itself the selection and pricing procedures and provides details of such selections and prices to subscribers.

The several matters itemised above are dealt with in some detail in Chapters 59 to 64 inclusive.

There are various weight-rating/selection services. *Punters' Choice Annual* (see Section 57.6) gives particulars of the background, services provided, and assessed performances of those rating selection services. Before entering into a contract for any service, punters are strongly urged to contact Punters' Choice for advice.

PART 24 WEIGHT RATINGS

CHAPTER 59 CALCULATION AND RECORDING OF WEIGHT RATINGS

Section 59.1
Method of Calculating Weight Ratings

The method of calculating the numerical measurement by weight, that is, the weight ratings for each horse that competed in a race and the various components of such ratings is indicated in the following table.

	kg
Weight Allotted .... +	
Less Allowance or Plus Overweight .... –/+	
Weight Carried .... +	
Less Losing Margin .... –	
Theoretical On-terms Weight .... +	
Barrier and In-Running Adjustments —	
Barrier Position .... +	
Running Mishaps, Interference, etc. —	
Missed the Start .... +	
Blocked, Pocketed or Other Interference .... +	
Running Wide .... +	
Hanging or Veering .... +	
Eased Down at Finish .... +	
Easy Win .... +	
Practical On-Terms Weight .... +	
Other Factors to make Rating Absolute —	
Race Class Relativity Value .... +	
Locality Quality Value .... –	
Field Strength .... –/+	
Time Factor .... –	
In Handicap Races — Excess of Bottom Limit Weight over common bottom limit weight of 51 kg. .... –	
Weight Rating .... +	

Penalty or bonus weight adjustments made about some of the components in this table depend upon personal, and therefore, subjective opinion. Accordingly, the following explanations of those items and the rules used to assign weight equivalents to facts and factors are general and flexible. It is impracticable to give positive and inflexible rules.

"As they come back to weigh... through a dense human lane that cheers them again and again". Here a large Flemington crowd cheers the triumphant jockey and horse as they come back to weigh-in.

(Refer to Section 50.6)   Photo courtesy Alan Peach Photography.

"A grim old stayer runs true to his breed". The seven-year-old Irish gelding Vintage Crop (by Rousillon from Overplay) was not hard pressed to win the 1993 VRC Melbourne Cup over 3 200 metres from Te Akau Nick and Mercator. Vintage Crop as a nine-year-old ran third in the 1995 Melbourne Cup won by Doriemus. A bronze monument of Vintage Crop has been erected at the Curragh, the headquarters of Irish racing.

(Refer to Section 43.13)   Photo courtesy Alan Peach Photography.

A small, not too busy bookmakers' ring. The financial viability of bookmaking has become increasingly difficult since the heydays prior to the early 1970's. (Refer to Section 53.6) Photo courtesy Alan Peach Photography.

"At the turn to the straight ... where every atom of weight is telling its tale." The field is shown spreading out for the most important part of the race — the run home to the winning post.

(Refer to Section 60.2) Photo courtesy Steve Hart Photographics.

Section 59.2
Losing Margin Adjustment

For weight-rating purposes it is necessary to determine what weight each losing horse should have carried in the race concerned so that theoretically all horses in the race would have finished on terms with the winner. This is done by accurately measuring losing margins and converting those margins to weights. A positive losing margin/weight equivalent is, therefore, needed.

There is a principle simply expressed that if two horses are evenly matched in all respects (ability, fitness, weight, and so on) they will finish a race on even terms. If, however, they are not evenly matched weightwise, the heavier weighted horse will lose, the losing margin being roughly one length (2.5m) for every 1.5kg of additional weight carried.

While some weight-rating authorities accept the above broad rule for races over all distances, others vary the rule according to their argument as to whether or not weight is more important over short or long distances. Using the losing margin and weight equivalent of 1.5kg per length up to 2200m and 1.0kg per length beyond that distance, losing margin adjustments would be as shown in the following table.

LOSING MARGIN		RACES Up to 2200m	RACES Beyond 2200m
Margin	Lengths	kg	kg
1/2 head	0.05	0	0
Head	0.1	0	0
1/4 length	0.2	0.5	0
1/3 length	0.3	0.5	0
1/2 length	0.5	1.0	0.5
2/3 length	0.7	1.0	0.5
3/4 length	0.8	1.0	1.0
1 length — head	0.9	1.5	1.0
1 length	1.0	1.5	1.0
2 lengths	2.0	3.0	2.0
3 lengths	3.0	4.5	3.0
4 lengths	4.0	6.0	4.0
5 lengths	5.0	7.5	5.0

Section 59.3
Barrier Position Adjustment

It is a mathematical fact that horses starting from wide barrier positions on a circuitous track cover more ground than horses starting from inside barrier positions. Accordingly it is necessary, in measuring performance, to allow for such extra distance and disadvantage. Recommended adjustments are indicated in the following scale.

BARRIER POSITIONS	ADJUSTMENT
	+ kg
1–9	0
10–13	0.5
14–17	1.0
18–21	1.5
22+	2.0

Section 59.4
Missed the Start Adjustment

If a horse missed the start or was hampered or slowly away, an estimate needs to be made of the number of lengths lost and such lengths converted to weight.

It does not mean that if a horse so missed the start that it would have finished such estimated number of lengths further in front if it had started normally. Because of the slower pace at the beginning of a race, it usually has an opportunity to overcome that disadvantage. The recommended adjustment to be made for such mishaps is, therefore, only 0.5kg per estimated length lost (and not the standard 1.5kg per length).

Section 59.5
Blocked-for-Room Adjustment

A horse may be blocked, pocketed, bumped, or otherwise suffer interference in running. As a consequence the horse may have to be vigorously restrained by the jockey from running into the horse in front; or where practicable and time permits, checked and switched around the field; or, where it blunders, steadied until it regains the rhythm of galloping.

If any such mishap occurs in the early part of a race the horse usually has time to regain all or part of the ground lost. If, however, the mishap occurs when making the home turn or when making its run in the straight, the horse may have little or no chance of recovery.

An estimate must, therefore, be made of the number of lengths lost by such interference in running, noting the number of such mishaps, their seriousness, and where they took place. The adjustment is usually reckoned as follows:

- in the early part of the race, 1/3 length or 0.5kg;
- on the home turn, 2/3 length or 1.0kg;
- in the straight, 1–2 lengths or 1.5kg to 3.0kg.

In the case of a very serious interference, greater weight adjustment should be made.

Section 59.6
Running-Wide Adjustment

In estimating the extra ground covered by a horse for running wide during a race, a number of facts and factors such as the layout and measurements of the track in question, the distance of the race, when and where it ran wide, and the number of runners the horse was from the inside rail must be noted. Some examples of adjustments for wide running are as follows:

(a) For running gradually and diagonally wide from the top of the straight to the winning post, about half-a-length (1kg).

(b) For every horse the runner was from the inside rail around the home turn, about one-third of a length (0.5kg).

(c) For running wide around the home turn and heading almost directly to the outside rail, much greater than (b).

(d) For running three-wide throughout a 1600m race on a large track with sweeping bends, about three to four lengths (5kg to 6kg); or on a small track with tight turns, about five lengths (7.5kg).

Section 59.7
Hanging or Veering Adjustment

The ground lost by a horse when hanging in or veering out in the straight is generally not significant. Runners that are under pressure or suffering fatigue are inclined to run erratically.

Section 59.8
Eased Down at Finish Adjustment

There is a rule of racing that every horse should be fully ridden out at the finish of a race, but it is common for many horses to be eased down by their riders near the winning post. A rider may ease down when of the opinion that the race is well and truly won; or that there is no chance of winning or running a minor place; or that the mount is tiring and should not be unnecessarily exerted; or otherwise.

If a horse is eased down, restrained, impassively ridden, or ridden with poor judgment and such an incident is detected, an adjustment must be made in the measurement of the horse's performance. It may be safely assumed that if fully ridden out the horse, if the winner, would have won by a greater margin; and, if a loser, would have lost by a lesser margin.

The estimated distance by which the margin would have been greater, or as the case may be, lesser, may vary from one-third of a length up to about two lengths (0.5kg to about 3kg) depending on how far from the winning post, the rider started to ease the mount.

Section 59.9
Easy Win Adjustment

Where a horse wins easily and with something in reserve, that is, where it could have won by a greater margin, an estimate is made of that extra margin. The estimate may vary from one-third length up to about two lengths (0.5kg to about 3kg) noting how easily the horse won.

Section 59.10
Race Class Relativity Value

For weight-rating purposes, relativity among race classes is based on handicappers' relativity scales (see Section 48.6). A rating service may provide for race class relativity values to be as indicated in those scales. On the other hand, the race class values used by a rating service may be only, say, half the values in those scales. The purpose of this approach is to keep rating figures as low as practicable to make workings easier.

Section 59.11
Horse Class Locality Quality Difference

Horses competing in the respective classes of races conducted at meetings held in Sydney and Melbourne on Saturdays are the highest quality horses of those race classes in Australia.

In order to make ratings "absolute", it is vital to make provision in terms of weight for the degrees by which the estimated quality of horses racing at other meetings held in Australia are comparatively less than that highest quality. Rating services provide for such quality differences using very detailed class weight tables that would be subject to change periodically. For our purposes, however, a broad overall picture of such table differences is indicated here.

MEETING	LOCALITY RATING
	kg
Metropolitan Saturdays and Public Holidays —	
Sydney and Melbourne	–0.0
Brisbane and Adelaide	–2.0 to –4.0
Perth	–3.0 to –5.0
Tasmania – Elwick and Mowbray	–5.0 to –7.0

Metropolitan Midweek —
    Sydney and Melbourne   −1.0 to −3.0
    Brisbane and Adelaide   −4.0 to −6.0
    Perth   −5.0 to −7.0
Provincial/Country TAB Meetings (Note 1) —
    NSW and Victoria   −3.0 to −5.0
    Queensland and South Australia   −6.0 to −8.0

Note 1:   Provincial TAB Meetings:
               NSW: Gosford, Hawkesbury, Newcastle, Wyong, Kembla Grange
               Victoria: Ballarat, Bendigo, Cranbourne, Geelong, Kilmore, Kyneton, Moe,
                                      Mornington, Packenham, Sale, Seymour, Werribee, Yarra Glen
               Queensland: Ipswich, Gold Coast, Sunshine Coast
               South Australia: Balaklava, Gawler, Murray Bridge, Strathalbyn.

Section 59.12
Field Strength

The number and quality of horses competing in a race of the same class or type at any meeting at any locality may vary significantly from the norm and it is, therefore, necessary for weight rating purposes to estimate any such variance and to express it in weight. Where the field of the race in question is assessed as being above average, the class value is increased by up to 3kg, or if particularly strong, by up to 5kg. Where, however, the field is assessed as being below average, the class value is reduced by up to 3kg.

Major variances in field strengths occur at annual carnival times when horses from other and stronger areas visit the district holding the particular carnival. Again, good quality races with attaching high prize money attract strong fields. On the other hand, for example, a class 6 race may comprise one class 6 horse and the rest lower class horses.

Section 59.13
Contingencies Affecting Race Times

Contingencies which may significantly affect the times taken for the running of races include such things as the following:

(a) Tracks differ markedly in shape and layout.

(b) The usual or advertised distances of races are often affected by the use of false or movable running rails and the location of barrier stalls depends on the state of the going or the need to save wear on a section of the track.

(c) The track condition or state of the going may vary for different parts of the same track and for races on the same track because of such things as changes in the weather, the effectiveness or otherwise of the drainage system, the length of the grass, and the nature of the materials used in track construction.

(d) The direction and velocity of winds are never constant.

(e) Every race is run differently, depending upon the distance of the race, the presence or absence of frontrunners, and the tactics of riders. Some middle-distance and staying events are run at a muddling pace.

(f) The winner of a race is often eased down nearing the winning post, causing the time to be greater than it would have been if the horse had been fully extended.

(g) Some races are both electronically and hand-timed, some are electronically timed only and, again, some are hand-timed only.

(h) In some cases, official times are obviously discrepant for reasons unknown or not officially recognised, and so on.

Section 59.14
Time Factor in Weight Rating

For weight-rating purposes where the official time for a race under review (or the adjusted or calculated time for that race), by comparison with the average or standard time:

- is about the same, no rating adjustment is necessary;
- is less (that is, better) to an important extent, a bonus adjustment is made to the ratings of all horses that competed in that race;
- is more (that is, worse) to an important extent, a penalty weight adjustment is made to the ratings of all horses that competed in that race.

Such bonus or penalty adjustments may vary from 0.5kg to 2.5kg.

Section 59.15
Speed Rating — Time Adjustment

In lieu of the time adjustment referred to above a more meaningful adjustment may be made by using the time adjustment as calculated for speed ratings.

If so used, the ratings simply described here as "weight ratings" would in fact be a combination of weight, class, and speed ratings.

Speed ratings only apply to races up to 1600m as the pace tends to be "on" over the whole course of the shorter races. They are not suitable for application to longer races because of the leisurely or muddling pace at which such races are run.

As demonstrated by the contingencies referred to in Section 59.13, the time factor is only of importance compared with average times that are calculated from research of past records for races of the same race class, run over the same distance, on the same track, and under somewhat the same conditions. Such Tables of Average Times are prepared by speed-rating services.

When estimating times of races at a race meeting, such rating services determine particulars of overall and sectional times of races, beaten margins, and other pertinent information from official sources and from studies of race photographs and video tapes.

Various adjustments are made to official race times considering such things as location of the starting stalls, use of the false or movable rail, and so on.

Some races are considered unsuitable for speed rating. These include races where the fields were small; where the pace was slow early; where there was a change in weather conditions; where there were hand-timing inaccuracies; and the like.

The times — or rather calculated or adjusted times — of races considered suitable for speed rating purposes are compared to the appropriate Table of Average Times — like being compared to like in all practical respects.

From the comparison, differences are decided and such differences in times, expressed in seconds, are converted to weight.

Time difference is converted to lengths using the standard of about six lengths generally being run in one second on a good track. Lengths are, of course, converted to weight at the standard of 1.5kg to one length. Accordingly, the conversion of time to weight is rounded off to 10 kilograms to the second.

If the calculated time of a race is faster than the average time, the time adjustment figure is a bonus; if slower, a penalty.

Such bonus or penalty is applied to the ratings of all competitors in the race irrespective of their losing margins. Losing margin adjustments, however, are applied as set out in Section 59.2.

Section 59.16
Recording of Weight Ratings for Future Use

After historical data about races run has been analysed and the performances of competing horses numerically measured by weight ratings, all such information is drawn together and recorded in computer databases for future use.

Certain data as set out in Chapter 60 is not included in the weight-ratings but is noted on the weight rating records for use by the punter when carrying out selection procedures for future races.

CHAPTER 60 DATA NOT INCLUDED IN WEIGHT RATINGS BUT NOTED FOR FUTURE SELECTION PROCEDURE

Section 60.1
Introduction

Certain weight-rating services do not make provision directly in their weight ratings for such matters as the manner of a horse's finishing run; likely improvement; signs of deteriorating form; defective racing equipment or gear; and so on. In such cases those matters are noted in the database during weight-rating procedures for consideration during future pre-race selection procedures.

Section 60.2
Manner of Horses' Finishing Run

The most important part of a race is the finish from the home turn to the winning post, a distance of some 400m to 600m.

The manner in which a horse finished the race under review is of vital interest to the reviewer.

Some horses tire and fall back or drift off the track. Signs of weariness or exhaustion include tail switching, shortening stride, open mouth, ears flat aback. These signs in a horse that has been "up" for some time may indicate that the horse is on the decline whereas in a horse having its first or second start since a spell the signs indicate that it is underdone and will improve.

On the other hand, some horses will be observed to finish full of running either winning, finishing close to the winner, or at least holding their position.

Where in its finishing run a horse overhauls or draws away from other horses that were tiring or below its class, or the race was run in slow time, the finishing run cannot be considered meritorious.

Where, however, the horse was overhauling or drawing away from horses that themselves were also full of running, then the finishing run of the horse was indeed meritorious.

If a horse just missed overhauling the winner it may have been because the rider wrongly timed the finishing run; it did not obtain an uninterrupted run; it needs a race over a longer distance; it could not do any better; or it was over-exerted and getting weary.

If, after considering the relevant facts and factors, it is decided that the finishing run of a horse is truly meritorious then, at its next start over the same or longer distance (but not over a shorter distance) it should, during the selection process for that race, be given credit for that impressive finish.

The arbitrary value attached to a meritorious finishing run is from 0.5kg to 1.5kg.

Section 60.3
Improvement

As indicated earlier, some horses are specially trained to be in top condition and to attempt to win at their first start in a race after a spell. In most cases, however, after trackwork and barrier trials, the preparation of a horse after a spell is continued by competing it against seasoned gallopers in races.

It is logical to expect that any such horse improving in condition will perform better in future races that it contests; therefore, it is rational when considering its chances in any such future race to credit it with a weight equivalent to the number of lengths by which it is expected to improve.

The estimated improvement depends a great deal on such factors as class and age of the horse; the duration of its spell or let-up; the manner in which it raced, particularly its finishing run in those conditioning races; and the distances of those races.

The improvement credit (usually 1.5kg, 3.0kg, or 4.5kg) is not a component of the horse's weight rating, but it is noted in the database for use if the horse starts again within four weeks. If the horse does not increase its rating, or does not increase its rating as much as anticipated, the improvement credit should be ignored or reduced for subsequent runs.

The rate of improvement is always a matter for personal judgment.

Section 60.4
Conditioning Runs

A trainer may, by nefarious practices, prepare a horse for a race of a suitable class, distance, and so on, and by such practices not only condition the horse, but also the bookmakers and the public.

This the trainer may do by:
- running the horse in a race of a class higher than that for which it is eligible;
- running the horse in a race over too short or too long a distance;
- engaging an unfashionable rider and, if necessary, instructing that rider to race the horse wide throughout or around the turns, or to allow the horse to run into dead ends, to be locked in on the fence and blocked for room;
- racing the horse in bandages.

These runs are noted as such and substantial improvement is expected when the horse is placed in a race of suitable class, distance, and so on; a good rider is engaged; the horse is left clean-legged; and the price is right.

Section 60.5
Horses on the Decline

If a horse shows signs of declining in condition and is considered to be "stale" or "over the peak" (see Section 32.10), the fact is noted in the database. Any such horse should be disregarded as a chance in any race until after it has been spelled.

Section 60.6
Casting a Plate

It is very difficult to assess what correction, if any, should be applied if a horse casts, spreads or twists a plate during a race.

A number of horses that cast a plate finish well down the track. Others win or finish close to the winner. Much depends on at what stage of the race the horse loses the plate.

Generally, when a horse casts a plate during a race, the run should be overlooked as any rating for that race may be sadly astray.

If the run in question is the only run to determine its qualification for a coming race, a minimum correction of 1.5kg should be added to its rating.

Section 60.7
Cut-Throat Tactics

When two or more horses vie for the lead almost from the start of a race they are said to cut at each other's throats by exerting themselves to the extreme. In most cases the vying front-runners tire before the winning post and are beaten by a horse more patiently ridden that quickly passes them when they shorten stride.

No correction is applied in the assessment of the weight ratings of a horse involved in cut-throat tactics. The dismal effort is the result of poor riding. It is better to forget the horse's run.

PART 25
APPLICATION OF WEIGHT RATINGS

Chapter	61	Preliminary Selection Procedure
Section	61.1	Introduction
	61.2	Reference Material
	61.3	Races to be Assessed
Chapter	62	Selection Procedure
Section	62.1	Explanatory Worksheet
	62.2	Qualifying Run
	62.3	Winners Come from Recent Starters
	62.4	Freak "Qualifying Run"
	62.5	Adjustments to Ratings of "Qualifying Runs"
	62.6	Weight to Carry
	62.7	Rider Eligibility
	62.8	Riders' Rating Adjustments
	62.9	Barrier Adjustments
	62.10	ADE Adjustments
	62.11	Adjustments re Data not Included in Ratings
	62.12	Distance Suitability
	62.13	Weight-Carrying Ability
	62.14	Dead Weight
	62.15	Bad Barrier Positions
	62.16	Liking or Aversion for Track
	62.17	Liking or Aversion for Track Condition
	62.18	Trainer Factor
	62.19	Performance Consistency
	62.20	Bandages
	62.21	Other Negative Factors
	62.22	Final Relative Handicap
	62.23	Final Relative Handicap on "0"
	62.24	Selections
Chapter	63	Framing a Market on Weight Ratings
Section	63.1	Assessment of Chances in Terms of Prices
	63.2	Calculation of Prices
	63.3	Amount of Stake and Price Limit

Chapter	64	The Flow of Weight Rating Data From Source to User
Section	64.1	Source of Race Results
	64.2	Source of Race Fields
	64.3	Supply of Race Results and Race Fields to Interested Parties
	64.4	Weight Rating Service Database
	64.5	Weight Rating Service Bulletin Board
	64.6	The Rating Bureau (TRB)

PART 25 APPLICATION OF WEIGHT RATINGS

CHAPTER 61 PRELIMINARY SELECTION PROCEDURE

Section 61.1
Introduction

Procedures for gathering and analysing historical data about horses' past performances, the numerical measurement or weight rating of those performances, and recording such ratings, have already been explained in some detail.

We now turn to the pre-race use of those established records to determine the main chances in a race and the most favourably handicapped of those chances.

Punters who subscribe to firms for the supply of weight rating historical records may, in some cases, subscribe to them for the weight rating selection procedures to be carried out on their behalf and particulars be supplied. Alternatively, they may carry out their own weight rating selection procedures using the weight rating records as the basis of such procedures.

Section 61.2
Reference Material

In carrying out the selection procedure about a race meeting, the selector needs to have manual or computerised reference data about:

- conditions of races;
- particulars of acceptors and of riders;
- riding weights of jockeys and of apprentices, and allowances of apprentices;
- jockey ratings;
- details of past performances of competing horses and of ratings of those past performances;
- ADE chart (see Section 62.10 for definition);
- design of the racetrack and of the relative barrier positions statistical table; and
- the likely state of the weather and the track, and official notification about the use, or otherwise, of a false running rail.

Section 61.3
Races to be Assessed

The programs of race meetings in which an astute punter is likely to be interested are those of metropolitan meetings held on Saturdays or public holidays. The prize money and conditions of races of those programs provide for and attract the best quality horses.

In determining which races of a selected meeting to consider, the punter in question would have regard to such factors as:

- race class, preference being given to the highest class of race, followed by the next highest class, and so on (see Section 48.6);
- field strength, preference being given to races with better quality horses;
- field numbers, preference being given to races with not less than eight nor more than 15 starters.

Races the punters would ignore would include maiden and standard restricted class races; special restricted races for horses that have not won a race or not won more than one race in a metropolitan area; other races being contested by low or poor graded horses; races restricted to jumping riders, visiting riders from overseas, apprentices, and so on; and races for two-year-olds or three-year-olds until horses competing in those races have raced often enough for weight ratings to reveal their ability and to indicate their pattern of improvement.

In summary, the good punter is looking for the better class races being contested by good quality horses.

PART 25 APPLICATION OF WEIGHT RATINGS

CHAPTER 62 SELECTION PROCEDURE

Section 62.1
Explanatory Worksheet

In order to explain the process of assessing the relative weights of horses contesting a race (called "doing the weights") a worksheet and explanatory notes are given in some detail in this chapter. In practice, worksheets as such are not prepared. The relative calculations are made in a race paper form guide or by computer.

EXPLANATORY SELECTION PROCEDURE WORKSHEET

	HORSE A	HORSE B	HORSE and so on C
Particulars of race under review			
Weight to carry			
Rider/Barrier position			
Particulars of qualifying run			
Weight carried/Distance			
Rider/Date			
	* kg	kg	kg
Rating of qualifying run . . . . –			
Adjustments re data not included in qualifying run rating —			
Improvement . . . . –			
Finishing run . . . . –			
Casting a plate . . . . –			
Weight to carry in race under review +			
Adjustments —			
Rider	–/+		
Barrier position	+		
ADE	–/+		
Corrected relative handicap	–		
Other positive/negative factors	–/+		
Final relative handicap	–		
Final relative handicap on "0"	0/+		

* Note re adjustments: Better or Bonus — Worse or Penalty+

Section 62.2
Qualifying Run

One of the elements of the handicapping procedure is to know whether or not any of a horse's past performances have qualified it for the race it is about to contest. Ideally, the qualifying run for that race should be the horse's most recent best effort:

- preferably within approximately two months;
- in the same or similar type or class of race;
- over the same or similar distance;
- on the same track;
- under the same or similar track conditions; and
- ridden by the same rider.

In determining the qualifying run much depends on the selector's own discretion and judgment. This is a matter of practice and experience.

Where a horse is to compete in its first race after a spell and is not a specialist first-upper or has not obviously been prepared for a first-up win; or in its second, third, or fourth race after a spell and its current ratings relate mainly to conditioning runs that are not truly indicative of its ability, the rule is to use a "qualifying run" before that spell and deduct a penalty condition correction from the weight rating of that run. The usual condition penalty is 1.5kg, 3.0kg, or 4.5kg having regard to the age and quality of the horse, the length of the spell, and the estimated number of lengths it needs to improve to attain top condition.

Note: A handicap is a good qualifying run for a welter, but the use of a welter as a qualifying run for a handicap should be avoided where practicable.

Section 62.3
Winners Come From Recent Starters

Statistics indicate that a predominant percentage of winners have their previous start in a race within three weeks of their winning effort. Particulars of those statistics are shown in the following table.

NUMBER OF WEEKS SINCE HORSE'S LAST START BEFORE WINNING EFFORT	% OF WINNERS	% CUMULATIVE
1	32	32
2	37	69
3	16	85
4	6	91
5	2	93
6 or more	7*	100

* first-uppers.

Sponsorships are an important part of race club revenue. Here Chief De Beers (by Hula Chief from Diamonds for Rosie) is shown easily winning the 1995 BTC Doomben 10 000 Handicap with sponsors' advertisements dominating the background. Placegetters All Our Mob and Cohort didn't make the photo.

(Refer to Section 69.3)   Photo courtesy Alan Peach Photography.

The finish of the 1997 AJC Doncaster Handicap run over 1 600 metres shows Secret Savings (by Seeking the Gold from Jurisdictional) winning from All Our Mob with Ravarda third.

(Refer to Section 60.2)   Photo courtesy Steve Hart Photographics.

Luskin Star (by Kaoru Star from Promising) was a brilliant sprinter who raced as a two-year-old and a three-year-old in the late 1970s. He started 17 times for 13 wins and 3 seconds before being retired to a very successful stud career.
Portrait courtesy South Australian Horse Artist Helen Krieg.

Todman (by Star Kingdom from Oceana) was a sensational sprinter during the late 1950's. He won ten races from twelve starts and established time records in six of them. He was also a sensation at stud.

(Refer to Section 34.5)   Portrait courtesy South Australian Horse Artist Helen Krieg.

As a general rule a horse should not be backed unless it has started in a race within three weeks of its current start.

Section 62.4
Freak "Qualifying Run"

Occasionally an ordinary horse will run an extraordinary race and will be credited with an extraordinary rating. These freak runs and ratings should be ignored.

Section 62.5
Adjustments to Ratings of "Qualifying Runs"

Ratings are "absolute" for handicap races but when a qualifying run of a set-weight race is used for selection procedures for a handicap race, or vice versa, certain adjustments must be made.

(a) If it is necessary to use a WFA event as a qualifying run for a handicap, the difference between the "given" weight of the horse in the WFA event (for example 58kg) and that for the handicap (for example, 54kg), that is, 4kg, should be deducted from the WFA rating.

Where a handicap is used as a qualifying run for a WFA event, no adjustment is required.

(b) Where a set-weight race is used as a qualifying run for a handicap and:
- there is a reduction in the "given" weights, the difference should be deducted from the set-weight rating;
- there is an increase in the "given" weights, the difference should be added to the set-weight rating.

(c) Where a handicap is used as a qualifying run for a set-weight race and:
- there is a reduction in the "given" weights, the difference should be added to the handicap rating;
- there is an increase in the "given" weights, the difference should be deducted from the handicap rating.

Section 62.6
Weight to Carry

The weight to be carried by a horse in any race is its allotted weight less apprentice's allowance (if the rider is a claiming apprentice and is permitted to claim by the conditions of the race) or plus overweight (if the rider's weight is in excess of the horse's allotted weight).

Section 62.7
Rider Eligibility

The dominant factor that decides the result of a race is the combination of horse and rider and their mutual understanding. Accordingly, a selection should be supported only when it is to be ridden:

- by any one of the top ten riders;
- by the regular rider provided that he or she is not a poor rider who has never won on the horse;
- by any rider, other than the regular rider, who has won or gone close to winning on the horse;
- by the stable apprentice who has ridden the horse in trackwork; or
- if the horse is a frontrunner, by any fashionable jockey or experienced apprentice.

Subject to rider eligibility assessed in accordance with the above condiions, rider-rating adjustments are made in the manner set out in the following section.

Section 62.8
Riders' Rating Adjustments

As indicated in Section 40.8, the Jockeys' Ratings express the ability of riders in kilograms from 0 to 5. The better the rider, the lower the rating.

The ratings provide a means of comparing riders should they differ between the horse's qualifying run and the race under consideration. The difference in ratings of such jockeys is regarded as an advantage or disadvantage to the horse in the coming race.

For example, if the rating of jockey A in a qualifying race is 0, and the rating of jockey B in the race under consideration is 2, then as B is an inferior rider, the horse is penalised with 2kg, expressing the difference in the riders' abilities. If, however, the circumstances were reversed because of the horse being ridden by a superior jockey, it would be granted a bonus of 2kg.

There are a number of circumstances where commonsense dictates that there must be some variation of the general rule. In the following cases the difference in rider ratings between that of a superior rider and that of an inferior rider should be halved: where the inferior rider (perhaps the regular rider) has ridden the horse for one or more wins; if the horse is a frontrunner; if the inferior rider is apprenticed to the horse's trainer; if both the superior rider and the inferior rider have ridden the horse for a similar rating.

In a case where a horse's regular rider in the country has ridden the horse for one or more wins and this rider is not listed in the riders' rating charts, the country rider should be given a provisional rating of 3.5. It should be noted well, however, that if a rider has never ridden on a particular city track and is thus a "stranger from the bush", it nearly always works out that the mount gets beaten — most likely because the horse and, more importantly, its rider, were not familiar with the track and its layout.

Section 62.9
Barrier Adjustments

Having regard to mathematical principles, the wider a horse is drawn at any starting barrier on any circuitous course, the greater the distance it has to run. A penalty must be imposed for such extra distance. Recommended penalties are indicated in the following table.

BARRIER POSITIONS	PENALTY (kg)
1–9	0
10–13	0.5
14–17	1.0
18–21	1.5
22+	2.0

Section 62.10
ADE Adjustments

The term "ADE" is an abbreviation of the words "Accelerating or decelerating effect of weight".

The theory is that weight carried by a horse has an influence on its galloping speed.

If, in a comparison between a coming race under review and the relevant qualifying race, a horse is required to carry (a) a greater weight over the same or longer distance or (b) the same weight over a longer distance, there will be a decelerating effect, or disadvantage. Conversely, if the horse is required to carry (a) less weight over the same or shorter distance or (b) the same weight over a shorter distance, there will be an accelerating effect or advantage.

As the result of research in this regard, various scales, graphs, or nomographs have been designed to express the relative ADE advantages or disadvantages that accrue, based on the various facts and factors. The following table is based on those designs. *Note:* Not all rating services accept or apply the ADE principle.

PART 25 APPLICATION OF WEIGHT RATINGS

ADE VALUES IN KILOGRAMS

WEIGHT				DISTANCE IN HUNDRED METRES								
kg	10	12	14	16	18	20	22	24	26	28	30	32
47	0	0	0	0	0.5	0.5	0.5	1.0	1.0	1.0	1.5	2.0
48	0	0.5	0.5	1.0	1.0	1.5	1.5	2.0	2.5	3.0	3.0	3.5
49	0.5	0.5	1.0	1.0	1.5	2.0	2.0	2.5	3.0	3.5	4.0	4.5
50	0.5	1.0	1.0	1.5	2.0	2.0	2.5	3.0	3.5	4.0	4.5	5.0
51	1.0	1.0	1.5	2.0	2.0	2.5	3.0	3.5	4.0	4.5	5.0	6.0
52	1.0	1.5	2.0	2.0	2.5	3.0	3.5	4.5	5.0	5.5	6.0	7.0
53	1.5	2.0	2.0	2.5	3.0	3.5	4.5	5.0	5.5	6.0	7.0	8.0
54	1.5	2.0	2.5	3.0	3.5	4.0	4.5	5.5	6.0	7.0	8.0	9.0
55	2.0	2.5	3.0	3.5	4.0	4.5	5.0	6.0	7.0	7.5	9.0	10.0
56	2.0	2.5	3.0	3.5	4.5	5.0	5.5	6.5	7.5	8.5	9.5	11.0
57	2.5	3.0	3.5	4.0	5.0	5.5	6.0	7.0	8.0	9.0	10.5	12.0
58	2.5	3.0	3.5	4.5	5.0	6.0	6.5	8.0	9.0	10.0	11.5	13.0
59	3.0	3.5	4.0	5.0	5.5	6.5	7.5	8.5	10.0	11.0	12.5	14.0
60	3.0	4.0	4.5	5.5	6.0	7.0	8.0	9.0	10.5	12.0	13.5	15.0

Examples on the application of the ADE principle follow.

(a) If a horse in its qualifying race carried 50.5kg over 1200m (a reading 1.0kg in the table) while in the coming race under review it is to carry 52.0kg over 1400m (a table reading of 2.0kg) there is a decelerating effect or disadvantage of 1.0kg.

(b) If a horse in its qualifying race carried 56.0kg over 2800m (a table reading of 8.5kg) while in the coming race under review it is to carry 54.5kg over 2600m (a table reading of 6.0kg) there is an accelerating effect or advantage of 2.5kg.

Section 62.11
Adjustments Re Data Not Included in Ratings

Adjustments should be made to ratings of qualifying runs for those matters dealt with in Chapter 60 that are noted on database, but not included in the ratings.

Section 62.12
Distance Suitability

Because of genetic or environmental reasons, each horse normally has a liking for a particular race distance range. Gallopers are divided into five categories as follows:

- "sprinters" that are suited by races up to 1500m;
- "milers" that excel in races run over 1600m;
- middle-distance horses that are suited by races in excess of 1600m up to about 2200m;
- stayers that are at their best in races beyond 2200m;
- versatile gallopers that can cope with almost any distance.

One of the basic requirements for selecting the "qualifying run" is that such a run be over the same or similar distance as the race under review. The term "similar distance" means where the race is over a sprint distance about 200m either way; over a mile (1.6km) about 300m either way; over a middle distance about 400m either way; and in the case of a stayer's race, within the staying range.

While the general rule is that no horse should be made a selection if it is in a race outside its pet distance range, there are exceptions. One is when a noted frontrunner goes back to a shorter distance.

Trainers often use races of unsuitable distance for conditioning purposes.

Section 62.13
Weight Carrying Ability

Having determined the weight a horse has to carry, an assessment then has to be made of the ability of the horse to carry that weight successfully over the distance of the race in question. That is to say the distance factor must be considered conjointly with the weight carrying ability factor.

Weight is the equaliser in racing and every horse can handle weight up to a certain limit over a certain distance. This is called the horse's "weight carrying ability". Reference to historical data will indicate the known weight carrying ability of a horse. Where it is required to carry weight significantly in excess of that known ability, it would be wise to omit the horse as a chance.

Section 62.14
Dead Weight

There is a marked difference between dead weight and live weight. Live weight is the weight of the rider fully dressed. Dead weight is the rider's gear, mainly saddle and, if necessary, lead bag used to make up the weight the horse is to carry.

The less dead weight a horse has to carry the better it can show its ability.

The fact that a selection has to carry dead weight in a race in excess of 1600m should be taken into account as a negative factor in determining whether to support that selection. The incidence of dead weight may be ignored in races up to 1600m.

Section 62.15
Bad Barrier Positions

The importance of barrier positions at the various starting points of various tracks has been explained in some detail in Part 18.

Tables provided there indicate barriers that are statistically rated as "good to fair" and those that are statistically rated as "poor to bad".

As a general rule horses that are average performers or slow starters and are to start from a barrier with a bad statistical rating should be discarded from selection consideration. Where a horse has a weight advantage, and the ability to begin smartly and take up and hold a good running position early without great effort, its barrier position is not of importance.

Section 62.16
Liking or Aversion for Track

Some horses have a special liking for one particular track at which they record most of their wins. Conversely, there are horses that have an absolute disliking for a certain track or tracks where they never run well.

These positive or negative factors are very important in the selection process. A contestant for a race at a particular track can be safely discarded from consideration if records indicate that it has consistently failed at that track.

Section 62.17
Liking or Aversion for Track Condition

Some horses show their best form on a fast or good track; some on a dead track; some on a slow or heavy track; and some, the versatile, on any type of track.

It is necessary to learn if the contestants for an event have a proven record of success or failure in the declared state of the going. Their ability cannot be taken on trust even though such ability seems to be genetic. Where the records indicate that a horse is unable to handle the going it can be safely discarded from consideration. Apart from a horse's ability to handle the going, it must also be currently fit in all respects.

In slow or heavy going, heavy weights are more burdensome than on good going and preference should be given to selections that are low in the weights.

Section 62.18
Trainer Factor

As indicated in Chapter 30, the quality of trainers varies considerably, from the very good to the very bad. A stable that produces winners tends to keep on producing them. Horses in the winning stable are trialled against each other, those improving in form against those in winning form. It is a positive factor if the trainer of a horse is one of the better ones.

Section 62.19
Performance Consistency

The degree of performance consistency of horses varies greatly — from the courageous, reliable and consistent performers to the erratic, unreliable unpredictable, inconsistent performers. Statistics in themselves (that is, number of wins, number of placings, total prize money won, average prize money per start) are not true indicators of consistency: Consider other factors such as the training program of the horse, the setting of the horse for a particular race, the pattern of its runs in previous preparations, and so on. Indeed, consistent horses display a predictable pattern which they tend to repeat throughout their careers.

Section 62.20
Bandages

A horse can race in bandages, provided that the Rules are observed in all respects.

Some of the disadvantages of bandages are discomfort to the horse; extra weight on the horse's legs, particularly in wet weather; impeding of action of horse's joints and hence galloping action if the bandages are applied too tightly; and hindering of the circulation.

A horse racing in bandages is generally not sound in all respects for racing. It may have tendon trouble or sore shins. Some horses race regularly in protective bandages, however, and become used to wearing them.

When a horse races for a period in bandages and then races clean-legged, there is usually significant improvement in its performance.

As a general punting rule, horses wearing bandages should not be backed unless they always wear bandages in their races. Remember the old adage not to back a horse wearing bandages on a heavy track.

Section 62.21
Other Negative Factors

Other horses that may be eliminated as chances include the following:
- Horses that have not won for twelve months or more, including any spell.
- Horses from overseas, except known horses from New Zealand, until they have shown their ability against Australian horses on Australian courses.
- Horses that have a disproportionately high rate of placings to wins. These horses lack the will to win, but may be good place-betting propositions.
- Horses used to running clockwise (or as the case may be, anti-clockwise) having their first start at a track where the running is anti-clockwise (or as the case may be clockwise).

- Horses that are unreliable and never run two races alike. These horses may occasionally win or run a place (invariably at long odds), but in the long term they are best avoided.
- Horses that are both aged and inconsistent.
- Horses five-years-old or older that are still contesting standard restricted class races.

During the mating season (spring and the early summer months) fillies and mares should be eliminated as chances from mixed-sex races, except those fillies or mares that have been showing consistently good form and are well weighted.

Section 62.22
Final Relative Handicap

When doing the weight-rating calculation relative to each horse:

(a) minus signs are used for the rating of the qualifying run and the better or bonus adjustments;

(b) plus signs are used for the weight to be carried and the worse or penalty adjustments.

The horse with the highest "minus" relative handicap is the first selection, the horse nearest to it is the second selection, and so on.

Section 62.23
Final Relative Handicap on "0"

Total relative handicaps may be levelled off on an "0" basis. The highest negative handicap figure is called "0" and this is the top-rated selection. Other handicap figures are adjusted accordingly. The minus and plus signs are omitted because all values other than "0" become positive. The relative difference between runners is then more easily seen. This is shown in the following example.

Horse No.	1	2	3	4	7	9	*5, 6, 8, 10
Final relative handicap (kg)	−7.5	−5.5	−10.5	−9	−9.5	−6	−
On "0"	+3	+5	0	+1.5	+1	+4.5	−
Selections			1st		3rd	2nd	*Eliminated

These final handicap figures on "0" can be used to calculate the chances of contestants in terms of price, that is, betting odds.

Section 62.24
Selections

After the handicap weights have been calculated for a particular race:

(a) Where a horse has an advantage of 3 or more kilograms, that horse becomes a standout selection;

(b) Where a horse has an advantage of less than 3kg, that horse becomes the selection, but in this case it would be wise to save on the second selection.

(c) Where no horse has a clear advantage or where there are a number of horses close together no selection can be made and the race should be bypassed.

(d) Again, where the first, second, and third selections are frontrunners the race should be bypassed. The horse that sits patiently behind them is likely to win.

PART 25 APPLICATION OF WEIGHT RATINGS

CHAPTER 63 FRAMING A MARKET ON WEIGHT RATINGS

Section 63.1
Assessment of Chances in Terms of Prices

Relative weight ratings have proved to be an important method of assessing chances of horses winning a race in terms of weight. and winning in terms of prices, that is, betting odds. This allows the person who uses the weight-rating method to determine what are fair prices about weight-rating predictions.

Section 63.2
Calculation of Prices

Here is a worksheet example followed by explanatory notes.

Horse no.	1	2	3	4	7	9	(*5, 6, 8, 10)
Final relative handicap on "0"	+3	+5	0	+1.5	+1	+4.5	
Allocation of points	44	17	130	80	95	21	(387)
Points expressed as %	10.2	4.0	30.2	18.6	22.1	4.9	10 (100)
Percentages converted to prices	9/1	25/1	9/4	9/2	7/2	20/1	

*Eliminated

In the example there are ten runners of which four are eliminated as having little or no chance.

The final relative handicap figures are ascertained as explained in Section 62.23. They indicate the weight disadvantage of each other horse compared with the winning selection on "0".

Points are allocated on a theoretical winning chance basis to each such final relative handicap figure as per the following table and totalled.

PART 25 APPLICATION OF WEIGHT RATINGS

kg	POINTS	kg	POINTS
0.0	130	4.0	27
0.5	112	4.5	21
1.0	95	5.0	17
1.5	80	5.5	13
2.0	67	6.0	10
2.5	55	6.5	7
3.0	44	7.0	5
3.5	34	7.5	3

The eliminated horses are allowed a guarded 10 per cent and the allocated points are expressed as a percentage of the total points, that is, the points for each individual horse are divided by the total points and multiplied by 90 (100 per cent minus the allowance for eliminated horses which in this case is 10 per cent. This allowance may vary from 0 to 20 per cent, depending on the estimated chances of eliminated horses, if any. The market is thus framed to 100 per cent to determine fair prices.

Percentages are then converted to prices as per the table to Section 53.5. If the price on-course is less than such calculated price it is under value.

The example above is worked to show the fair prices of runners, based on their relative weight ratings, while the opening market used by bookmakers is framed well over-round — usually to about 130. This means that prices are quoted below real price-chances. This guarded opening is a protection against unanticipated or heavy betting for a particular runner or runners. What happens to the opening prices is determined by the circumstances of the betting ring.

Section 63.3
Amount of Stake and Price Limit

Having assessed the chances of horses in a race, in terms of both weight and betting odds, the amount of the betting stake and the acceptable price limit should be related to the quality of horse selected and the class of race. For example, it is suggested that the stake be related to the quality of horse as follows: champion × 3 units; high × 2; good × 1; medium × 0.5; poor, no bet.

It is also suggested that the price be not less than from 2/1 to 4/1 considering the class of race assessed (see Section 61.3) and the relevant facts and factors about that race and the quality of the horse selected. The arithmetical average of winners' prices is about 4/1

The term "weight ratings" is thus seen to be linked by its very nature with the terms "betting to prices", "betting to percentages" and "value betting".

CHAPTER 64 THE FLOW OF WEIGHT RATING DATA FROM SOURCE TO USER

Section 64.1
Source of Race Results

As mentioned in Section 51.1, after a race meeting is held anywhere in Australia the race club holding that meeting and the stewards of that meeting prepare and forward through the relevant District Racing Association to the relevant State Principal Club, reports setting out prescribed information about the meeting and the races that were conducted.

The club's report is required to set out particulars about:

- the class or type of each race, actual distance over which the race was run, the official time taken by the winner, the state of the track at the time the race was run, prize moneys;
- horses that competed in each of those races, that is., name, age, sex, colour, allotted weight, allowances and overweights, barrier positions;
- position in which each horse finished in each race, margins between those positions;
- pedigrees of placed horses; and
- owners and trainers of placed horses.

The stewards' report is required to set out particulars of anything that may have affected the running of a horse in a race; any loss or breakage of gear during a race or any unusual happening in connection with it; all objections or complaints made to them; offences dealt with; fines or other punishment inflicted; and any action taken by them.

The abovenamed reports are, in turn, relayed to the Racing Services Bureau referred to in Chapter 51 which promptly makes that information available to Bureau subscribers.

Section 64.2
Source of Race Fields

After race days have been allotted to race clubs, the administrators of those clubs prepare programs for the meetings to be held on those days and advise their District Racing Association and State Principal Club of this. The Principal Clubs approve the programs which they then advertise in their monthly *Racing Calendars* for the information of owners, trainers, and other interested parties.

In due course the clubs receive nominations, allot weights, declare acceptances, draw barriers and record details of declared riders.

All this information about race fields for coming meetings throughout Australia then flows through official channels to the Racing Services Bureau and is recorded on its computerised Bulletin Board.

Section 64.3
Supply of Race Results and Race Fields to Interested Parties

Access to the various components of the Racing Services Bureau database and Bulletin Board is available to officials of race clubs and associations (handicappers, stewards, and so on), officials of the Totalisator Agency Boards, and to any interested person who subscribes for any such information.

The Australian Associated Press Racing Services supplies from its database and Bulletin Board, particulars of fields and relative form guides to newspapers, to specialist racing papers, and to any interested person who makes arrangements and subscribes in that regard.

Section 64.4
Weight Rating Service Database

This information is referred to as foundation rating data which the weight rating services, described in Chapter 58, can obtain from the Racing Services Bureau, or other appropriate source, on the performances of horses that competed at all or selected race meetings (say, all metropolitan meetings and the more important provincial and country meetings of one or more States).

These services then analyse and assess those performances in the light of pertinent facts and factors as revealed by: the foundation data referred to above; stewards' reports; video tape replays; quality pictures taken at various stages of a race, particularly at the home turn, leger and finish; and any other information to which the service may have access.

That relevant information is assigned weight equivalents and the weight ratings calculated along the lines explained in Chapters 59 and 60. All that information is then recorded in the computer database of the relevant weight rating service.

Section 64.5
Weight Rating Service Bulletin Board

There are several organisations (for particulars refer to Punters' Choice) that now offer computerised weight rating services to subscribers. While they all start with the same basic rating data (supplied by the Racing Services Bureau) their rating assessment input depends upon their personal opinion, whether objective or subjective. Punters may choose whichever system suits them personally for costs, accessibility, simplicity, and easy assimilation of the form of presentation of information.

Having established and maintained timely information in its computer database, a weight rating service will also maintain a Bulletin Board and display

(a) particulars of fields for upcoming race meetings for which it provides a service to subscribers;

(b) particulars drawn from the database about the past performances (including weight ratings) of horses competing in races to be run at those meetings;

(c) in cases where the service also provides a selection service, comparisons of relative weights of horses in each such race indicating the chances and their prices for the weight rating system.

In other words, a weight rating service may supply to subscribers details of the rating database about competitors in specified events, leaving it to those subscribers to carry out their own selection procedures or, alternatively, the service may itself carry out the selecting and pricing procedure and provide details of its selections and prices to subscribers — at a price, of course.

Section 64.6
The Rating Bureau (TRB)

Earlier I acknowledged that this book is, in fact, an updating and expansion of Rem Plante's 1964 publication *Australian Horse Racing and Punters' Guide*. While there are several people or companies offering various rating services to punters it would be remiss of me not to comment, albeit briefly and broadly, on the rating services started by Rem and continued and developed over the years by his son Marcel and his associates.

In the days of manual recording Plante and Associates prepared and issued to subscribers weekly Weight Rating Charts. (I was one of the many people who successfully used these charts over the years.)

In time, Plante and Associates formed a private company called "The Rating Bureau Pty Ltd" (TRB) and moved into the field of modern technology. Its first computerised service was named *Formline* which was upgraded in 1993 to *Formline Gold* and further upgraded in 1996 to *Wingold*.

In addition to *Wingold,* the Bureau through Trackform Marketing, a Division of TRB, also markets a service called Winline. This is basically a "speed" rating service developed and maintained by Dennis Walker. At the time of writing, a new service called *Winline GT,* a combined class, weight and speed rating service, is also being introduced. (See Section 59.15.)

The TRB also maintains a most comprehensive master database with a correlated Bulletin Board at its headquarters at Sydney. Data for every race conducted at every meeting in Australia on which the TAB provides a betting service is available to subscribers from the Bulletin Board 24 hours a day.

Subscriber installation requirements for any of the TRB services are a compatible PC and a floppy manager program. Hook-up to the TRB Bulletin Board is by telephone via modem. The subscriber may accept TRB final selections and odds or alternatively display on the PC the available options and apply his or her own modifications to determine final chances and their odds.

PART 26

ADMINISTRATION OF THE RACING INDUSTRY

Chapter	65	Origin of Racing and Racing Administration
Section	65.1	Origin of Racing
	65.2	Origin of Racing Administration in England
	65.3	Development of Racing in Australia
	65.4	The Racing Industry
	65.5	Racing Areas and Hierarchical Orders
Chapter	66	Structure of Racing Control
Section	66.1	Australian System of Control Modelled on English System
	66.2	Structure of Control
	66.3	Regulation by State Governments
	66.4	Government Revenue from Racing
	66.5	Racing Development Funds
Chapter	67	The Role of Principal Clubs
Section	67.1	Australian Rules of Racing
	67.2	Local Rules of Racing
	67.3	Functions and Powers of a Principal Club
	67.4	Racing Calendars
	67.5	Accountability of a Principal Club
	67.6	The Role of Racing Stewards
Chapter	68	The Role of District Racing Associations
Section	68.1	Constitution of District Racing Associations
	68.2	Powers and Duties of a District Racing Association
	68.3	Accountability of a District Racing Association
Chapter	69	The Role of Race Clubs
Section	69.1	Constitution and Registration of Race Clubs
	69.2	Dissolution of a Race Club
	69.3	Race Club Revenue and Expenditure
	69.4	Race Club Capital Expenditure
	69.5	Application of Race Club Profits
	69.6	Accountability of Race Clubs
	69.7	Some Racing Industry Statistics

PART 26 ADMINISTRATION OF THE RACING INDUSTRY

CHAPTER 65 ORIGIN OF RACING AND RACING ADMINISTRATION

Section 65.1
Origin of Racing

The origin of racing in one form or another probably dates back to soon after the horse was first domesticated — probably between 7000 to 5000 years ago.

Hittite cuneiform tablets indicate that those ancient people of Asia Minor raced horses about 4000 years ago.

Some 2600 years ago there was horse racing in Greece. Mounted horses competed in events staged at the Twenty-third Olympic Games held about that time. The Romans probably learnt of the sport from the Greeks because, soon after that Olympiad, chariot races were held at the Circus, a large arena in Rome. The Romans and Egyptians also staged mounted races on the flat.

The Romans seem to have introduced racing into Britain. For about 1000 years following the Roman occupation of the country, racing was practised in a limited way — publicly in market places or privately as matches between patricians.

In the early part of the seventeenth century King James I built a palace at Newmarket and members of his Court soon established the sport of horse racing there. During his reign from 1603 to 1625 good horses were imported to improve the speed and stamina of the British horses.

Racing continued at Newmarket under Charles I who reigned from 1625 to 1649. After the Civil War Oliver Cromwell was the lord protector of the Commonwealth from 1653 to 1658 and horse racing was prohibited.

In 1660 England and Ireland saw the restoration of the monarchy and the return of Charles II. Charles had a passion for horse racing and during his reign from 1660 to 1685 the sport flourished at Newmarket. Whereas previously most races had been match races, the monarch organised stamina-testing races over four miles (6.4 km) for horses five-year-old and upwards with most races decided after three or four heats with half-hour rests between heats. These races were called "Royal Plates".

About the middle of the eighteenth century four-year-old racing was introduced which was soon followed by three-year-old racing. It was towards the end of the eighteenth century that two-year-old racing began.

Associated with the development of forms of racing was the development of a better class of racehorse from native mares and imported eastern stallions. This culminated at the end of the eighteenth century with the development and establishment of the thoroughbred as an independent breed.

In about 1790 the handicap race was introduced to be followed many years later by weight-for-age races.

Section 65.2
Origin of Racing Administration in England

Racing for many years had been the sport of the wealthy and gradually it won the interest of the general public and burgeoned.

The professional jockey and the professional trainer emerged. Many racecourses were constructed, particularly during the early part of the eighteenth century — including, during the reign of Queen Anne, the Royal Ascot Racecourse in Berkshire.

Overall control of racing was lax and there became a pressing need for the protection of the public to regulate and control the growing industry. In the Newmarket area this became the function and responsibility of the Jockey Club which had originated in the 1750s as a social club for gentlemen interested in breeding and racing horses.

Not only was the Jockey Club's aim to regulate and control the racing industry in the Newmarket area eventually achieved but in time the Club's influence spread and it became, and still is, the principal racing authority in Britain with such powers as the sanctioning of racecourse construction, licensing of participants in the industry, approving of race meetings and programs, and the framing of racing rules. Indeed, it became the model for the constitution of Principal Clubs in Australia and similar authorities established in other countries for the regulation and control of thoroughbred racing.

Section 65.3
Development of Racing in Australia

Like most features of Australian life horse racing was imported from Britain. During the first 100 years, however, the sport was somewhat primitive, unordered and, indeed, unrestrained with a distinctly Australian character. Race meetings were mainly social gatherings with novelty events and heavy drinking bouts.

By the latter half of the nineteenth century, horse racing was a national sport — a sport that had a great effect upon our social and cultural life. By that time race clubs had been formed throughout the length and breadth of the country. These clubs not only constructed racecourses and conducted race meetings, but also organised the associated social functions such as dinners, dances, balls, carnivals, fairs, and so on. Communities in the cities, towns, and bush were brought together by racing for the highlights of social life.

The story of the development of racing in Australia is well documented.

Section 65.4
The Racing Industry

For most of us racing is a sport, a recreation, or a pastime. We pursue racing for pleasure, relaxation, enjoyment, and possible gain. And it has been so since the days when horses were introduced into the early colonial settlements to assist settlers in most fields of their endeavours.

Over the years, however, the emphasis has moved from racing's contribution to our social and cultural life to racing's contribution to the economy, particularly its huge contribution to the coffers of the State Treasuries. State governments now see racing only as an "industry".

Apart then from being a very large entertainment activity, thoroughbred racing is also a very large-scale business undertaking or industry. It encompasses such activities as the breeding, owning, training, management, riding and racing of thoroughbreds; on-course and off-course betting; race club operations; and Principal Club and government administrative control. In terms of employment it involves all the people or associations of people directly or indirectly, full-time or part-time, permanently, or casually, in the above activities.

A very large and complex industry, it contributes very significantly to the economy of the nation in various ways including the following:

- It makes an important contribution to the nation's Gross Domestic Product.
- It is one of the nation's largest employers and provides income and, therefore, spending ability to employees in the industry.
- It generates high levels of turnover or revenue for breeders, race clubs, totalisator operators, bookmakers, and so on.
- In particular, for State governments, it generates substantial revenues from totalisator turnover tax, bookmakers' turnover tax, and betting ticket tax.

The industry is of significant national importance and it is vital that all its aspects be properly controlled.

Section 65.5
Racing Areas and Hierarchical Orders

Racing in Australia is divided into three administrative areas, namely, metropolitan, provincial, and country areas. In terms of hierarchical orders of racing, the four orders are metropolitan, provincial, country, and picnic. The distinction between provincial and country and between country and picnic is sometimes vague.

CHAPTER 66 STRUCTURE OF RACING CONTROL

Section 66.1
Australian System of Control Modelled on English System

Broad patterns of control and administration that had been established for thoroughbred racing in England were transplanted by the early European settlers to the Australian colonies. Indeed most countries modelled their thoroughbred racing organisation on the English system.

Section 66.2
Structure of Control

The structure of regulation and control of the racing industry in Australia is one where the dominant roles are played (a) by the State governments exercising broad control through legislation, and (b) subject to that legislation, by the Principal Club or clubs of each State exercising detailed operation, control and supervision of racing in their respective areas of responsibility.

The Commonwealth Government is not involved directly with any regulation or control of the industry.

Section 66.3
Regulation By State Governments

The governments of the States of Australia, through various Acts of their Legislatures, have provided for the broad regulation and control of the racing industry within the separate areas of their responsibility.

The objects of that legislation and subsidiary legislation include such matters as administration of the racing industry by a Minister of the Crown or a government department or statutory body assisting the Minister; control over Principal Clubs, racing clubs and other racing bodies; regulation of bookmakers, totalisators and betting; suppression of unlawful betting; the raising of taxes and other revenue; and so on.

Section 66.4
Government Revenue From Racing

Revenue collected by each State government from the racing industry is substantial. Such revenue comprises taxation on turnovers of bookmakers, on-course totalisators and off-course totalisators and, in addition, tax on betting tickets of bookmakers.

Section 66.5
Racing Development Funds

A Racing Development Fund has been established by the government of each State to assist race clubs improve their facilities.

The income of the Fund consists mainly of levies on turnovers of all totalisators; the unpaid fractions, unpaid dividends, unpaid refunds, and surplus moneys of totalisators; instalments of interest and redemption; and grants from TAB profits.

Payments are made from the Fund to race clubs by way of low interest or interest-free loans or, as the case may be, non-repayable grants, to assist clubs to meet the cost of capital or special requirements; and in some cases to the government department or agencies assisting the Minister for Racing.

PART 26 ADMINISTRATION OF THE RACING INDUSTRY

CHAPTER 67 THE ROLE OF PRINCIPAL CLUBS

Section 67.1
Australian Rules of Racing

Subject to the broad controls of State legislation the Australian racing industry is self-regulated through Principal Club control.

To provide uniformity in control throughout Australia, all Principal Clubs have adopted rules called the "Australian Rules of Racing". These rules were made some decades ago by the Conference of Principal Clubs and have been amended from time to time at regular or special meetings of the Conference.

At the present time the Principal Clubs of Australia for the purposes of the Australian Rules of Racing and their voting power at a Conference are as shown in the following Table.

STATE	VOTING POWER	PRINCIPAL CLUB	LOCATION OF SECRETARIAT
New South Wales (Incl. A.C.T.)	6	*NSW Thoroughbred Racing Board	Sydney
Victoria	6	Victoria Racing Club	Melbourne
Queensland	5	*Queensland Principal Club	Brisbane
South Australia	4	South Australian Jockey Club	Adelaide
Western Australia	4	Western Australian Turf Club	Perth
Tasmania	2	*Tasmanian Thoroughbred Racing Council	Hobart
Northern Territory	1	Darwin Turf Club	Darwin

*A body created by Act of Parliament. Not a race club.

Legislation of the States and Territories listed in the table provide for, and underpin, the principle of self-regulation of the thoroughbred racing industry by Principal Club control. Further the Australian Rules of Racing provide that no member of a Principal Club shall be directly appointed by a government.

The committees of the race clubs indicated in the table are also ex officio the committees of the relative Principal Clubs. Members of the committees are experienced professional or business persons having long association with the racing industry who give their services on a part-time basis.

At times there have been proposals or threats to abrogate the powers of a Principal Club and to vest such powers in a State government agency or instrumentality under the control of the Minister for Racing. Those occasions were usually during periods of disagreement between the Minister and office-bearers of the clubs or during periods of scandal in the industry. Any proposal to remove control, however, to politicians, bureaucrats, or political appointees and so empowering those persons to administer regulations made by themselves, is fraught with danger. History shows that almost without exception business enterprises conducted by State governments have ended in dismal administrative and financial failure.

With reference to scandals, these have always been associated with racing, and the industry, rather than suffering any damage, has not only emerged unscathed, but seemingly thrived on them.

Section 67.2
Local Rules of Racing

In addition to adopting the Australian Rules of Racing, each Principal Club has adopted local Rules to meet the specific needs of local circumstances. The Rules governing racing in the territory of each Principal Club are, therefore, an amalgamation of the Australian Rules and the local Rules which as so amalgamated are called "The Local Rules of Racing of (the Principal Club concerned)".

Section 67.3
Functions and Powers of a Principal Club

A Principal Club is a body corporate or unincorporate, constituted by legislation or under the authority of State legislation and charged with functions:

(a) to control, supervise, regulate and promote racing within its area of jurisdiction being a State, Territory, or part thereof; and

(b) to initiate, develop, and implement policies it considers conducive to the development and welfare of the racing industry within that area, and the protection of the public interest in relation to that industry.

A Principal Club is vested with powers to do all such things as are necessary, incidental, or convenient to be done for, or in connection with, the performance of its functions referred to above.

Included in its functions and duties are such things as these:

- to consider and report to the Minister for Racing on matters that may be referred to it by the Minister or that it may raise on its own initiation;
- to make or amend the Local Rules of Racing;
- to allocate to race clubs or, as the case may be, to recommend to the Minister, the days and times on, and the places at which, race clubs may hold race meetings;
- to investigate, determine or, as the case may be, make recommendation relative to any application for the construction of a new racecourse or the alteration or renovation of an existing racecourse;
- to register, refuse to register or suspend the registration of a race club; supervise the activities of race clubs; where necessary appoint an administrator to conduct the affairs of a race club; direct or supervise the dissolution of a race club;
- to license (a "licence" includes a permit), cancel or suspend the licence of a trainer, jockey, bookmaker, bookmaker's clerk, apprentice jockey, stable foreman, stablehand, farrier or other person associated with racing; and supervise the activities of such licensed persons and all other persons engaged in or associated with racing;
- to renew licences annually;
- to register or refuse to register a racehorse; or disqualify or exclude a horse from participating in a race;
- to impose fees and charges for its services with respect to licensing, registration, etc;
- to impose a penalty on any licensee or owner for a contravention of the Rules of Racing;
- and so on.

The licensing process for the people referred to above, among other things, forms certain barriers to entry into each licensed group. These barriers, by restricting the number of licences of each group, influence the level of earnings of people in each such group and protect them from unreasonable competition.

Section 67.4
Racing Calendars

Each Principal Club issues monthly *The Racing Calendar* (of the Principal Club concerned) and publishes therein details of matters relating to racing, including particulars of future race meetings; the registration and licensing of horses and participant people; riding weights of jockeys and apprentices; allowances of apprentices; amendments to the Rules of Racing; and various other racing information.

Section 67.5
Accountability of a Principal Club

Expenditure is incurred by a Principal Club for salaries of administrative staff and stewards; insurance of jockeys and stablehands; publication of the monthly *Racing Calendar*; and other relevant items. Expenditure is financed from recovery of costs of providing services to race clubs; licence and registration fees; sales of the *Racing Calendar*; in some cases, contribution from the Racing Development Fund; and other relevant sources.

As soon as practicable after the close of each financial year, the Principal Club must prepare a report on its activities and financial transactions during that year and its financial position at the end of that year. The Principal Club is also required to furnish a copy of that report to the Minister of the Crown responsible for racing who, in turn, has responsibility for reporting to the Executive Government and to Parliament.

Section 67.6
The Role of Racing Stewards

Stewards are officials appointed by a Principal Club (or by a District Racing Association acting under delegated power of the Principal Club) to assist in the control and promotion of racing within the territory of the Principal Club (or as the case may be, District Racing Association). Their particular function is to act at every race meeting held in that territory. When so acting at a race meeting they are the stewards of the race club holding that meeting.

Stewards are termed or grouped as "stipendiary stewards" or "honorary stewards". Stipendiary stewards are those who are employed on a full-time basis and who are paid a fixed remuneration for their services. Honorary stewards are those who, under certain circumstances, serve gratuitously, carrying out such duties as betting steward, photo-finish steward, and so on.

Again, under certain circumstances, persons may be appointed as deputy stewards or assistant stewards to assist stewards in the performance of their duties.

In the case of country race meetings, the Rules of Racing are sometimes relaxed for the number of stewards required to act so as to permit one or a limited number of stipendiary stewards to act at a meeting with assistance from deputy stewards. Where, however, no stipendiary stewards or deputy stewards are available, three members of the committee of that race club may act as stewards for the meeting.

Stewards are vested with powers and charged with duties under the Rules of Racing and the Rules of Betting. Their main duty is, as stated earlier, to act at every race meeting in the area for which they are appointed and to observe that races are run, and the meeting conducted, in accordance with the Rules. In cases where they observe breaches of the Rules, they are authorised to take disciplinary action against the person or horse concerned.

Stewards of a race meeting confer after each race is run, carry out necessary inquiries, view closed-circuit video coverage, and make necessary decisions. For the purpose of good public relations — to assure the public that every horse, every jockey and every happening in every race is subject to close scrutiny — they prepare a report as soon as practicable after the event and release it to the media.

The stewards' race report sets forth particulars of anything that may have affected the running of every horse in that race; any loss or breakage of gear during the race; any objections or complaints made to them; any offences dealt with; and any other action taken by them.

After the race meeting, the stewards of that meeting prepare and forward to the Principal Club concerned (or the District Racing Association being the agent of the Principal Club) a report setting out prescribed information about that meeting and the races conducted there.

The electronic media plays an important role throughout race day via radio, and television — including on-course closed-circuit television.

The print media uses the stewards' report as the basis of racing copy. It is also published verbatim in some newspapers and specialised racing publications. Relevant excerpts are also recorded in the databases of past performances of horses and published in form guides for future races in which they compete.

The responsibilities of stewards are onerous and multifarious. Their role is a vital one and needs to be undertaken in a fully professional manner in order to maintain public confidence in racing.

CHAPTER 68   THE ROLE OF DISTRICT RACING ASSOCIATIONS

Section 68.1
Constitution of District Racing Associations

Principal clubs have found it effective and expedient to discharge their responsibilities throughout the large area of their territory, being a State or part of it, by decentralising their administrative control.

Decentralisation has been accomplished by each Principal Club by: (a) dividing the areas outside the metropolitan area into districts; (b) grouping all race clubs holding registered race meetings within each such district into an association with respect to that district; (c) delegating certain powers and duties conferred or imposed on the Principal Club to those associations; and (d) ensuring that the powers and duties so delegated are properly incorporated into the constitutions or articles of the district associations.

Section 68.2
Powers and Duties of a District Racing Association

Powers and duties of an association usually include such matters as the following, that is, the power or duty (a) to license or register participants in the racing industry in its district; (b) to fix dates upon which racing meetings may be held by affiliated clubs; (c) to appoint stewards to assist in the control of racing within its district; (d) to hear first-level appeals from decisions of stewards; (e) to investigate and deal with any matter about racing within its district; and (f) to do such other things necessary or convenient to be done for, or in connection with the performance of its functions.

The powers and duties of a district association are exercised or performed for, and on behalf of, the association by an executive committee.

Section 68.3
Accountability of a District Racing Association

The committee of each District Racing Association is required to report annually on its activities and financial operations to its associated race clubs, to its Principal Club, and through the Principal Club to the Minister for Racing of the State concerned.

CHAPTER 69 THE ROLE OF RACE CLUBS

Section 69.1
Constitution and Registration of Race Clubs

In earlier history of racing in Australia private investors owned racecourses and held race meetings for personal profit. Today, however, all racing is conducted on a non-proprietary basis. Proprietary and unregistered racing is prohibited by law.

A race club is a body or association of persons, corporate or unincorporate:

- that is formed to promote, hold or control race meetings for galloping horses;
- that is non-proprietary (See Section 69.5); and
- that is registered by a Principal Club.

A race club may conduct race meetings only on the dates allocated to it by the Principal Club or other authorised body.

When a race club that is not a body corporate acquires land for use as a racing venue the title to such land is vested in trustees. The relationship in which the trustees hold the land for the benefit of members of the race club is fiduciary.

Section 69.2
Dissolution of a Race Club

Under certain circumstances, a Principal Club may dissolve the committee of a race club, appoint an administrator of the club for a period, and arrange for the election of a new committee of that club.

The race club itself may be dissolved under certain circumstances in accordance with its constitution, the Rules of Racing, and the relevant state law.

Section 69.3
Race Club Revenue and Expenditure

Sources from which revenue is derived include: membership subscriptions; bookmakers' fielding fees and levies; on-course totalisator commission; TAB profits distribution; public admission charges; radio and television rights; sponsorships; nomination, acceptance and various other prescribed fees; and so on.

Expenditure is incurred under headings such as: racing expenses being prize money, race-day wages and ancillary costs, closed-circuit television costs, stewards' fees, swabbing fees, rebates, and so on.; racecourse maintenance expenses being wages and ancillary costs, materials and services; administration and miscellaneous expenses being staff salaries and ancillary costs, maintenance of office equipment, stationery, printing, telephones, postage and the like; interest on loans; depreciation of assets.

Clubs aim to keep prize money at the highest possible level so that race fields will be as large as practicable and comprise the best available horses.

Sponsorships, that is, large contributions by sponsors towards capital works programs and prize money are significant and directly benefit the sponsors and the clubs and the racing industry generally.

Section 69.4
Race Club Capital Expenditure

Expenditure of a capital nature, that is, for the acquisition of assets may be financed by the raising of loan moneys from private sources. Clubs may apply for financial assistance from the government-controlled Racing Development Funds, however, by way of low interest or interest-free loans, or non-repayable grants, to meet capital expenditure for certain purposes. Those purposes include the acquisition of land for racing or the improvement of facilities on racecourses.

Section 69.5
Application of Race Club Profits

Every race club is non-proprietary, that is, the constitution of the club must (a) provide for the application of its profits, if any, to the promotion of racing and (b) prohibit the distribution of any profit directly or indirectly among members of the club. That prohibition does not, of course, prevent payment by a club to a member for such things as prize money won or professional services rendered. Nor does it prevent expenditure for reasonable entertainment of members.

Section 69.6
Accountability of Race Clubs

As soon as practicable after the close of each financial year, a race club is required to furnish to its Principal Club or, as the case may be, District Racing Association, a report on its activities and financial transactions during that year and its financial position at the end of that year.

Section 69.7
Some Racing Industry Statistics

The Appendix that follows gives some Australian thoroughbred racing industry statistics about the 1992 – 1993 season. Relative statistics for the 1989 – 1990 season are also quoted for comparison. Such figures were compiled from data published by the Victoria Racing Club.

APPENDIX

SOME AUSTRALIAN THOROUGHBRED RACING STATISTICS — 1992–1993 SEASON

1989–90				1992–93
492	Race Clubs	No. registered at 31 July 1993		480
412	Racecourses	No. registered at 31 July 1993		410
3 715	Racemeetings	No. conducted		3 589
25 214	Races	No. of races run		24 390
7		Av. no. of races per meeting		7
$7 534		Av. prize money per race		$8 158
243 021	Starters	No. of starters in those races		239 560
10		Av. no. of starters per race		10
37 264	Horses	No of individual horses started		36 707
7		Av. no. of starts per horse		7
$5 098		Av. prize money won per horse (Note 1)		$5 420
$15 000		Av. cost of racing and training a horse		$16 000
$29.2m	Prize money	65 Group 1 Races	$27.5m (Note 2)	
$10.0m		69 Group 2 Races	$9.1m	
$7.5m		96 Group 3 Races	$7.2m	
$11.4m		284 Listed Races	$13.4m	
$131.8m		23 876 Other Races	$141.7m	
$189.9m		24 390 races		$198.9m
$754.9m	Betting Turnover	On-course Totalisators	$753.5m	
$7 059.1m		Off-course Totalisator	$7 962.5m	
$2 088.6m		Bookmakers	$1 470.1m	
$9 902.6m		Total Betting Turnover		$10 186.1m
2 890	T.A.B	No. of TAB Agencies and Pubtabs		3 400
428 800		No. of TAB telephone betting accounts		450 000
--	"Licencees"	No. of trainers		7 350
		No. of (flat) jockeys		1 200
		No. of apprentices		400
		No. of registered stablehands		7 000
39 201	Australian Studbook Returns	No. of mares "returned" 1993		35 120
3 260		No. of stallions "returned" 1993		2 473
21 983		No. of foals bred 1993		18 627
--	Attendances	No. of persons that attended race meetings		6.2m

Note 1: "Veandercross" (NZ) won $1.7m while seven other horses won in excess of $1m in the season.
Note 2: Two races had prize money in excess of $2m and five others in excess of $1m.

BIBLIOGRAPHY

Anderson, C. W. 1963, *Complete Book of Horses and Horsemanship*, Macmillan Publishing Co., New York

Brander, Michael *The Complete Guide to Horsemanship*, 2nd edn, Adam and Charles Black, London.

Hayes, M. Horace 1983 *Veterinary Notes for Horse Owners*, Anchor Press Ltd, Great Britain

Johnson, J. W. G. 1982, *The Crumbling Theory of Evolution*, Queensland Binding Service, Brisbane, Australia.

Lasley, John F. 1981, *Genetic Principles in Horse Breeding*, (rev edn) Horseman Books (Cordovan Publications) Houston USA

Lemon, Andrew 1987, *The History of Australian Thoroughbred Racing*, Classic Reproductions, Melbourne, Australia.

Low, Sampson 1980, *The World Atlas of Horses & Ponies*, Purnell and Sons Limited and Chris Milsome Limited, Berkshire, England.

Macdonald, Janet W. 1982, *The Right Horse—An Owners' and Buyers' Guide*, Methuen London Ltd, Suffolk.

McLeod, Neil & Skinner, Alan 1986, *Horse Australia*, Dorr/McLeod Publishing, West Heidelberg, Australia.

Paterson, A. B. 'Banjo' 1984, *Song of the Pen*, Lansdowne Press, Sydney, Australia.

Plante, Rem, 1974, *Australian Horse Racing and Punters' Guide*, Horwitz Publications, Sydney

Pollard, Jack *the Pictorial History of Australian Horseracing*, Lansdowne Press, Sydney, Australia.

Robinson, Harry 1984, *The Bookie Book*, Griffin Press Limited, South Australia

Rossdale, Peter 1981, *Horse Breeding*, David & Charles Inc, Vermont, USA

Sauter, Frederick J. & Glover, John A *Behaviour, Development, and Training of the Horse*, Arco Publishing, Inc., New York

Sayer, Angela 1982, *The World of Horses*, Hamlyn Publishing Group Limited, Middlesex, England.

Scott, Don 1990, *Winning in the '90s*, Horwitz Grahame Pty. Ltd, Sydney, Australia

Schuster, Simon 1990, *A Portrait of Racing*, Simon and Schuster, Brookvale, Australia.

Taylor, Peter 1986, *Thoroughbred Studs of Australia & New Zealand*, Allen & Unwin, Sydney, Australia.

Willis, Larryann C. 1979, *Horse-breeding Farm*, Thomas Yoseloff Ltd, London, England.

Wright, Maurice 1983, *The Jeffery Method of Horse Handling*, Griffin Press Limited, South Australia.

Australian Jockey Club 1993, *Thoroughbred Breeders' Guide to the Australian Stud Book*, Guilfoyle Printing Pty Ltd, Australia.

CHAPTER 37 STABLES AND STABLECRAFT — 146
- Section 37.1 Training Stables — 146
- Section 37.2 Care of the Stabled Racehorse — 146
- Section 37.3 Stable Routines — 147
- Section 37.4 Grooming — 147
- Section 37.5 Bedding — 147
- Section 37.6 Mucking-Out — 148
- Section 37.7 Clipping — 148

CHAPTER 38 SADDLERY — 149
- Section 38.1 Meaning of Term — 149
- Section 38.2 Racing Gear — 149
- Section 38.3 Some Items of Saddlery — 149

CHAPTER 39 STABLE AND OTHER VICES OF THE RACEHORSE — 152
- Section 39.1 Causes of Vices — 152
- Section 39.2 Common Vices — 152

CHAPTER 40 JOCKEYS — 156
- Section 40.1 Authorised Riders — 156
- Section 40.2 Jockeys — 156
- Section 40.3 Apprentice Jockeys — 156
- Section 40.4 Apprentices' Allowances — 157
- Section 40.5 Restrictions on Jockeys and Apprentices — 158
- Section 40.6 Jockeys' Dress and Equipment — 158
- Section 40.7 State Jockey Poll — 158
- Section 40.8 Assessment of Jockeys' Ability — 158
- Section 40.9 Never Bet on Jockeys — 159
- Section 40.10 At the End of a Jockey's Career — 159

CHAPTER 41 FINANCIAL VIABILITY OF JOCKEYSHIP — 160
- Section 41.1 Income of Jockeys — 160
- Section 41.2 Riding Fees — 160
- Section 41.3 Retainer Fees — 160
- Section 41.4 Other Income of Jockeys — 160
- Section 41.5 Matters Affecting Earning Capacity of Jockeys — 161
- Section 41.6 Conclusion — 161

CHAPTER 42 JOCKEYSHIP — 162
- Section 42.1 Jockey and Horse Must Act as Combined Unit — 162
- Section 42.2 Horsemen and Mere Riders — 162
- Section 42.3 Qualities of Top Jockeys — 162
- Section 42.4 Stirrup Lengths — 163
- Section 42.5 Race Tactics — 163
- Section 42.6 Use of the Whip — 163
- Section 42.7 Use of Spurs — 164

CHAPTER 43 CLASSES AND TYPES OF RACES — 166
- Section 43.1 Definitions of Terms — 166
- Section 43.2 Division of Races into Classes — 166
- Section 43.3 Races for Two Year-Olds — 167
- Section 43.4 Races for Three-Year-Olds — 167
- Section 43.5 Standard Restricted Class Races — Old Format — 168
- Section 43.6 Standard Restricted Class Races — New Format — 168
- Section 43.7 Statistics Underpinning Scheme for Restricted Class 1–6 Races — 169
- Section 43.8 Special Restricted Races and Special Condition Races — 170
- Section 43.9 Open Fillies and Mares Races — 170
- Section 43.10 Open Class Races — 171
- Section 43.11 Group and Listed Races — 171
- Section 43.12 Classic Races — 172
- Section 43.13 The Melbourne Cup — 172
- Section 43.14 Picnic Races — 173

CHAPTER 44 WEIGHT-FOR-AGE SCALE — 174
- Section 44.1 Weight-for-Age Scale — 174
- Section 44.2 Use of WFA Scale for Handicapping — 176

CHAPTER 45 RACETRACKS GENERALLY — 178
- Section 45.1 Meaning of Terms "Racecourse" and "Racetrack" — 178
- Section 45.2 Racetrack Design — 178
- Section 45.3 Horses for Courses — 179
- Section 45.4 Barrier Stalls — 179
- Section 45.5 Barrier Positions — 180
- Section 45.6 Importance of Barrier Positions — 180
- Section 45.7 Limitation on Size of Fields — 181
- Section 45.8 Meaning of Term "Distance" — 181
- Section 45.9 State of the Going — 182
- Section 45.10 Cutaway Rail — 183

CHAPTER 46 METROPOLITAN RACE TRACKS AND BARRIER GUIDES — 184
- Section 46.1 Diagrams of Tracks and Barrier Tables — 184

CHAPTER 47 RACE MEETINGS GENERALLY — 206
- Section 47.1 Registered Race Meetings Held By Registered Clubs — 206
- Section 47.2 Other Registered Race Meetings — 206
- Section 47.3 Unregistered or Unlawful Race Meetings — 206
- Section 47.4 Postponement or Abandonment of Race Meeting — 206
- Section 47.5 Phantom Race Meetings — 207
- Section 47.6 Novelty Events at a Race Meeting — 207

CHAPTER 48 PRE-RACE DAY PROCEDURES — 208
- Section 48.1 Race Programs — 208
- Section 48.2 Nominations — 208
- Section 48.3 Allocation of Weights — 209
- Section 48.4 Bottom Limit Weight — 210
- Section 48.5 Minimum Top Weight — 210
- Section 48.6 Race Class Relativity Weight Scale — 210
- Section 48.7 Weights to be Raised — 212
- Section 48.8 Declaration of Weights — 212
- Section 48.9 Declarations of Acceptance — 212
- Section 48.10 Division of Races and Rejection of Entries — 212
- Section 48.11 Emergency Acceptors — 213
- Section 48.12 Barrier Draw — 213
- Section 48.13 Declaration of Riders — 213
- Section 48.14 Withdrawals (Scratchings) — 214

Section 48.15	Cancellation of Race	214
Section 48.16	Race Books	214

CHAPTER 49 RACE DAY PROCEDURES BEFORE THE RACE — 216

Section 49.1	Horses Held in Saddling Paddock	216
Section 49.2	Weighing-out	216
Section 49.3	Weight to be Carried	216
Section 49.4	Weight Penalties	217
Section 49.5	Apprentices' Allowances	217
Section 49.6	Substitution of Riders	217
Section 49.7	Saddling and Mounting	218
Section 49.8	The Preliminary	218
Section 49.9	Barrier Positions	219

CHAPTER 50 THE RACE — 220

Section 50.1	The Start	220
Section 50.2	Running	220
Section 50.3	Finishing Positions	221
Section 50.4	Dead-Heats	221
Section 50.5	Losing Margins	221
Section 50.6	Weighing-in	222
Section 50.7	Correct Weight	222
Section 50.8	Protests	222
Section 50.9	Other Objections and Complaints	223

CHAPTER 51 POST RACE MEETING PROCEDURES — 224

Section 51.1	Reports on Race Meetings	224
Section 51.2	Payment of Prize Moneys	224
Section 51.3	Offences and Punishments	224
Section 51.4	List of Disqualifications	225
Section 51.5	Forfeit List	226

CHAPTER 52 BOOKMAKERS — 228

Section 52.1	Introduction	228
Section 52.2	Licensing of Bookmakers	228
Section 52.3	Bookmakers' Clerks	229
Section 52.4	Bookmakers' Associations	229
Section 52.5	Indemnification of Bettors	229

CHAPTER 53 BOOKMAKING — 230

Section 53.1	Services Provided by a Bookmaker	230
Section 53.2	Betting Tickets	230
Section 53.3	Betting Sheets	230
Section 53.4	Betting Ring Strategies	231
Section 53.5	Bookmakers' Percentages	231
Section 53.6	Financial Viability of Bookmaking	233

CHAPTER 54 BETTING WITH BOOKMAKERS — 235

Section 54.1	Betting Law	235
Section 54.2	Play or Pay Principle	235
Section 54.3	Dead-heats	236
Section 54.4	"Win Only" Betting	236
Section 54.5	"Place Only" Betting	236
Section 54.6	"Win and Place" Betting	236
Section 54.7	Doubles Betting	236
Section 54.8	On-course Starting Price Betting	237
Section 54.9	Compulsory Maximum Amount of Bet	237
Section 54.10	Disputes or Claims Relating to Bets	237

CHAPTER 55 TOTALISATORS — 240

Section 55.1	Meaning of "Totalisator"	240
Section 55.2	Off-course Totalisator Operators	240
Section 55.3	On-course Totalisator Operators	240
Section 55.4	Classes of Totalisators	240
Section 55.5	Modes of Investing on Totalisators	241
Section 55.6	Totalisator Investments	243
Section 55.7	Totalisator Pools	243
Section 55.8	Deductions from Totalisator Pools	243
Section 55.9	Calculation of Dividends	244
Section 55.10	Fractions	244
Section 55.11	Amalgamation of Pools	244
Section 55.12	Payment of Dividends and Refunds	245
Section 55.13	Unpaid Dividends and Refunds	245
Section 55.14	Government Control	245

CHAPTER 56 TOTALISATOR ADMINISTRATION BOARDS (TABS) — 246

Section 56.1	Constitution of State TABs	246
Section 56.2	Service Provided by TABs	246
Section 56.3	Achievements of TABs	246
Section 56.4	TAB Operations Predominantly Relate to Thoroughbred Racing	247
Section 56.5	Operating Results of TABs	247
Section 56.6	Distributions of TAB Profits to Clubs	247
Section 56.7	Accountability of TABs	247

CHAPTER 57 PUNTERS AND PUNTING — 250

Section 57.1	Punters	250
Section 57.2	Marks of an Astute Punter	250
Section 57.3	Historical Data Basis of Selection Procedure	251
Section 57.4	Selection Systems	251
Section 57.5	Selection Services	251
Section 57.6	The Consumers' Annual Guide to Punting Publications and Services	251
Section 57.7	Relevance of Probability to Punting	252

CHAPTER 58 INTRODUCTION TO WEIGHT RATING — 254

Section 58.1	Weight Rating — Definition	254
Section 58.2	Weight-Rating Service — Definition	254

CHAPTER 59 CALCULATION AND RECORDING OF WEIGHT RATINGS — 256

Section 59.1	Method of Calculating Weight Ratings	256
Section 59.2	Losing Margin Adjustment	257
Section 59.3	Barrier Position Adjustment	258
Section 59.4	Missed the Start Adjustment	258
Section 59.5	Blocked-for-Room Adjustment	258